Possibility's Parents

Politics, Literature, and Film

Series Editor: Lee Trepanier, Saginaw Valley State University

The Politics, Literature, and Film series is an interdisciplinary examination of the intersection of politics with literature and/or film. The series is receptive to works that use a variety of methodological approaches, focus on any period from antiquity to the present, and situate their analysis in national, comparative, or global contexts. Politics, Literature, and Film seeks to be truly interdisciplinary by including authors from all the social sciences and humanities, such as political science, sociology, psychology, literature, philosophy, history, religious studies, and law. The series is open to both American and non-American literature and film. By putting forth bold and innovative ideas that appeal to a broad range of interests, the series aims to enrich our conversations about literature, film, and their relationship to politics.

Advisory Board

Recent titles in the series:

Possibility's Parents

Stories at the End of Liberalism

Margaret Seyford Hrezo
and Nicholas Pappas

LEXINGTON BOOKS
Lanham • Boulder • New York • London

Published by Lexington Books
An imprint of The Rowman & Littlefield Publishing Group, Inc.
4501 Forbes Boulevard, Suite 200, Lanham, Maryland 20706
www.rowman.com

6 Tinworth Street, London SE11 5AL

British Library Cataloguing in Publication Information Available

Library of Congress Cataloging-in-Publication Data

Library of Congress Control Number:2019950757
ISBN: 978-1-4985-9882-8 (cloth)
ISBN: 978-1-4985-9883-5 (electronic)

To our families

Contents

Preface

This book's approach to the human search for communal order is unusual. It definitely is not the approach to writing political science taught to this work's authors in graduate school. We write from the perspective of teachers of political philosophy. Our work is anchored in the fact that human beings are puzzlers, questioners, seekers of meaning. That is why each chapter begins with a question asked by one of our grandchildren. We did this because this child's questions are the same that most children and adults face. The difference is that a child demands answers; many adults either believe that they already hold the answers or that the questions are impossible to answer or are not worth bothering about. For hundreds of years Western democracies have taken their answers primarily from classical liberalism developed by myriad thinkers from the sixteenth century until today. We think it may be time to re-examine the assumptions and intellectual structures that produce and support such answers.

In each chapter, we move from the initial question to discussion of a myth related to that question which many in the contemporary world believe and some hold sacred. Classical, or Lockean, liberalism provides the foundation for each of these myths. Finally, in each chapter we examine the initial question and the myth related to it through the lens of works of late twentieth and early twenty-first century novels—in particular, works written in the form of myth. We are neither conservatives nor liberals in the sense with which today's world is familiar. However, we do believe that classical liberalism, the political theory of John Locke through today, is no longer viable and that political philosophy must begin searching for new possibilities in answering the questions posed by human existence.

Our many years of reading, writing, and teaching have led us to believe that mythopoesis (or writing in the form of myth) provides the best contemporary insights into what any new meta-narrative needs to include. We do not believe in totalizing narratives—those that attempt to include all aspects of existence and whose adherents view them for ultimate truth. Totalizing narratives serve no purpose other than to develop or sustain entrenched power. However, meta-narratives do not need to be totalizing. They can reflect preliminary answers to the unending search for the truth of human existence. Further, meta-narratives do not need to foster exclusion. Rather, they may and should demand inclusion.

Our writing style reflects our belief that political theory needs to do a better job of making itself accessible. Following Theodore Lowi, we think political science (and in our view especially political theory) is in danger of making itself irrelevant in the discussion of politics. Theorists write for and speak to each other. There are many reasons for this, primarily the increasing demand that they produce scholarly publications in order to receive tenure and promotion and the overspecialization this demand generates. We seek to engage our readers and write in a fashion that promotes their understanding (if not their agreement), while at the same time providing enough academic political theory to pique interest and further exploration on the part of graduate students and academics. To help bridge the gap we have done three things. The first is this foreword. Second, there is an attached glossary to help with unfamiliar terms. Finally, we believe that one way of fostering understanding and engagement with the text is by using literature to think about political issues and ideas. Only the reader will know whether we have been successful. Thus, with apologies to our graduate school professors, we begin. [1]

NOTE

1. Many thanks to Pam Pappas for her support and to William Hrezo for his patience and willingness to serve as first reader. His help was invaluable.

ONE

Did You Ever Wonder What the World Would Be Like Without You in It?: An Introduction

Questions, Stories, and Possibility

Coming from a nine-year-old "did you ever wonder what the world would be like without you in it?" was an eye-popping question.[1] What this question suggests is that human beings begin trying to sort out their place in the world at a very young age. That was not Kai's first interesting question and it is not likely to be his last. He also has asked: Where do you think the world comes from? Why is the world so cruel? Do you believe in God? Do you believe in magic? Do you believe in dragons? What do you think happens to people when they die? What is our purpose in life? What about the purpose of other people? And, why can't people get over racism? Not only are these some of the perennial questions on whose answers depend the choice between an orderly or a disorderly life; they also are the questions on whose answers human beings build either orderly or disorderly social and political communities. They are the beginning of the stories human beings tell one another. As Neil Gaiman writes, storytellers are creators and "when we begin, separately or together, there's a blank piece of paper. When we are done; we are giving people dreams and magic and journeys into minds and lives that they have never lived."[2] Stories implant possibilities in the mind—offer a vision, or visions, of change for an individual human life or a communal one. They are the parents of possibility, challenging humanity to analyze, evaluate, and, if needed, change its vision and actions.

This book is about politics and literature. It is about the questions people ask and the societal myths they develop and teach to organize their communal lives. It also is about the need for change in Western societies' current organizing concept, classical liberalism. Finally, this book surveys some of the hints at new possibilities and directions mytho-poets, writers whose stories include the form and/or texture of myth, have to offer political theory at the end of Liberalism.

The book is part detective story and part argument. We have taught extensively most of the novels included in it. As we read them, we caught glimpses of ideas related to the authors' critiques of the world they expe-rienced. The more we taught them, the more questions they raised, and thus began our research. That research has led to three arguments. First, as have many others over time, we argue that all human beings live some myth and that myth is part of the search for order. Myth expresses the "truth"—the felt and lived experiences and values—of a particular peo-ple, place, and time. Next, we maintain that the myths held dear by contemporary Western liberal societies since the onset of modernity need more radical overhauls than current political science can accomplish on its own. Finally, we suggest that it is writers of mythopoesis who, in every age, have used the form of myth to point out the cracks in domi-nant cultures and values. Mythopoets, we believe, have much to offer contemporary Western societies in their attempt to imagine their way out of social disorder into a new sense of what it means to be human and to live together in communities, and in the world.

The foci of each chapter are Kai's questions and Sheldon Wolin's com-ment in *Politics and Vision* that the genuine problem facing classical liber-alism is not the individual versus the state or freedom versus authority; rather it is "authority and community."[3] Eric Voegelin also saw new ways of defining political space and addressed the alienation of citizens from public life and their withdrawal into "private worlds centered around trivial distractions" as a threat to democracy.[4] How do/should human beings balance the nation-state with their sense of community? Our book focuses on a certain type of late twentieth- and early twenty-first-century novel that perhaps offers clues to forging better answers than those offered by classical liberalism—a better myth, if you will, with which to reflect upon the perennial questions of both life and political philosophy and their relation to the problem Wolin and Voegelin posed.

LOGOS, MUTHOS, AND *MANA*: RESPONDING TO MYSTERY

Myth has a universal appeal and a universal importance. It draws human beings into something. People may never be quite sure what that some-thing is, but they do understand that myth invites participation and helps in making meaning. That is why myth is just as much a part of the contemporary world as of the "primitive" worlds that preceded moder-nity. Human beings also appear to intuitively grasp that by inviting participation and assisting in the search for meaning, myth has a place in the human search for individual and communal order. Although various authors and various disciplines perceive myth's form and function differently, they seem to agree that the study of myth is essential to the human search for meaning and order. In today's highly rationalized world and highly quantitative political science, myth and myth-making are underrated. This book seeks to study the importance of reintegrating the study of myth and mythopoesis into political philosophy and to examine some examples of how this task has been accomplished.

What is myth and how is it related to the mystery of existence in space and time? That question is both very easy and very difficult to answer. In the contemporary world, myth often is considered "just an old story," a delusion, or a flat-out lie. Thus, any book relying on mythopoesis for its analyses needs to be careful in defining its understanding of myth. For most scholars of the subject, myth is *muthos*, or *logos* — a word, statement, or tale. Many current scholars also accept Robert Segal's definition of myth, stories about personalities who are agents or objects of action. Those stories, whether true or untrue "accomplish something significant" for their adherents and are believed tenaciously.[5] He argues that although traditional myths often took the sacred as their background or subject matter, today's myths are purely secular. Others argue that all myths have some religious element. Still others maintain that the key to understanding myth is the concept of *mana*, or sacred power, which although extraordinary and often preternatural, is not necessarily religious.

Disagreement attends every aspect of the study of myth.[6] Scholars in the field disagree about whether mythic thinking is rational. For some myth is both illogical and irrational.[7] In contrast, Lévi-Strauss argued that "the kind of logic which is used by mythical thought is as rigorous as that of modern science."[8] In his view, the difference between myth and science lies in the topics to which each is applied. Science and myth have the same job and each approaches its object of study with the tools most appropriate to that object. Both are logical and rational. The realm of scientific understanding and knowledge is the physical world, and myth rules the equally important world of metaphysics (that which is real, but outside our physical examination).

Is there a difference between myth, folklore, and legend? In what ways do communal and individual myths differ? Is there a difference between primary myths of origin and myths that reflect on that culture at a latter point in time? Is myth real or something manufactured by scholars? Does myth live on in contemporary society or is it solely the product of primitive humanity? Does myth support the social order?[9] Scholars have given multiple and contradictory answers to each of these questions. Yes, no, and maybe say the sources. Most twentieth-century students, however, argue that myth, although often in a different form, pervades "modern" just as much as "primitive" societies. Marshall Sahlins, for example, writes about the dominance of Hobbesian myth in American society. He argues that Thomas Hobbes developed the origin myth of capitalism in which "the competitive and acquisitive characteristics of Western man have been confounded with Nature, and the Nature thus fashioned in the human image has been in turn reapplied to the explanation of man."[10] In other words, Hobbes put the cart before the horse. Instead of studying human beings and developing a theory based on experience, he developed a theory and then molded human nature to support it.

Complete analysis of this immense corpus is beyond the scope and purpose of this book. What seems evident, though, is that a comprehensive meta-narrative of myth is impossible. Thus, it behooves anyone who ventures into the field to heed the warning of Lessa and Vogt that they should consider myth a general label that covers myriad narrative styles, forms, and function.[11] The novels discussed in this book are examples of this multiplicity. Myths, however, do tend to manifest certain key characteristics. (1) heroes and quests; (2) encounters with the preternatural; (3) a weakening of the boundaries between existent and nonexistent reality; and (4) a bending or breaking of modernity's notion of time. Each novel contains one or more of these characteristics.

Further, these works pose the protagonist with the choice between participation in or closure to a universal human story that requires looking for meaning in all levels of reality. The key element in these works, what sets them apart from other works of literature, is the emphasis on the choice between participation in and closure to a universal human story. *Mason & Dixon* presents the reader multiple chances to contemplate the American experience and reorient thinking. In *Phantastes* Anodos' adventures in Faerie demand a response on his part both there and when he returns to his own world. The woman who does not go blind in *Blindness* demands *opsis* (both personal and social) of every reader. And at the end of McCarthy's border trilogy the character of the Mexican Stranger makes one last attempt to get Billy to understand and live the one tale. Each one is a piece of the human search for individual and communal order.

We do want to briefly address five generalizations, related to our overall argument for the book, that we see arising out of the scholarly literature. These are: (1) the function of myth as participation in and response to question and mystery; (2) the relation of myth to the search for meaning and order; (3) the relation of myth to the lived world of the time; (4); the demands myth places on the hearer for immediacy, engagement, and answerability; and (5) the continued existence of myth in the contemporary world. We believe that agreement could be found among most scholars of myth concerning the first four of the points above. Only the argument for the continued existence of myth, even in highly technological societies, would be likely to provoke disagreement.

All theories of myth seem to rest on the same premise: human beings face a mysterious world, are made anxious by that mystery, and ask questions in order to assuage that anxiety of existence and express their sense of awe and wonder at the world. Whether a given scholar agrees with the way in which myths work toward that goal is immaterial. The assumption underlying what scholars of widely divergent opinions say about the nature and purpose of myth is that these stories are responses to question and mystery. As peoples ask questions like those asked by Kai and search for answers, they incorporate them into their search for meaning and order at both the individual and communal levels. Myths help them respond to their existential situation, to the world as they experience it. This world is partly open to the human senses, banal, and capable of being changed according to human intention. However, that lived world also seems part of some larger and more comprehensive reality which is outside human understanding and control. Myth attempts to respond to both aspects. In addition, myths make demands on the hearer to learn certain lessons, to understand the reasons for those lessons, and live as witnesses for those lessons by incorporating them into their lives—to immerse themselves in a drama of being, a story in which they often do not know either their role or even the nature of the whole experience. We argue that these generalizations transcend the many differences among scholars and schools of thought in the field of myth.

The final generalization would not be accepted easily by some scholars, although it is certainly more commonly made today than at other times in the history of myth scholarship.[12] We argue that myth and mythopoesis pervade human social life. The myths are different because the understanding of the gods, human beings, social life, and the cosmos (what political philosopher Eric Voegelin called the community of being) they embody is different from that of other places and times. But even the most industrialized and rationalized societies use myth to aid their understanding of the mystery of the universe and to advance their search for meaning and order. We agree with Eric Voegelin that there really is no answer to the questions that face human existence except through the symbols of theory and myth.[13] The myths that order the contemporary Western world are about "liberal man," "socialist man," race, consciousness, science, reason, the nature of reality, the individual as an autonomous subject, the administrative state, and so on. Because these myths are so familiar and so deeply embedded in contemporary life, human beings do not view them as myths. Human beings view the narratives that guide today's world as basic and self-evident truths. In this respect, today's myths are no different than any myth system in the past. In this generalization, we agree with a long list of scholars from literary theory, philosophy, and anthropology[14] who argue that myth is just as much a part of our world as it was of the primitive world.

Here, however, it is important to differentiate between myth and ideology. To us, they are not always the same phenomena. Ideologies tend to be closed systems that prohibit questions. They attempt to give final answers and argue for the absolute truth of those answers. They close off mystery rather than opening it up for human participation. Some myths do that as well. Other myths do not. The answers found in "good" myth tend to be far more provisional. They are true at that time for that culture. However, they recognize that as human consciousness changes, so too will ideas about meaning and order. Thus, there will be new insights that at some point will augment or replace older visions and ideas.

Incorporating these five generalizations into our thinking, we argue that myth is the human response to mystery. For a time, myths fulfill the human need for meaning. Myth attempts to encompass all human experience of the world by bridging reason and imagination. Following C. S. Lewis, we maintain that myth resonates with the soul, the organ of truth in the psyche of a given society in a given historical period. Somehow myth finds the symbols that can express a society's understanding of itself. Ultimately, we agree with Weber that myth is complicated. In myth, economic, political, religious, social, and psychological factors all play a role. Similar external forms among cultures may not mean the same internal "ethic" applies and similar external forms may not produce the same historical results. Although religion and ritual play some role in myth, myths are not determined by them. Thus, we cannot agree with the late René Girard that the transference over time of divine status to a sacrificial scapegoat is the source of ritual, myth, and human culture.[15] Myths do delineate between the sacred and the profane. They are full of *mana,* of numinous dread, of the sacred. But, as Hatab points out (following Cassirer), the "sacred does not mean exclusively the supernatural or otherworldly, but simply the *extraordinary,* the uncommon, both wondrous and terrifying. The profane, therefore, does not mean something sacrilegious but simply the *ordinary,* the common."[16] Myth expresses the mystery of existence. Myth does not intend to eliminate mystery. Instead, myth opens mystery to human participation and engagement.

THE MYTHS OF LIBERALISM AND MODERNITY

Over time, human beings develop frameworks that pull together their answers to the perennial questions into a code that can guide their personal and communal lives. That code becomes the society's myth. As Harari states in *Sapiens,* "any large-scale human cooperation. . . . is rooted in common myths that exist only in people's collective imagination."[17] Further, none of these myths exist "outside the stories that people invent and tell one another."[18] A society's political myth embodies and safeguards certain answers to those questions, questions such as those Kai has asked. Human beings ask questions. In the attempt to answer those questions, they tell stories. If enough members of the group like and retell one story, a myth expressing the commonly held "truth" of the group's place in and experience of living develops. That myth will encompass a society's actual conditions, values, and ideals.

However, just as all myths are true, reflecting the experiences and values of their time; all myths also are false. As they age, they change. For once an idea is let loose in the world, it develops a life of its own, one separate from what the original thinker of that idea could ever have foreseen. There are new accretions to meet changing conditions. Other parts fall away and are forgotten. Further some myths are "better" than others from the start. Better myths understand they are not the truth for all times and all places. In addition, we maintain that better myths realize they are part of what political philosopher Eric Voegelin called the "one tale"—a story of the interaction of an ineffable reality not visible to the human eye with the reality of will and intention in our physical world. They look to guarding the sum of things—all of life's multiple planes. Such narratives, "*require* the embrace of the full range of human otherness . . ."[19] They look to the borders of life and integrate human intention and participation in some larger and mysterious story. Who knows what that ineffable, transcendent something is—God? Some Life Force? Love? Chaos? The music of the universe? Something that is neither being nor Being? Ultimate Mystery? Whatever IT is, it is real but ever unknown to its full extent. We argue that transcendence does not necessitate a belief in any God. The transcendent is the ineffably mysterious that goes beyond the "conditions of space and time and our direct or substantive understanding."[20] It is a part of reality that is ultimately unknowable. As Voegelin argues, myths are the "provisional answers" to the questions posed by human experience of the world.[21] Their truth is True only so long as it fits human experience of questions such as why do things exist? Why are things the way they are and not different? It seems that the answers posited in the contemporary world no longer quite fit with human experience of those questions.

Despite the attempts of numerous insightful political thinkers, the myth of classical liberalism—like Humpty Dumpty—has developed so many cracks and fault lines that it cannot be put back together again. If not failed, it is at this point unsalvageable in its present form, although not necessarily for the reasons suggested by Patrick Deneen.[22] It should not surprise anyone that classical liberalism is not the end of the history of political thought. Never the thought of just one person, the liberal model of individual religious, political, and economic freedom developed over hundreds of years from Martin Luther's dictum that every man should be his own priest through Rawlsians, Libertarians, Communitarians, and postmodernists. Lockean liberalism is not one thing, or even the same thing to all people. At its most basic level, this model sees human beings as individuals who exist prior to government and have rights over government and the social good; that is, the individual right always trumps the moral and social good.[23]

Still, although old myths seldom die, fresh ideas from different perspectives develop to meet the challenges presented by new understandings of the ineffable mystery surrounding all of life, of humanity, of the place of humanity in the universe (or multiverse as Terry Pratchett or Douglas Adams would have had it), and of what it means for human beings to live in community. These new ideas confront the weaknesses of the old myths and are the seeds of new ones. It is in this situation that Western liberal democracies find themselves today. Political liberalism is a myth that is showing its age. It has not failed. It is like the old (and usually untrue) stereotype of the ancient professor who still uses class notes from twenty years ago despite the wealth of changes in their profession over that period.

Classical liberalism remains part of Western societies' cultural and intellectual landscape. However, even the best scholars of the myriad ideas and accretions that have come to symbolize Western liberalism seem unable to tell a story that provides convincing answers to the perennial questions as they arise in the present. In response to classical liberalism's inability to meet the challenges of twenty-first century life, come social turmoil and new ideas. The old order becomes disordered and the search for an order more attuned to a changed concrete historical situation must continue. Today everyone believes they hold absolute truth in the face of a corrupt system and that their opinions should not only be respected but also dominate political decision making. The result is stalemate and the end of compromise and civil discourse. They have forgotten that no right, no matter how precious to one or the other individual or group, is absolute and that rights always must be balanced.

In the face of the disorder haunting the contemporary world, it is fruitless to assert the need to defend Western civilization, or any modern trope. As usual, political philosophy is not the product of happy times. Rather, political philosophy is humanity's attempt during times of seeming disruption and chaos to return to the perennial questions about where things come from and what can be changed or not changed in the world in which human beings live. It lets in the light of new thinking and allows human beings, as Hannah Arendt put it, to make miracles by coming together to begin something new. The attempt to harden one creative spiritual or mental outburst into truth for all time is fruitless; yet in all times and places there will be many who try to do so.

In summary, the experience of facing question and mystery propels humanity on a quest for some ground of happiness, meaning, and order. Myth remembers and tells the story of history and reality "as an unfinished tale . . ."[24] Through the power of language and story, it evokes and communicates a feeling of participation in the whole of experienced reality. The societal tale expressed through myth pervades a society's sense of individual and communal order and disorder. Even the bawdiest of myths and folktales imply some vision of an orderly or disorderly individual and/or communal life. Disorder in a society severely limits the search for personal and communal meaning and order. Yet the search for individual meaning can produce highly equivocal results for a concrete political order. That search for meaning may reinforce existing institutions and social values; it also may undermine them by revealing some hidden disorder at the heart of the existing pattern of order and/or suggesting alternative readings of the lived world. So, too, may myth. As a variety of scholars have noted, certain kinds of myth are one way in which societies teach about and replace visions of order.

MYTHOPOESIS AND THE SEARCH FOR ORDER

The genuine question is: "What comes next?" Whatever comes next, it will be the work of human imagination combined with noetic reason. Mythopoesis, writing in the form of a myth, provides the imaginative spark human beings need to pay attention to and reflect upon possibility. Applying noetic reason to imagine possibilities is the task of political philosophy. They are like Terry Pratchett's witches who "look to the 'edges. . . . There's a lot of edges, more than people know: Between life and death, this world and the next, night and day, right and wrong . . . an' they need watching. . . . We watch 'em, we guard the sum of things. And we never ask for any reward. That's important."[25] Mythopoets watch the borders between two realities, a reality of physical things and a reality composed of non-physical things, illuminating the cracks and their effects on human life. They hint at new possibilities, new answers to old questions. It always has been this way. Often, they reveal the flaws in their society's understanding of the world. Homer's *Iliad*, for example, chronicles the cracks that brought about the demise of Mycenaean civilization. The Old Testament YHWH signaled a true ancient *Gotterdammerung* by exposing the dark side of its competitors in the Middle East. The truth of the Old Testament gave way to that of Christianity when Old Testament truths no longer appeared to fit the circumstances of Christ's lifetime. When cracks appeared in Christianity in the Middle Ages, the Enlightenment began, and classical liberalism arose out of it. The story repeats itself again and again.

Politics, like mythopoesis, is an act of evocation. The reality of the political order is called into being by the magical power of language as some human being (or beings) continue the search for communal order through writing that takes the form of a myth. Such writing shares with philosophy a sense of awe and wonder that motivates a quest for understanding. Human beings want to understand their world. They want their world and their lives to be intelligible and meaningful. This is as much a communal concern as an individual one. In today's world, it is mythopoesis that leads the way in assisting citizens' understanding of their world. For the novelist, imagination and reason combine to achieve a vision of a flourishing and meaningful individual and communal life.

Mythopoesis prepares the way for that shared evocation of a community's sense of meaning and order. Mythopoesis (to make a story) refers to the use of the myth to communicate ever more differentiated experiences of the truth of existence. Rather than a literal interpretation of a myth, the term suggests the use of myth to explore the ground of human existence and the interaction of the human and transcendent in the world. Today, political philosophy seems to have lost its ability to participate in the deep knowing of the lover of the beautiful that Socrates accords to both philosophers and poets in *Phaedrus* (298d-e).

Human beings seem to have come full circle in terms of the symbols they use to express their experience of their lives, their place in the world, and their search for meaning and order. Pre-language societies expressed those experiences in signs and drawings. The discovery of language and writing allowed the use of another type of symbol—words and sentences—to evoke those experiences. However, as the scientific revolution advanced, the symbols used to discuss the political in political science turned to formulas, statistics, and computer models. Calculus truly did become the universal language. But calculus is not the language of the lived world of human consciousness. Thus, while pre-linguistic societies still could express their understandings of meaning and order, post-linguistic societies, which depend on data analysis and equations, have increasing difficulty in doing so. This is what makes the work of the mythopoets so important. Our readings of the works included in this book demonstrate that mythopoets continue to be wary of universal political truths and principles and distrustful of institutions and power, especially supposedly neutral ones. In this, mythopoets may reveal this age's hopes, aims, and worries (its consciousness) better than do standard works of politics.

Mythopoesis uses the form of the myth to pry open the human experience of life in the middle. It lays bare the consequences of human and societal choices. It offers examples of orderly and disorderly individual and communal lives. Mythopoesis often takes liberties with the physical world to highlight truths that are felt but cannot be seen. It accepts the reality of non-physical things, and in the face of mystery, ask a thousand important questions. Some scholars label these writers "Postsecularists" because they see in these writers a turn away from secularism to a religion-less religion. Although the authors we have chosen for this volume exhibit the criteria these scholars call Postsecularist, we do not think the term fully encompasses what our authors are about.

There are similarities between our approach and that of postsecular scholars. McClure defines the postsecular movement in literature as "a mode of being and seeing that is at once critical of secular constructions of reality and of dogmatic religiosity."[26] In such fiction, he argues, there is a "disruption" of the laws of physics and "an opening up of spiritual possibilities."[27] Both these statements apply to the novels explored in this book. There is the reawakening of a sense of awe and wonder in the face of life's mystery. Gods and goddesses may appear, but only McCarthy and MacDonald suggest God per se.

However, there are important differences in our approach that make this work unique. First, we rely on very different thinkers in pursuing our argument. McClure relies on Gianni Vattimo, William Connolly, Richard Rorty, Jacques Derrida, William James, and Mircea Eliade to present a picture of "weak" religion. In his analysis, characters, who in the past were purely secular in their thinking, react to critical junctures in the story with a halfhearted turn to an ambiguous "and dramatically partial" religiosity linked to "progressive values and projects."[28]

The sources for our analyses of Cormac McCarthy, Thomas Pynchon, Neil Gaiman, José Saramago, J.M. Coetzee, and Nnedi Okorafor, on the other hand, include Plato, Simone Weil, Eric Voegelin, G. K. Chesterton, Albert Camus, Emmanuel Levinas, Michael J. Sandel, and Sheldon Wolin and the theology of Dietrich Bonhoeffer, Pavel Florensky, and Miroslav Volf. Nods to the late work of Jacques Derrida and to William E. Connolly also appear in this book. Pynchon is the only writer we analyze who also appears in McClure's *Partial Truths*. Our analysis suggests that characters do not head toward religion, even the "weak" religion McClure borrows from Vattimo. The writers we have chosen are neither postsecular, nor post doctrinal. Instead, they use myth to explore a vision of life as lived in-between physical reality and some ineffable transcendent reality.

McClure's view leaves individuals as sole creators of their lives and world. Our authors appear, on the other hand, to see human beings as co-creators of reality who never fully oversee and control the events in which they partake. Second, McClure argues that the authors he labels postsecularist lead readers to a progressive and more inclusive politics. Politics would still be Easton's authoritative allocation of values for society. In our reading of the authors examined here, the concern is more about certain characteristics that should be cultivated in order to address the issue of authority and community that haunts the contemporary world than about the political implications of those characteristics. The political comes in only through our contentions that (1) the quality of a city depends on the quality of its citizens and (2) politics, as Simone Weil suggested, is a composition on a multiple plane—not just numbers and power, but also justice, inclusion of the mystery that surrounds human existence, the presence of some unknowable and unexplainable reality within the physical world, clear-sightedness, noetic reason, and obligations of solidarity. Close readings of the novels indicate to us that their authors are more interested in these concepts than in actual political outcomes.

The six contemporary mythopoets (and one late nineteenth-century theologian) whose works we analyze share several commonalities. All these authors are moralists with deep concerns about the current Western political fascination with liberalism's materialist vision, the role of human beings in mass society, and the totalizing and totalitarian aspects of the Enlightenment and the Modern Project (or modernity). Over hundreds of years, the Modern Project came to mean that the desires for wealth, power, and survival are the sole goals of human life and action. Under its influence, the job of the State is to provide its citizens with the means of achieving these goals. The myth of modernity rests upon a certain type of consciousness—the belief that human beings can order their physical and personal environment according to will (intent) and that progress is the result of the imposition of human will on the world and on social relations. Freedom, thus, is the ability to impose one's will and achieve one's desired ends.

Among the authors we have chosen are atheists, agnostics, puzzlers, and believers concerning the existence of a supreme being or beings. At least one does not give the question much thought. All of them, however, acknowledge that human beings face mystery and ask questions. These mythopoets use the questions to form their stories and frame those stories in the form of myth. They accept the reality of an ineffability that humanity can glimpse periodically, but never grab onto. They do not claim to have answers. For, as Gaiman writes, "Things need not to have happened to be true. Tales and dreams are the shadow truths that will endure when mere facts are dust and ashes, and forgot."[29] Thus, they challenge their readers to question the myths that permeate modernity and to continue the search for new ways to think about what it means to be human, the place of human beings in the universe, how human beings should relate to the ineffable mystery that surrounds them, and how they should relate to one another. Mythopoets offer glimpses of what needs to come—no more.

These authors seem to agree that human beings experience life as occurring with the *metaxy*—an experience of always living in the middle—and accept what Eric Voegelin called the paradox of consciousness—the feeling of being a subject in a world of will and intention *and* an actor in a play that takes place within a mystery participants cannot understand. Thus, all explore boundaries and borders. These authors layer story upon story exploring the forces of dissatisfaction with and revolt from the myths of the administrative state, of the American founding, of nativism, racism and tribalism, and of instrumental reason. They include moments of grace, or presence (*Parousia*). Further, evidence suggests that Plato has influenced each of them.

We argue that, for these authors at least, any new political vision should include acknowledgment of a paradox of consciousness. But acceptance of mystery is not enough. These authors suggest that also needed are acceptance of mystery's presence in the world (grace), reliance on some form of reasoning that is more than instrumental, *opsis* (clear-sightedness), and response to the call for witness, that is, recognition and acceptance of obligations of solidarity.[30] They point a direction for political philosophy as it struggles to deal with the problem of authority and community. Ultimately, these authors offer the imaginative seeds of a political philosophy that not only would be different in emphasis from classical liberalism, but also is somewhat outside the bounds of contemporary political science. We make no judgement concerning the real-world applicability of their offerings. We do argue that they tell us something important, whether we believe their ideas will work, for always "the quest for truth speaks the language of the tale." [31]

All the authors chosen for this book create characters who engage in quests, come of age, and/or sacrifice their lives or careers to witness what they see as some larger principle. They confront one myth and suggest important aspects of new ones. Our mythopoets provide no final solutions to the mystery that surrounds human life. If anything, they leave us with more questions. Each explores the complexities of human existence in the middle—in between an unknown beginning and an unknowable future, between the beginning and end of human life or some stage of human life, between ideals and current reality, between physical reality and whatever unseen and ineffable reality exists. They unearth and share the lived reality of the wide variety of human experiences and allow readers to live those unending questions about why things exist and why they are the way they are. If Eric Voegelin is correct (and we believe he is) that life is "an adventure of decision on the edge of freedom and necessity," [32] then it is mythopoesis that roams the edges guarding the sum of things and searching for the places where the balance between freedom and necessity has been lost and must be redeemed before political philosophy can suggest a workable blend of community and authority. On those edges they find possibility.

THE MYTHOPOETS

Chapters 2-6 of this book focus on Cormac McCarthy, Thomas Pynchon, Neil Gaiman, José Saramago, J.M. Coetzee, and Nnedi Okorafor. The chapter on Gaiman also includes thoughts on a late nineteenth-century writer, George MacDonald whose understanding of reason is similar to Gaiman's. These authors engage their protagonists in adventures that critique old myths and evoke aspects of what the novelists see as important in the development of a myth better suited to the contemporary world.

Chapter 2: "Did you ever notice that there are stories within stories" relies on Cormac McCarthy's Border Trilogy (*All the Pretty Horses, The Crossing*, and *Cities of the Plain*) to explore the multiple layers of reality experienced by human beings. We argue that McCarthy's conception of the Real and of transcendence most fully reveal themselves when approached from the perspective of Eric Voegelin's paradox of consciousness. In the contemporary world, the real is what human beings can see, taste, and touch. The sense of the real pervading the Border Trilogy is different and paradoxical. For McCarthy, reality includes both the physical and the metaphysical and both need to be remembered and honored. Human beings experience life as occurring in the *metaxy*, in the middle and live with the tensions that experience imposes.

In chapter 3, Do You Believe in God? we examine the myth of America as a city upon a hill and the implications of accepting life in the middle. Over the course of his prolific career, Pynchon has offered a mythic history of the United States—a vision of Americans at work and play, trying to act out their part in a drama of being whose plot is unknown. *Mason & Dixon* skillfully symbolizes the almost incommunicable experience of life in the *metaxy* and *metalepsis*, the joint participation of something unseen and humans in a drama of being in which we sometimes are "the Slate" and sometimes "the Chalk."[33] In Pynchon's presentation of pre-founding America, he may be showing his readers that grace/presence is ubiquitous and needs to be recognized in the formation of any polity that accepts the paradox of consciousness. Without such consideration no political community should receive the title of "city upon a hill."

Chapter 4 begins with the question: "Do you believe in magic?' Its focus is coming-of-age myths and the contemporary myth of instrumental reason. Instrumental reason has become modernity's magic incantation for decision making. Close readings of the coming-of-age quests in *Phantastes* and *Anansi Boys* reveal that, despite their many differences, both George MacDonald and Neil Gaiman are critics of the Myth of Instrumental Reason and call for inclusion of reason in the classicl sense, or *Nous*. Further, for MacDonald and Gaiman the essence of order is justice, and justice requires witness and self-sacrifice. Growing up involves development of noetic reason and the will to make sacrifices for others. Magical creatures and experiences become guides in the human need to develop a "wise" imagination.

In chapter 5, Do You Believe in Dragons? we argue that J.M. Coetzee's *Waiting for the Barbarians* and José Saramago's *Blindness* suggest that the Myth of the Administrative State allows free rein to the dragon of building dream worlds and blindness to reality. These works suggest the need to develop horizons that encompass the whole of reality and, most importantly, they portray *opsis*, clear-sightedness, as an essential requirement in discerning the demands of life in the *metaxy*. These works give us a hint about the most important constituent of order—the ability of an individual to see clearly and deeply into all levels of reality and to use that insight to participate in the drama of being as co-creators, not sole authors of reality.

Finally, "Why Can't People Accept Each Other?" (chapter 6) examines the universal question of why human beings create tribes and believe they cannot live with those who are not like themselves. Nnedi Okorafor's *The Book of Phoenix* and *Who Fears Death* examine those themes. Her books are excellent examples of new trends in science fiction/fantasy that elucidate important considerations for any attempt to reconcile authority and community. *The Book of Phoenix* and *Who Fears Death* contain themes of the paradox of consciousness, inclusion/exclusion, cultural change, oppression, alterity, necessity/freedom, reason, *opsis* and weakness, justice and self-interest. In fact, most of the themes we evoke in the other chapters are present in these two books. Okorafor's work, the most overtly political included, testifies to the importance to any political community of witness.

The final chapter begins with the question "What Can I Do? I'm only one person." Thomas Mann offers a clue to the implications of this question in *Joseph the Provider* when Joseph says, "I don't know, Mai, what sort of man I am. One does not know beforehand how one will behave in one's story; but when the time comes it is clear enough and then a man gets acquainted with himself." [34] It suggests that Albert Camus and Alyosha Karamazov both were correct in asserting that human beings are responsible in some manner to all and for all—at least for each human being's small corner of the world. The conclusion summarizes the insights of the authors canvassed and their call for human humility, imagining possibility, and listening to other's stories. Their themes make them the parents of possibility. These authors and their stories do not ask human beings to go back to some previous time when life and values were "better." They imply, instead, that political philosophy needs to move forward beyond Lockean liberalism and develop political thinking that includes the entire community of being, both the knowable physical and the mysterious and ineffable transcendent. Their message to political philosophy is to expand its understanding of reason and embrace new possibilities. Such a change in political philosophy would start with recognizing the paradox of consciousness.

NOTES

1. Thanks to Radford University's Faculty Development Leave Program for supporting an initial draft of this work.

2. Neil Gaiman, "A Speech Given to Professionals Contemplating Alternative Employment, Given at PROCON, April 1997," in *The View from the Cheap Seats* (New York: William Morrow *An imprint of* HarperCollins *Publishers*, 2016.

3. Sheldon Wolin, *Politics and Vision: Continuity and Innovation in Western Political Thought* (Princeton: Princeton University Press, 2004), 314.

4. John Ranieri, "Grounding Public Discourse: The Contribution of Eric Voegelin," in Glenn Hughes, ed. *The Politics of the Soul* (Lanham, MD: Rowman & Littlefield Publishers, 1999), 35.

5. Robert Segal, *Myth: A Very Short Introduction* (Oxford University Press, 2004), 6.

6. Excellent synopses of the history of myth scholarship are available in the work of Eleazar Meletinsky, Raphael Patai, Fiona Bowie, Robert Segal, and J. Van Baal. Full citations for these works can be found in *Chapter 1: Works Consulted* for this volume. Here we provide only the briefest synthesis of a fascinating scholarly conversation. Herodotus and Euhemeris viewed myth as an explanation of the transformation of an individual into a god. During the Medieval and Renaissance periods students interpreted myths as allegories designed to illustrate moral principles. Nineteenth-century romantics saw myth as an aesthetic that depicts the universe through nature. The turn of the century was dominated by those who saw myth as explanations of ritual (Edward Burnett Tylor, Sir James George Frazer, Lord Raglan, Walter F. Otto, Wilhelm Wundt). Emile Durkheim and Lucien Levy-Bruhl moved away from the emphasis on ritual, but still considered myth the building block for religious belief. Over the course of the twentieth century, scholarship tended to move away from the ritualist school and to include ideas from philosophy, linguistic studies, psychology and literary criticism. Those viewing the topic through the lens of literary criticism focus on myth as a work of art and imagination, as mythopoesis (Richard Chase, Northrop Frye, C. S. Lewis). The philosopher Lawrence Hatab considers myth to be culture. The psychologists and psycho-analysts follow Freud and Jung in arguing that myth is the attempt of the psyche to integrate the conscious and unconscious or explain the psychic life of the tribe. Anthropologists seem to fall into one of six general points of view. Some follow Malinowski's view that myths are charter stories; that is, they function to reinforce religious and/or social mores, institutions, and power relationships. Others support the idea, first suggested by Giambattista Vico in the eighteenth century, that myths are illogical or pre-logical explanations of natural phenomena that are replaced over time by reason and science. A third group supports Claude Lévi-Strauss' characterization of myth as a vehicle through which a culture can logically reconcile contradictions experienced in individual and social life. Still others agree with Eliade that myths are explanations of the origins of something, usually something sacred, or of the morality of certain actions. In the late twentieth century Ernst Cassirer's argument that myth is a vehicle for symbolic truth has attracted many followers. Finally, popular audiences have responded favorably to Campbell's thesis that myths are hero stories, and a variety of scholars are studying René Girard's vision of mimetic desire, ritual scapegoats, and the development of myth in the formation of human culture.

7. David Bidney argues myth is a kind of delusional thinking that is beyond truth and falsity and that disappears as human reason develops. Giambattista Vico considered myth both irrational and illogical and rejoiced in its replacement by reason and science. Ernst Cassirer and Lucien Levy-Bruhl believed that myth is a kind of knowledge, but that science is better.

8. Claude Lévi-Strauss, *Myth and Meaning* (New York: Schocken Books, 1978), 197.

9. Some, including David Bidney, Joseph Campbell, Richard Chase, Kathryn Hume, and Max Weber, say yes; others argue not necessarily.

10. Marshall Sahlins wrote several pieces in which he discussed the illusory Western vision of human nature that he traced to Thomas Hobbes and Hobbes' understanding of the Thucydides. Hobbes provided the first translation of Thucydides' *The Peloponnesian War*. See, for example, Marshall Sahlins, "The Western Illusion of Human Nature," *Michigan Quarterly Review* XLV, no. 3 (Summer 2006), accessed December 18, 2018, http://hdl.handle.net/2027/spo.act2080.0045.306; and Marshall Sahlins,

The Sidney W. Mintz Lecture for 1994: "The Sadness of Sweetness: The Native Anthropology of Western Cosmology," *Current Anthropology* 37, no. 3 (June 1996): 395–428, accessed December 19, 2018, DOI: 10.2307/536765, https://www-jstor-org.lib-proxy.radford.edu/stable/536765.

11. William A. Lessa and Evon C. Vogt, *Reader in Comparative Religion: An Anthropological Approach* (New York: HarperCollins, 1979), 168.

12. See, for example, Mircea Eliade, Robert Segal, Ernst Cassirer, Fiona Bowie, G. S, Kirk, Lawrence J. Hatab, Max Weber, Paul Ricoeur, David Bidney, and Northrop Frye.

13. Eric Voegelin, "In Search of the Ground," *The Collected Works of Eric Voegelin, Vol. 11: Published Essays 1953–1965*, ed. Ellis Sandoz (Columbia: University of Missouri Press, 2000). 225–226.

14. See, for example, Ernst Cassirer, Northrop Frye, Eleazar M. Meletinsky, Raphael Patai, Harry Slochower, Robert Segal, J. Van Baal, Max Weber, and Lawrence J. Hatab.

15. See for example, René Girard, *Deceit, Desire, and the Novel* (Baltimore: Johns Hopkins University Press, 1976); *Violence and the Sacred* (W.W. North & Company, 1979); *The Scapegoat* (Baltimore: Johns Hopkins University Press, 1989); and *I See Satan Fall Like Lightening* (Orbis Books, 2001).

16. Lawrence Hatab, *Myth and Philosophy* (LaSalle, IL: Open Court, 1990), 22.

17. Yuval Noah Harari, *Sapiens: A Brief History of Humankind* (Harper, 2015), 27.

18. Ibid., 28.

19. Glenn Hughes, *Transcendence and History* (Columbia and London: University of Missouri Press, 2003), 37.

20. Ibid., 20.

21. Eric Voegelin, *Order and History, Vol. IV: The Ecumenic Age* (Baton Rouge: Louisiana State University Press, 1974), 304.

22. Patrick Deneen, *Why Liberalism Failed* (Yale University Press, 2018). In this work, Professor Deneen suggests that the only way out of liberalism is the building of small, local cultures with different sets of values than those of today's dominant liberal culture (18). Simone Weil suggested something similar during World War II in *The Need for Roots* (New York: Harper-Colophon, 1971). More recently, Kyle Scott's *The Limits of Politics* also explores the importance of moral imagination in developing new political ideas that include the possibility of more localized political cultures and the requirement of concurrent majorities. These are fascinating ideas that deserve consideration and genuine reflection. In our view, however, implementing them would lead to the ultimate break-up of the United States—an idea with which the old novel *Ecotopia* plays. See Ernest Callenbach. *Ecotopia* (Bantam Books, 1990). Scott's concurrent majorities really is no remedy for that.

23. See, for example, Michael Sandel, *Democracy's Discontent: America in Search of a Public* Philosophy (Belknap Press, 1996).

24. Eric Voegelin, *Order and History, Vol. V: In Search of Order* (Baton Rouge: Louisiana State University Press, 1987), 1.

25. Terry Pratchett, *The Wee Free Men* (HarperCollins, 2015), 314.

26. John McClure, *Partial Faiths: Postsecular Fiction in the Age of Pynchon and Morrison* (University of Georgia Press, 2007), ix.

27. Ibid., 4.

28. Ibid., 6.

29. Neil Gaiman, *The Sandman, Vol. 3: Dream Country* (DC Comics, 1995), 21.

30. See Michael J. Sandel, *Justice* (Farrar, Straus & Giroux, 2010) and Alasdair MacIntyre, *After Virtue*, 2nd edition (Notre Dame, IN: University of Notre Dame Press, 1984).

31. Voegelin, *In Search of Order*, 65.

32. Eric Voegelin, *Order and History, Vol. I: Israel and Revelation* (Baton Rouge: Louisiana State University Press, 1956), 1.

33. Thomas Pynchon, *Mason & Dixon* (Picador, 2004), 442.

34. Thomas Mann, *Joseph the Provider* (New York: Alfred Knopf, 1944), 352.

TWO

Have You Ever Noticed That There Are Stories within Stories within Stories?

Consciousness and Modernity's Myth of Reality in Cormac McCarthy's Border Trilogy

STORIES WITHIN STORIES

Then 10, Kai asked: "Have you ever noticed that there are stories within stories?"[1] That question led back to a high-school experience in Washington, D.C. Through the end of the 1960s teams still played baseball on the Ellipse behind the White House. Almost every weekday evening one could find an Industrial League or American Legion game to watch. It was in some ways a place of wonder because, if the observer cared to open themselves, the Ellipse made visible a variety of levels of reality. There was the reality of the individual game. For a center-fielder focused on the interaction of the pitcher and the batter, the reality that mattered was the pie-shaped boundaries of the playing field. However, behind him was the reality of another game. Beyond that was the reality of a tourist city and then of Washington, D.C., as a seat of power. Yet the White House, the monuments, the museums, the Capitol, and the Supreme Court building were not all of reality either. Transcending them was a city in which average people went to work and school, raised their families, and interacted with friends, neighbors, and enemies. In a very real way the order of that city depended on the order of each of those smaller realities. However, the city's order also depended on the attunement of those realities to each other and to any other realities that transcended them, even if they were unrecognized by denizens who were intent on their own little worlds. Truly there were stories within stories and multiple realities in this city. Yet in the end, all these stories participated in one overall tale, one overall Reality that, although not totalizing, encompassed them.

You had to pay attention to see it, but those nights watching ball on the Ellipse allowed one a momentary glimpse of the paradox of consciousness—the experience of participating not only in a physical reality one can see, touch, and manipulate by will and intention but also in a nonphysical reality not subject to human manipulation. It is a paradox, yes, but one that Cormac McCarthy suggests all inhabit and few recognize. Standing there, it was impossible not to understand that human beings participate in some comprehensive reality that is composed of many layers. Not every evening, but some evenings it was a place where the things of God and men were of a piece—a place where one could experience stories within stories in multiple worlds.

Why is that experience important to this book? To answer this question, we ask the reader to remember the argument outlined in the Introduction. The books included in this volume share five elements. First, they accept the paradox of consciousness, the feeling that life is lived on several levels within some ineffable and encompassing reality. Next, acceptance of the paradox of consciousness opens these authors' characters to the presence of mystery and grace as a ubiquitous part of life. In turn, they become aware of a different sort of reasoning than the instrumental version that dominates the contemporary world. The authors appear to suggest that reason in the classic (or noetic) sense is the best tool available to those who accept the paradox of consciousness for navigating a world enveloped in mystery. Further, the outcome of employing reason in its classic sense is what Camus called "clear-sightedness" and the Greeks called *opsis*. *Opsis* calls the characters in these novels to action. Finally, living in the paradox of consciousness, acceptance of presence, the use of reason in its older sense, and clear-sightedness demand a response. The circumstances in which the characters find themselves require that they witness what they have seen and experienced. Some characters respond; others do not. However, all are called upon to witness one story—a story that accepts ineffable mystery and contains myriad political implications.

The question of a perceptive child and this experience on the Ellipse provide the starting points for our exploration of Cormac McCarthy's Border Trilogy. The Border Trilogy, *All the Pretty Horses, The Crossing,* and *Cities of the Plain,* requires its readers to open themselves to many different levels of reality, and, especially, to the first part of our argument—the paradox of consciousness. Of all the late twentieth-century authors included in this book, McCarthy is the one most interested in God. Yet one does not need the idea of God to accept the paradox of consciousness. All the authors presented here, including those who either do not believe in a personal God or just do not care about whether such a God exists, portray the paradox in their stories. This paradox asks human beings to open themselves to some mystery that is unseen but real and which comprehends all the other levels of reality in the human world. The paradox confronts humanity with both a physical reality in which human beings are subjects able to make choices and control events and a non-physical reality in which they are predicates who must accept Necessity. As McCarthy puts it, besides will and intention, individuals have a "predicate life." From this paradox McCarthy draws the language that evokes his sense of the Real, one that is very different from the dominant myth of modernity, the Modern Project.

According to the Modern Project, the desires for wealth, power, and survival are the sole goals of human life and action. Under this model the job of the State exists to provide its citizens with the means of achieving these goals. The myth of modernity rests upon a certain type of consciousness—the belief that human beings can order their physical and personal environment according to will (intent) and that progress is the result of the imposition of human will on the world and on social relations. Freedom, thus, is the ability to impose one's will.[2] McCarthy, sometimes sounding much like Simone Weil, exposes his readers to the disastrous consequences of subscribing to the Modern Project and its trinity of science, instrumental reason, and absolute individual freedom. The Border Trilogy grants readers a very different perspective, one in which the paradox of consciousness allows some of his characters a reflective distance (an attunement to all of reality) and larger perspective that can culminate in order. Others, rejecting this paradox as "unreal," choose egoism, isolation, and disorder. Yet others are continually torn between accepting and rejecting the paradox and trying to exist as outside observers. The Border Trilogy produces moments of both the movement of the human soul out of itself to others and to a mysterious Beyond and moments of the irruption of the luminosity of Beyond into human reality. It also produces moments of horror, spiritual sickness, and depravity. In these books, "two worlds touch." [3] From the perspective of the Border Trilogy, decision and choice about what is Real—about whether to accept or reject the paradox of consciousness and the consequences resulting from that choice form the essence of the human condition. Everything follows from that choice.

In his western novels McCarthy dissects the consequences of several myths concerning the American West, among them the reality of the cowboy versus the romanticized version, civilization versus nature, and freedom versus social control. Certainly, there are stories within stories contained in the Border Trilogy: the stories of John Grady Cole and Billy Parham, the story of America's development into a world power, the story of manifest destiny, the story of the passing of the cowboy, the story of Mexican history, the story of a providential (or not) god. Each story has its own reality founded on some underlying myth. In each story ethnic, metaphysical, and physical borders are crossed, violated, re-crossed.

Some scholars have seen McCarthy's stories as criticisms of the cow-boy myth, and they have a point. However, the center of his work is the problems generated by the myth of modernity, especially the under-standing of what is Real incited by the discovery of Lucretius' *On the Nature of Things* in 1417.[4] Once found, Lucretius' poem celebrating the beauty and elegance of nature and the human body and arguing that everything is built of atoms that follow no intelligent design or divine plan changed the way human beings viewed themselves and the world around them.[5] The poem influenced Francis Bacon, Richard Hooker, Leo-nardo da Vinci, Machiavelli, Montaigne, Cervantes, Michelangelo, Botti-celli, Spinoza, William Harvey, Copernicus, and ultimately Thomas Hobbes.

The quests undertaken by Billy Parham and John Grady Cole in the trilogy illuminate the violence at the heart of this myth. Those quests, which always end in failure, demonstrate the disastrous consequences that can occur when modernity exercises authority over human life and refuses the paradox of consciousness. Rejection of the paradox results in isolation, solitary egoism, the failure of community, and disorder. Only consciousness of all of reality, McCarthy maintains, allows humanity to remember what it means to be a human being living in-between two poles of one story and thus able to get past themselves as individuals and participate in and act as witnesses to all Reality, to the one story com-posed of stories within stories. Only such participation produces order in both individuals and societies. We are not the first to examine the anti-modern strain in McCarthy's writing.[6] What we contribute is an excava-tion of McCarthy's critique of this myth to its foundation and his vision of a better theory of consciousness.

A THEORY OF CONSCIOUSNESS

McCarthy's vision in the telling of each of these stories and in his explora-tion of each myth is spiritual. This spiritual vision has led several scholars to suggest he is a post-secularist.[7] However, the post-secularist trope fails to help a reader understand the ground beneath McCarthy's sense of the sacred, of personal responsibility, and of an ethics of intentions. There are many influences on Cormac McCarthy's work. However, we argue that philosophers influenced by Plato, such as Eric Voegelin and Simone Weil, provide the best entry into Cormac McCarthy's dark and labyrinthine world and to his spiritual sense.[8] For one can never understand how to make the things of God and man of one piece without accepting what Voegelin termed the paradox of consciousness. That paradox is central to

McCarthy's Border Trilogy. It also can be seen in his other western novels, *Blood Meridian* and *No Country for Old Men*. A theory of consciousness based on that paradox, on the belief that human beings exist in the *metaxy*, in the experience (for *metaxy* is an experience, not a place) of living in-between two realities—one of will and intention and the other of the ineffable pull of something that is real but not a thing in the physical sense—undergirds each of McCarthy's stories within stories.

Certainly, recognition of the need for attunement of all levels of reality to some ground of being—some comprehensive reality that transcends the world of things—and the ability of language to evoke an understanding of that common and comprehensive reality—are the common threads that bind together *All the Pretty Horses, The Crossing,* and *Cities of the Plain*. In them, McCarthy calls for answerability and witness (participation in the one tale) on the part of human beings who understand themselves as participants and co-creators of reality rather than lords of creation. Yes, humans are beings with reason and will. However, each work suggests that as important as each individual story is, all stories take place in the theatre of transcendence. Thus, "Ultimately every man's path is every other. There are no separate journeys . . . there is no other tale to tell."[9] It is that tale which is the ultimate reality to which human thought and action must be attuned and which human language and politics must seek to evoke. The Border Trilogy rails against the politics of pure power and insists that politics requires a certain way of looking at the world—a certain paradoxical consciousness of human beings existing in the experience of *metaxy*.

Further, for McCarthy consciousness is not the same as interiority; consciousness is located not in us, but in the comprehending reality. Many McCarthy scholars equate consciousness and interiority.[10] That is a start, but McCarthy's understanding of consciousness is much more expansive. The Border Trilogy's understanding of consciousness is like that of Voegelin. Reality in both McCarthy and Voegelin is not an object of consciousness "but something in which consciousness occurs as an event of participation between partners in the community of being."[11] Both It-Reality, a reality full of non-physical things, and Thing-Reality, a reality where facts are facts, must participate in consciousness. Not only must intention and will be present, but also an understanding that will and intention form only part of life's story. Consciousness occurs in the border experience of both tensional poles of reality. For Voegelin and for McCarthy, human beings feel that border experience but often ignore it. Billy Parham and John Grady Cole are not learned or religious men. They do not philosophize; they have only their experience and that experience is of a life lived in-between. They live in-between cultures, nations, races (Billy's part Mexican heritage and John Grady and his two Mexican love relationships), beauty and the ugliness of human depravity, life and death, justice and the will to power, love and loss, the beginning and the beyond. They are not knowers; they are puzzlers. They ask questions about the existence of God, about the nature of the Real, and about justice that they cannot answer. Yet, they always answer the call to participate. They resist any one symbolism as wholly adequate to understanding reality and instead respond to some unseen metaphysical call.

They stand witness to what Voegelin describes as the luminosity of consciousness, the experience of participation in a drama of being encompassing all reality that shines brightly (but momentarily) into the physical world, a luminosity located somewhere in-between, at the edge of all the middles in which they exist. John Grady Cole cannot agree with the realist worldview of Dueña Alfonsa, the great-aunt and godmother of his lover, or of Eduardo, the pimp who "owns" the epileptic prostitute he seeks to save. Yet he also cannot accept completely the paradox of consciousness. Because he is "ardent-hearted" John Grady merely responds, often without understanding, to the pull of the luminous but mysterious Beyond. Billy crosses borders and responds to luminosity through friendship.

COMING OF AGE STORIES

McCarthy's Border Trilogy takes place in Mexico and the southwestern United States from 1939 (*The Crossing*) to 1952 (*Cities of the Plain*). Each book is set against the backdrop of a worldwide disorder, what Thucydides called a *kinesis*. Each evokes the same spirit of futility and despair that gripped Polybius in *The Histories* when he realized that the real purpose of Roman expansion during the Punic Wars was nothing more than the expansion itself, or, more bluntly "Why not?" By the end of the trilogy, the great Mexican revolutions have come and gone, the American conquest of the continent is complete, and the United States has just emerged victorious from the greatest war in history. The country is on the eve of becoming a nuclear superpower. But what does this mean in terms of order and consciousness? How does it change the traditional coming of age story? In McCarthy's vision—not for the better.

John Grady Cole is the heart of *All the Pretty Horses* and *Cities of the Plain*. In *All the Pretty Horses* he and a friend, Lacey Rawlins, ride away from the divorce of John's parents, the death of his grandfather, and the prospective sale by his mother of the grandfather's ranch. It is 1949 and John Grady is sixteen. They cross the Texas border to find adventure, romance, and meaning in Mexico. John Grady Cole possesses not only a seemingly magical ability to understand and train horses, but also great integrity and passion. Yet trouble befalls the two friends almost as soon as they leave home.

Jimmy Blevins, thirteen and riding a stolen horse, joins them. In turn, Blevins' gun and horse are stolen from him. Jimmy's first attempt to get them back leads to recovery of the horse, a chase, and Blevins' separation from John Grady and Lacey. A second attempt to recover the gun by Blevins alone leads to the killing of a Mexican official and Jimmy's ultimate capture. In the meantime, John Grady and Lacey get jobs at a Mexican ranch, the *Hacienda de Nuestra Señora Purísima Concepcion* owned by Don Héctor Rocha y Villareal, where he falls in love with the owner's daughter.

Crossing this forbidden ethnic and cultural border proves disastrous for both him and for his friend Rawlins. They are arrested, falsely accused of stealing horses, and sent to prison in Saltillo. On the way to prison they are reunited with Jimmy Blevins whom guards execute in the desert. In Saltillo they are abused and a hired killer attacks John Grady but is killed by him. Mysteriously released, John Grady returns to the ranch where he finds that Dueña Alfonsa has paid for their freedom once Alejandra has promised never to see John Grady again. In one final meeting, Alejandra says she will honor her promise to her great-aunt and leaves. John Grady goes after the Captain who took his and Lacey's horses and, retaking the horses, crosses back into Texas with them although chased and wounded by the corrupt Captain. He returns Lacey's horse to him and, finding that his father also has died, "rides on."

Billy Parham is the main character in *The Crossing*. In 1939 Billy, also sixteen, leaves home and makes three quixotic journeys across the border: first in an attempt to return a pregnant she-wolf to her home in the mountains; next, to pursue with his brother, Boyd, those who murdered their parents and stole their horses; and, finally, to find his brother who disappeared with a young Mexican girl encountered during their wanderings. Like John Grady Cole, Billy and Boyd Parham seem to meet violence, blood, and suffering more than meaning on these journeys. During Billy's first crossing the she-wolf is stolen by men to use in dog fights. Death in one of those fights is a certainty. To save her from the indignity of such a death, Billy kills her himself and returns home to find his parents murdered and his brother and himself orphans.

Billy crosses a second time, taking Boyd with him, to search for the horses stolen when their parents were killed. They find them, take them, but then are accused of stealing them. Boyd is shot but recovers and decides to leave Billy and remain in Mexico with a young Mexican girl they rescued during their search. Billy returns to New Mexico but crosses into Mexico a third time to find Boyd. He finds Boyd has died and that he and his brother have become the stuff of heroic *corridos*, ballads. Billy searches for Boyd's grave and returns his body home. Crossing the border with Boyd's bones, Billy views in the distance the light from the Trinity Project. He is home, but he is not Home. Riding into town he is a stranger to all who see him. A stray dog approaches him. Afraid of any connection after the deaths of the she-wolf, his parents, and Boyd, Billy shoos him away.

However, Billy's conscience won't let him rest. He searches for the stray, cannot find it, and sits crying in the road. He has become the *huérfano* (orphan) an old Mexican warned him he might become. Billy, like John Grady Cole, rides on, seemingly unwilling to "make for himself some place in the world" so that he would not become "estranged from men and so ultimately from himself."[12] Still, the old Mexican was correct in telling Billy that he contained "a largeness of spirit which men could see . . . and that the world would need him even as he needed the world for they were one."[13] Billy becomes a wanderer with a strong ethical core built from interaction with a consciousness he cannot accept, but also cannot ignore.

The most overtly metaphysical of the three books in the trilogy, *The Crossing* sees Billy encounter three important figures in understanding McCarthy's sense of life in the middle: an ex-priest, a man who had his eyes sucked out for participating in the Mexican Revolution, and a gypsy. Each has a story that stays with Billy and influences him even though he does not understand them. Billy remains an unwitting participant in consciousness—always torn between a desire to believe the real is what he can see and the continued irruption into his life of ineffable mystery.

John and Billy's lives come together in *Cities of the Plain*. It is 1952 and Billy is twenty-nine and John Grady nineteen. They work together on Mac McGovern's ranch near Alamogordo, New Mexico. The ranch's continued existence is precarious because the older model of cattle ranching is dying and because the US government is considering taking ranches in the vicinity to expand its nuclear test site. When the men have free time, they cross the border between El Paso and Juárez to visit its bars and brothels. On one of these visits John Grady Cole meets a young prostitute named Magdalena and falls in love. John Grady's competitor for Magdalena is her pimp, Eduardo. John Grady's attempt to marry Magdalena and its effect on Billy drive the plot. After restoring a small cabin with the help of Billy and other ranch hands, Billy and John Grady cross the border to Ciudad Juárez to free Magdalena and bring her back to New Mexico to live. Before they can arrive, Eduardo has Magdalena killed. Then Eduardo confronts John Grady in a knife fight. John Grady kills Eduardo but is mortally wounded himself. Billy finds John Grady just before his death.

CONSCIOUSNESS AND THE ORDER OF REALITY

The quests of John Grady Cole and Billy Parham provide insights into the "order of reality." Billy is the Everyman critics find him to be, just not in the way they expect. Much of the literature on McCarthy's novels stresses the view that his main characters believe that freedom is the ability to create one's own narrative through the control of language, people, and events. They argue that his characters attempt to control reality through the exercise of their reason and facility with language. The opposite is true of the Border Trilogy. Those who, like Eduardo and Duéna Alfonsa, attempt control through language neither convince nor appeal. McCarthy's message is not that we must accommodate ourselves to reality as hard facts and power politics. Neither is his point that Billy and Boyd Parham or John Grady Cole suffers in the world because of a failure to realize the mistakenness of any idealism. They are endlessly disappointed, but never cynical. They find that neither life nor the world always bends to human will and intention and recoil from the examples of freedom as will to power they meet along the way.

Billy Parham and John Grady Cole are far from being intellectual in their choices and actions. However, at some gut level, they understand that human beings are bound up with each other and with all aspects of life (especially the natural world). Transcendent mystery, humanity, world, and society form one interconnected experience. Their initial choices—John Grady's to leave for Mexico in hope of continuing a cowboy lifestyle that he associates, somewhat romantically, with the order of nature and the mystery of the old Comanche trail, and Billy's quixotic attempt to capture a pregnant she-wolf and return her across the mountains to Mexico—mark them for the rest of their lives as participants in some mystery of being they barely glimpse. From love for his brother and a sense of justice, Billy goes back. For friendship he crosses the border between Texas and Mexico with John Grady Cole first in search of a good time and later to support John Grady's disastrous attempt to free the prostitute Magdalena. They puzzle over the existence of a provident God, but they always respond to the call of some Beyond expressed as justice. The order of nature they see around them and the mysterious pull they feel from some luminous Beyond, prevents them from total atheism. Throughout they believe in friendship, community, justice, and love. They remain men of order—an order that goes beyond that glorified in either the romanticized myth of the cowboy or in modernity's myth of consciousness as will and intention.

McCarthy's western novels strongly suggest that human beings need to re-imagine their understanding of freedom. Freedom is not the ability to control people, the physical world, events, and so forth, to produce some end in accordance with a human will. Freedom is human choice that takes place within the constraints of necessity, the web of life that stretches from a Beginning that human beings cannot know to an End they cannot predict. And where is this web-of-life conducted? In the middle, always in a middle touched by both human choice and some Beyond which is not a thing even though it becomes luminous from time to time in everyday things and relationships. When Billy looks into the eyes of the she-wolf he sees that luminosity—that place where everything fits together. Consciousness becomes luminous in the kindness of peasants, the wisdom of the Judge to whom John Grady confesses his experiences in Mexico, the ex-priest's ramblings about God, the gypsy's warning about the fleetingness of life and fame as he tells the story of the father who searches for the remnants of the plane crash in which his son died, the Mexican Stranger's dream of mortality and immortality, and the warnings of two blind men. In effect, for McCarthy, as for Plato, freedom is the ability to choose whether to participate in all of reality and in the one tale. Without such an understanding of freedom, a person is cut off from reality and becomes alienated from everything and everyone. In McCarthy's novels being an orphan is the ultimate alienation from self and others. It is failure to participate in all of reality. Billy is warned about that alienation in *The Crossing* and almost succumbs after John Grady's death. "He rode on," becoming the Wanderer. Yet, despite almost fifty years of wandering after John's death, he is never fully severed from a reality that is larger than human will.

Implicit in Cormac McCarthy's Border Trilogy is an argument that contemporary political philosophies are destructive of the very human flourishing they purport to engender. McCarthy sets his stories in the West, but he is not mourning the passing of a lifestyle; his tragedies mourn the rejection of the human condition. In his works the reader sees a movement going on in the soul that parallels the structure of history as an intermediate reality. As does St. Augustine, McCarthy reminds us here that human constructions are not all that is real. He suggests that human creations and relationships are limited, ephemeral, and rooted in humanity's fallen condition. Cormac McCarthy's vision of consciousness is quite different from that of most contemporary political theorists, whether conservative, liberal, or postmodern. McCarthy holds out neither personal autonomy nor self-creation as the goal. His response to life's contingency, mystery, and pain is not self-protection, rage, or despair. Life is not meaningless in McCarthy's works; life is ordered by death as it is in Plato's "Myth of Er" from *Republic* and the "Judgment of the Dead" from *Gorgias*. This is what the old trapper told Billy he would see in the eyes of the she-wolf.

There is much in these stories that mirrors the work of the French mystic and philosopher Simone Weil—especially her thoughts on life in the *metaxy*, necessity, grace, and freedom. Weil believed that human beings live in the *metaxy*, Plato's metaphor for the ground of human-divine interaction, the tensional push-pull of existence that reflects the order of the universe and provides the setting for a quest for the good that will never reach an end. We cannot escape the *metaxy* because it is reality. And because it is reality, the *metaxy* is cluttered and messy. For her, the best tool for a messy reality is not ideology. She argued that ideology is closed, asserting it has the truth and everyone should acknowledge it. Rather philosophy is the best tool because it follows the pull of transcendence on the imperishable part of every human being because philosophy is open and seeks the truth while agreeing with Thomas Mann that the truth is "endlessly far." [14]

An inexorable part of experiencing life in the middle is necessity; it is the backdrop of human life. As Plato put it: "From the extremities stretched the spindle of Necessity, by which all the revolutions are turned." [15] Necessity frightens humanity. They perceive it as an arbitrary, fearsome, unintelligible, and uncontrollable *strength* controlling their lives. Human beings will never overpower Necessity. They can transform it through love in the form of *agape*, the choice to care for others. *Agape* is unconditional love that is a matter of hearing a command and being willing to carry it out. Necessity conditions the melody line so that human existence is part of the order of the world. Individuals compose their songs; necessity merely sets some limits to the composition. In the end each selects their Demon through the choices they make. For, "A demon will not select you, but you will choose a demon. Let him who gets the first lot make the first choice of a life to which he will be bound by necessity. Virtue is without a master; as he honors or dishonors her, each will have more or less of her. The blame belongs to him who chooses; god is blameless." [16] For Weil, it is *agape* that gives human beings choices — that makes them free. This sort of love is "a direction, not a state of the soul," [17] manifested as love of neighbor, love of the order of the world, and love of religious practice. It is participation in a drama of being whose plot (and each person's role in it) one will never totally know. As Betty suggests in the final moments of *Cities of the Plain*, no one is anything special. *Agape* demands human beings love each other anyway. For Weil, humanity is most capable of choice when its members love and cease looking only at themselves. It is then that humans experience freedom.

In the end, Weil argues, power is love and love is consent to participation in the one story of life in the theater of God. Here it is important to remember that for Weil, the love of religious practice means a commitment to *dikē* (righteousness, justice). It is not synonymous with acceptance of the Christian God. For Weil, all religions contain "treasures of the purest gold" [18] and God is not a "person" who exists in some place one could call "heaven." Her life took her beyond the symbol of God to the mystery that underlies it.

Consciousness is that luminous moment when one becomes aware of both the reality of intention and the reality of the human experience as predicates, a part of some drama of being — what McCarthy calls "our predicate life" in *Cities of the Plain*. Consciousness occurs at those moments when human beings catch a glimpse of the joint participation of a mysterious nonphysical reality and of humanity in the world. These are the moments of grace. Human beings pull those glimpses of luminosity into their lives through remembering and acting on them in their personal and political lives. These moments of consciousness are the source of

any true order, an order that has both personal and political consequences. These luminous moments both allow human beings to participate in the story despite its mystery and contingency and are their reward for participation.

This is the understanding of consciousness as a paradoxical interaction of human beings and transcendence that illuminates *All the Pretty
Horses, The Crossing,* and *Cities of the Plain.* Reality as a thing intended
confronts the mystery and contingency of life. In the Border Trilogy the
"seeing," who often are physically blind, understand that most people
see dream worlds rather than reality. "Between their acts and their cere-
monies lies the world and in this world the storms blow and the trees
twist in the wind and all the animals that man has made go to and fro.
Yet this world men do not see. They see the acts of their own hands . . . ,
but the world is invisible to them."[19] They cannot see the proverbial
forest for the trees.

During their journeys, Billy and John meet strange messengers that
cease to be strange when the reader finally realizes that they "speak" the
paradoxical word of some transcendent mystery that is tremendously
thick and theophanic and at the same time very human, small, silent, and
clear. These messengers, who see clearly the reality invisible to most, call
Billy and John to consciousness. The priest believed that "the truth may
often be carried about by those who themselves remain unaware of it."[20]
Everywhere they go, they are asked to participate in some mystery. They
have their own goals and plans, but they cannot escape the call to participate in transcendence. At every turn they find evidence of these words:
"The world takes its form hourly by a weighing of things at hand." Try as
one might, there is no way of seeing what the future holds, for "We have
only God's law, and the wisdom to follow it if we will."[21] They always
answer the call.

In the works of Cormac McCarthy, the world always is the same and
always tells the same story. Humans are challenged to understand the
fact that reality "is no longer an object of consciousness but the something in which consciousness occurs as an event of participation between
partners in the community of being."[22] Or, as the old man tells Billy in
The Crossing, if he wants to catch the wolf he must find that place "where
the acts of God and those of man are of a piece."[23] Consciousness is
participation in an all-encompassing reality that consists of the primor-
dial community of ineffable mystery and humanity's need to construct
understandable and meaningful lives, worlds, and societies.

All three stories within the Border Trilogy occur in some middle place
where moments of luminosity are remembered and either acted upon or
ignored. As the protagonists proceed, they often appear mute and confused among the many deformed states of consciousness they encounter.
They seem like helpless toys in a world of dogma, atomic testing, and
war. But John and Billy are not helpless at all. They encounter help every-

where. That help consistently takes the form of a call to them to be awake and aware and to participate with others in the story of order and disorder going on around them. They are constantly called to consciousness — to stand for order against disorder.

CONSCIOUSNESS AND POLITICS

How human beings define reality has political implications. If the real is only physical and human beings are no more than a random array of atoms, then a society's politics will be David Easton's authoritative allocation of resources. The result often is disorder, oppression, and injustice. What the Border Trilogy teaches us is that the field of politics is the soul of man. Individuals know their "selves" as part of a story. Individuals create themselves, as individuals and collectivities, through participation in the story. The mysterious sacred is the ground where the story takes place. McCarthy suggests that if communities participate in the paradox; they will be more orderly. Simone Weil provides some insight into the effect of consciousness on communal life. She saw politics as "forming an art governed by composition on a multiple plane." [24] For her, composition required balancing "a series of relations and mediations between God, humans, and matter." [25] Thus, politics is the attempt to harmonize the mental, physical, and moral/ethical planes to allow the individual the widest scope for thoughtful, creative, caring action through love of the order of the world, love of religious practice, and love of neighbor. Above all, balancing the various planes encompassed by the political requires individuals to "give up being the center of the world in imagination." [26] Is not that what McCarthy implies in the Border Trilogy? Is that not where the things of God and man are of a piece?

Where and how do human beings find order? They find order through nurturing an ability to understand there is only one story. Their story is part of it; their lives *are* only an instant and that their path has been trodden by millions in the past and many more millions to come. They realize that all stories ultimately are one. They must make those lives and stories what they can. Participation in the one story, the drama of being, makes demands. One of those demands is that human beings stand witness for one another.

Stories founded on the paradox of consciousness show their hearers and readers whether the storyteller is awake and aware or asleep and blind. In the Border Trilogy the folks who live closest to nature, closest to necessity, closest to death seem to be the most awake and aware. They see best the interplay of transcendent reality and human will in life and the impossibility of pulling apart the threads of the story to analyze whose part is whose. The point of looking into oneself is imaginatively to see both the forest and the trees — to learn how one's individual story affects and is affected by other stories and, ultimately, by what McCarthy calls the one tale. In doing so, individuals achieve reflective distance and are better able to remember the moments of irruption of the Beyond into the physical world and act upon them. Without some understanding that life takes place within the experience of *metaxy*, it is very difficult to achieve that perspective. In extreme situations, an individual may fall into ignorance, resistance, or Gnosticism. It appears that for McCarthy those individuals become as truly orphaned metaphysically as is Billy Parham.

McCarthy most eloquently summarizes all this in the Epilogue to *Cities of the Plain*. Like Plato's Myth of Er, the epilogue is a carefully constructed work on the art of measuring life from the perspective of death. And if the measure of life is death, the measuring line is immortality. The story of Er is a symbol of man, existing in time and experiencing himself as participating in the timeless.

The Epilogue is immediately preceded by the death of John Grady Cole. Billy holds his friend in his arms and calls out to God to look at what has happened and see. Billy wants to know the reason for the meaningless death of his good friend. He wants an answer. He wants to know why a provident God would allow the existence of cruelty and evil. But no one looks and no one provides answers. The chapter ends with a group of children crossing the road and the town going about its business as if nothing had happened. For Billy, John's death seems to demonstrate the futility of participation and the importance of resistance. Nothing ever has changed or ever will change.

In both *The Crossing* and *Cities of the Plain* Billy wants to stand outside the drama of being and not get involved. Involvement hurts. He wants to think people's lives are made easier, less dangerous, less complicated by resistance to the call. But he is too awake, too in-tune with reality, and too honest to be fooled. Billy wants to forget, but he always stands witness. However, he is never comfortable with either choice. Thus, he never seems to find a place in the world. Billy can never fully commit himself to the middle. But he is wise enough to love the men who can and do. He does honor their path and listen to their tales. He never realizes it, but he carries order within him and shares it freely with those whose hearts he recognizes whether human or beast. But he is never at peace and he is always alone.

After John's death Billy kept riding, "Till he was old."[27] This is consciousness as madness in the sense of the Aeschylean *nosos*, a loss of personal and social order through loss of contact with reality. The atomic testing is a reminder that prudence as wisdom is reduced to the maxim "if something can be done, it shall be done." Where in this madhouse is there room for a rational discussion of immortality that presupposes the very contact with reality that has been lost? Perhaps, somewhere in the middle of Arizona, underneath the overpass of an interstate, where cranes fly north from Mexico. There Billy meets his messenger, his Er, in the person of "The Mexican Stranger." The stranger will reinforce a lesson from the old trapper Billy sought out in *The Crossing*: "the wolf is a being of great order and it knows what men do not; that there is no order in the world save that which death put there."[28] Billy has been chasing the meaning of the old trapper's words for years; he will receive an answer in the story told by this man.

The stranger seems to just materialize—without history, without introduction, without beginning or end. They begin a conversation about death as they share some crackers under the rumbling traffic. The stranger said that in the middle of his life he had drawn a map that he hoped would show him his life's pattern and how he should continue. He thought that such a map would aid him in planning the rest of his life.[29] Through his map, the stranger tried to assert control. He believed instrumental reason and good planning would result in a straight line to his goal. In his dream, he found that this was futile.

From this intense meditation of remembrance, the Stranger only concludes that it is very hard to see things as they are rather than as one would want them to be. The wisdom he offered Billy was that, although planning ultimately is futile and much of life is beyond human control, one can learn a great deal from experience by freely participating in the story rather than by trying to write its script completely on one's own. To Billy, this is nonsense. Human beings see what is right in front of them. The Stranger, however, disagrees.

Now the reader knows where Billy has been throughout The Trilogy—conflicted. He has thought of himself as firmly rooted in the world of will and intention. Yet, he acts ardently when friendship or a sense of justice requires it *despite* the spiritual wasteland through which he has been riding. And now, at seventy-eight, he still cannot *see* in the sense of the "deep-seeing" of Heraclitus and Aeschylus. He will act, but he cannot commit to the paradox of consciousness. That lack of commitment has eaten him alive. Viewing himself as a subject ordering a world full of objects, he accounts himself a failure.

The stranger continues by telling Billy a dream, a dream that made him know it was the middle of his life and draw the map that he thought could show him where he had been and where his future lay. In the dream a traveler is making his way through the mountains. He comes to a certain demonic place, like the spirited and numinous location at the end of Plato's Myth of Er, where pilgrims take their rest. The place was high in the mountains, sky and flat land's in-between. And at the place was a table of rock that had been used to slaughter victims to appease the gods. In the end, the old man observes "I'm guessing every man is more than he supposes."[30] Each of us is more than a subject, more than an object. Life, the stranger says, is participation in some dream or drama from outside the rims and edges of the world that is also a place in a dream or drama. By the stranger's method of accounting, Billy is more than the failure he supposes himself to be.

But during the night the dream man is having a dream. What kind of reality can a dream within a dream possess? Not much, thinks Billy, who considers it superstition. The stranger points out that the map is more than a picture. It is an effort through remembrance to constitute the full reality of consciousness. But consciousness is shrouded in the very mystery it seeks to comprehend. The missing piece is knowledge of the point at which "the seen becomes the remembered. . . . And yet it is all we have."[31] The best we ever will be able to muster is memory of truths within us but long forgotten.

Yet that might be enough. Now the dream traveler finds himself at the intersection of the paradox of necessity and free will, of Thing-Reality and It-Reality. The Stranger insists that the dream traveler is real, that he must have a history even though neither the Stranger nor Billy knows what it is. Further the Stranger's story suggests that the history of the figure in his dream, the reality which grounds that history and gives it substance "is not different from yours and mine for it is the predicate life of men that assures us of our own reality and that of all about us."[32] "This predicate life" is the tension between human choice and blind Necessity. It is *only* a paradox and that paradoxical juxtaposition is the tang and smart of reality, which stands ever ready to be penultimately pulverized and hypostatized by our incomprehension or unwillingness to participate in its flux. This is what keeps Billy "movin' on" or perhaps the "movin' on" is the assertion of the paradox and the unconscious effort to escape the imaginative blindness that has robbed him of "deep seeing."

The story continues as the man on the mountain composed himself for sleep. There was a storm in the mountains and the lightning cracked and the wind moaned. In the flare of the lightning the traveler saw a procession descending through the rocky arroyos singing some kind of chant or prayer. In a long passage the procession is described in language that evokes the lines of *The Republic* where the dead are assembled in a great plain, with dreadful and beautiful sounds of sirens singing their single note, all together sounding the harmony of the cosmos. The traveler finds himself in the position of a sacrificial victim, is beheaded, and does not die. Here the Stranger evokes the experience of immortalizing that has a historical index going at least back to the ancient Egyptians and who knows how far into the paleolithicum and beyond.

Billy still wonders whether the Mexican Stranger's tale is just a "made-up" story. The Stranger responds that the story of the dream traveler is like every other story because all stories begin with a question.[33] A why? A what if? A why did that happen? The stranger has told Billy how myth is both an expression of the experience of participating in immortalizing and part of a story told by an unseen other, who seems bent on obliterating human beings as subjects to involve them in some mysterious but hard-felt process of transfiguration. That is why myth remains important in the world. And it is the experience of immortalizing (living into whatever is immortal in the universe) that keeps humanity poised on the edge of myth, ready to be drawn into its depth, which flows out of eternity into time, into consciousness, into the one story of all humanity. The dream traveler finally saw that every man was always and eternally in the middle of his journey, whatever his years or whatever distance he had come. He thought he saw in the world's silence a great conspiracy and he knew that he must be a part of that conspiracy and that he had already moved beyond his captors and their plans. This is the moment of consciousness—of conspiracy or "breathing together" between transcendent mystery and the human desire for facts.

And then, like Er, the Stranger has a message to transmit, a saving tale from a demonic place. After this long meditation on an intra-cosmic experience of immortality, the reader is taken quite off guard by its power. "Every man's death is a standing in for every other. . . . Do you love him, that man? Will you honor the path he has taken? Will you listen to his tale?"[34] No one will escape death. In that one characteristic, one individual is just like every other. The only way to lessen the fear of death, then, is to love every person because every human is "all men and stands in the dock for us until our own time comes."[35] Is there any real choice but to stand for the person who stands for you, to listen to their story, to love them?

Up until now the Epilogue has been mythic in the sense of some ineffable presence writing the story with whatever bits of material ranged through the unconscious of the writer. Now, suddenly, the strangers' myth becomes the message of the Gospel written in the hearts and actions of actual humans, lived out where two worlds meet—or possibly Camus' conclusion that all humans are the first man.

The Trilogy ends with a simple mystic insight of a God *like* a woman yet not a woman, full of love and grace. Billy, who has been taken in by a family in New Mexico, is about to go to bed. The wife, Betty, comes in and asks him if he wants a glass of water. Billy assures her that he is fine, and Betty takes his hand: "Gnarled, rope scarred, speckled from the sun and years of it. . . . There was map enough for men to read. There God's plenty of signs and wonders to make a landscape. To make a world."[36] As she left Billy said: "I'm not what you think I am. I ain't nothin'."[37] She answers that she does know who he is, and she does "know why." [38] I ain't nothin'." That is the same thing John Grady Cole tells the Judge with whom he shares his adventures in Mexico. The Judge responds to him the same way Betty does to Billy.

The Border Trilogy is an artist's meditative exercise on existence and consciousness as an in-between reality. Rather than hypostatize one pole or the other of consciousness as *the reality*—rather than treat only one aspect of reality's presence as all of it—McCarthy portrays the characters in the trilogy as existing in a tension between life and death, being and becoming. Through McCarthy's mythopoesis, the reader can see politics as the process of people living together in their attempt to participate in that mystery and question. "The events of the waking world . . . are forced upon us. . . . It falls to us to weigh and sort and order these events. It is we who assemble them into the story which is us."[39] Human beings cannot live in the middle without living with each other. They make not only personal stories, but also communal ones.

What the traveler in the old Stranger's dream saw was that human life was brief indeed, especially when seen from the perspective of time's eternity. Therefore, "every man was always and eternally in the middle of his journey."[40] And what human beings learn from their individual stories is part of that middle place. Every human story begins with some question. Each of those stories must bear witness: ". . . a life can never be its own. Only the witness has power to take its measure. It is lived for the other only."[41] What would a political order look like that allowed itself to participate in the paradox of consciousness? What semblance would it bear to the feverish movement of war, revolution, and ceaseless diversion of the past three centuries? Aristotle may have put the whole thing best when he noted that as he got older, the truth of the myth became more and more enjoyable and edifying.

In his masterpiece of mythopoesis, Cormac McCarthy has demonstrated consciousness as the central issue of a theory of politics. McCarthy pushes his readers to move from the obliteration of consciousness that is part of the disorder dominating contemporary politics to a place where they again can raise the question of humanity's mysterious participation in a reality that brings forth the turkey and deer, the flowers and birds, the jagged rims of the world, and ultimately humanity and human consciousness. The Border Trilogy demonstrates how the personal truly is the political. Both the personal and political rely upon and are tied together through the paradox of consciousness—through awareness of life as an adventure of decision that takes place surrounded by some ineffable reality, through understanding that wisdom may sometimes be the gift of the powerless, the alien, and the outsider. It is a story within a story—a composition on a multiple plane and any truly new politics that could replace classical liberalism would have to accept that fact and try to find balance and proportion among all the planes of existence. Implicit in the paradox of consciousness is the idea that the Real calls human beings to understand that they are one piece of a larger whole and toward community with others—to the political in the sense that Weil describes and toward obligations of solidarity in order to find a balance between authority and community. It calls citizens to build societies based on all levels of reality, as messy as that will be, but not to theocracy, because the ineffable mystery cannot be pinned down or institutionalized. The paradox of consciousness pushes us toward individual order and individual order is a prerequisite of communal order.

How does Cormac McCarthy represent life? Look into the eyes of the she-wolf. Listen to the tale of the Mexican Stranger. Neither the wolf nor the Stranger offers the politics of a contemporary Western liberal democracy that honors the ideas McCarthy disputes—consciousness as purely human will and intention backed by power. The Border Trilogy consistently reinforces the idea that consciousness is the keystone of an orderly society—a consciousness in which human beings live (often uncomfortably) in-between and must consider two tensional poles of It-Reality and Thing-Reality and face demands for participation and acceptance of obligations of solidarity. If consciousness is the keystone of any myth, then the Border Trilogy asserts the need to replace liberal democracy's reliance on will, intention, rugged individualism, and power with the paradox of living in-between with its call out of isolation and into participation. To respond to this call, however, it is necessary to include "presence" in the one tale that encompasses all humanity's stories within stories.

NOTES

1. An earlier version of this chapter appeared as Margaret Hrezo and Nicholas Pappas, "The Things of God and Man: The Paradox of Consciousness in Cormac McCarthy's Border Trilogy," *Voegelin View* (April 2, 2018). Available at https://voegelinview.com/author/margaret-hrezo-and-nick-pappas/. The authors also thank their colleague Craig Waggaman for his time discussing these works with us and his own writing on the subject.

2. Modernity rests on four foundations. First, "community" means the modern state, an artificial creation designed to meet the needs of the rulers (whether one, few, or many). See Machiavelli, Hobbes, Rousseau, Marx, Rawls. Next, "justice" is a convention. Designed to mask the harsh realities of power politics, it consists in the practice of actions useful to the greatest number and the decisions made according to accepted procedures. See Hobbes, Locke, Helvetius. Third, there is no "Good." God is either a human artifact or the deists' clock winder. See Hobbes, Helvetius. Finally, human beings are motivated only by self-interest, fear, and the will to power. Isolated and inwardly directed, we are morally neutral creatures who seek meaning in the world. See Hobbes, Locke, Helvetius, Comte. Modern ideologies, whether liberalism, conservatism, or Marxism, and the idolization of science, instrumental reason, and the state blind humanity to the tension inherent in living and confine us to a world defined by the limited categories of political realism.

3. Cormac McCarthy, *Cities of the Plain* (New York: Vintage Books, 1993), 280; hereafter abbreviated *COTP*.

4. Stephen Greenblatt, *The Swerve: How the World Became Modern* (New York: W.W. Norton & Company, 2011).

5. Ibid., 5

6. See, for example, Edwin T., "'Go to Sleep': Dreams and Visions in the Border Trilogy," in Edwin T. Arnold and Dianne C. Luce, ed. *A Cormac McCarthy Companion: The Border Trilogy* (Jackson: University Press of Mississippi, 2001, 37-72 and Nick Monk, "An Impulse to Action, an Undefined Want: Modernity, Flight, and Crisis in the Border Trilogy and *Blood Meridian*" in *Sacred Violence, Vol 2: Cormac McCarthy's*

Western Novels, ed. Wade Hall and Rick Wallach (University of Texas El Paso: Texas Western Press, 2002), 83-103.

7. See, for example, Matthew Potts, *Cormac McCarthy and the Signs of Sacrament: Literature, Theology, and the Moral of Stories* (New York: Bloomsbury Press, 2015) and Robert Metcalf, "Religion and the 'Religious': Cormac McCarthy and John Dewey," *The Journal of Speculative Philosophy* 31.1 (2017): 135-154, accessed November 2, 2017, https://muse.jhu.edu/. For a primer on postsecularism see John A. McClure, *Partial Faiths: Postsecular Fiction in the Age of Pynchon and Morrison* (Athens: University of Georgia Press, 2007).

8. For more on Plato's influence on Cormac McCarthy, see Ty Hawkins, *Cormac McCarthy's Philosophy* (Palgrave Macmillan, 2017).

9. McCarthy, *TC*, 156-57.

10. See, for example, Lydia R. Cooper, *No More Heroes: Narrative Perspective and Morality in Cormac McCarthy* (Baton Rouge: Louisiana State University Press, 2011).

11. Eric Voegelin, *Order and History, Volume V: In Search of Order*, introduction by Ellis Sandoz (Baton Rouge: Louisiana State University Press, 1987), 3.

12. Cormac McCarthy, *The Crossing* (New York: Vintage Books, 1994), 134; hereafter abbreviated as *TC*.

13. Id.

14. Thomas Mann, *Joseph the Provider* (New York: Alfred A. Knopf, 1944), 133.

15. Plato, *The Republic*, Trans. Allan Bloom (New York: Basic Books, 1968), 616d.

16. Plato, *Republic*, 617d.

17. Simone Weil, *Waiting for God* (New York: Harper and Row, 1973), 135.

18. Simone Weil, *The Need for Roots* (New York: Harper-Colophon, 1971), 243.

19. Ibid., 46.

20. Ibid., 158.

21. McCarthy, *COTP*, 195.

22. Voegelin, *In Search of Order*, 15.

23. *TC*, 46-47..

24. Weil, *The Need for Roots*, 216.

25. Diogenes Allen and Eric O. Springsted, *Spirit, Nature, and Community: Issues in the Thought of Simone Weil* (Albany: State University of New York Press, 1994), 44.

26. Weil, *Waiting for God*,160.

27. Ibid., 264.

28. McCarthy, *TC*, 46.

29. McCarthy, *COTP*, 268.

30. Ibid., 271.

31. Ibid., 274.

32. Id.

33. Ibid., 277.

34. Ibid., 288.

35. Id.

36. Ibid., 291-292.

37. Id.

38. Id.

39. Ibid., 283.

40. Ibid., 293.

41. McCarthy, *TC*, 158.

THREE

Do You Believe in God?

Presence, the Anxiety of Existence, and the Myth of
America as a City upon a Hill in Thomas Pynchon's
Mason & Dixon

Thomas Pynchon, like Cormac McCarthy in The Border Trilogy, writes myths of quest, self-discovery, and the paradox of consciousness to attack the prevailing myths of contemporary life. McCarthy replaces one myth of reality with another that he believes better fits human experience. In *Mason & Dixon*, Pynchon's concern is grace and its implications for the myth of America as a "city upon a hill." Pynchon's mythopoesis reinforces McCarthy's image of life lived in the *metaxy*—in the middle of some ineffable mystery or drama of being that demands recognition in all spheres of life, including the political. The corollary of the paradox of consciousness is that grace, the presence and possibility that accompanies mystery, pervades every aspect of life and is available to all. For Plato, "the Being of the cosmos derives its existence and essence . . . from the presence, from the Parousia, of the divine Beyond."[1] In fact, grace becomes the pre-condition for participation in the *metaxy*. As Voegelin wrote, there is a "flux of presence endowing all the phases—past, present, and future—of external time with the structural dimension of an indelible present."[2] Without acceptance of grace one may believe that human life is part of some drama of being, but one will be unable to act on that belief. Grace, that momentary experience of the numinous (that which evokes awe and wonder), provides the necessary fuel for action in response to understanding.[3] Call it grace; call it something else. Without it, any idea of bringing metaphysics to bear in the real world is dead on arrival.

In the grocery store parking lot one day Kai asked: "Do you believe in God? What God do you believe in?" He averred a preference for the Greek gods over those of the Romans, the Norse, and the Christian because they seem to interact more with human beings. They were present. He recognized the presence of some ubiquitous and ineffable mystery in the world. If one accepts the paradox of consciousness, then some aspect of nonphysical reality always is present, and always demands respect. Christians might call it grace. However, grace (a moment when the world lights up and presence is felt) is slippery, and one would be wrong to consider grace a concept or a thing. That, perhaps, is the greatest flaw in Paul's epistles and is the difficulty with many of the myriad definitions of grace. Definitions transform grace into a specimen on a tray. It is too easy to get caught in differentiating between actual grace and sanctifying grace, earned and unearned grace, and cheap grace and costly grace.[4] Even if such distinctions are made and communicated successfully, they really mean nothing to human beings' lived experience of grace.

If it *is* anything, grace is the experience of transcendence and mystery that allows a human being to be unconscious of self and participate fully in the drama of being. Free and permeating all of existence, it is evidence of human praise for joint participation of the human and the mysterious Beyond in the *metaxy*. Grace is not a physical force, but it is a force that one can feel with their senses—a real substantive experience and realization that participation in the drama of being is Tolkien's joyous turn. Like the dynamo, it does little of itself, but it powers action. It is easy to misread that force as emotion and ignore it. It is grace that allows one to successfully reach what Flaubert called "the soul of things." It is not earned, and it cannot be bought. It is a part of existence in the world—the gift of the presence that surrounds all human life and is always open to human recognition. In the end, grace is a word that human beings have devised to evoke the experience of presence—the irruption of nonphysical reality into the physical world, an experience of presence that motivates human beings toward *dikē*.

Aldous Huxley suggested that the quest for grace is humankind's essential problem.[5] But is the problem the difficulty of the quest or the fact that human beings view questing as the only way to find grace? The search for grace indicates how little human beings understand and/or accept the paradox of consciousness. They search for grace as if they were searching for some lost object, like one's glasses or the Holy Grail. When human beings search for grace, they search for an experience that has not been lost. Grace does not need to be found. It is in plain view if only people open themselves to participation in the drama of being. In the world of purpose and intention, human beings must search for what is hidden, undiscovered, or lost. Mysteries exist to be solved and human beings strive courageously and conscientiously to solve them. In the reality of nonexistent experiences, mystery cannot be eliminated.

Openness to mystery, however, does allow a kind of seeing that momentarily dissolves mystery and allows the light of understanding to shine through it. Only faith, hope, and love—the orienting forces of the psyche—allow that openness to the ground which enables understanding. Without them, as Heraclitus knew, human beings are blind sleepwalkers who cannot see the common world of reason and, instead, live in the private dream world of their passions. *Mason & Dixon* suggests vast numbers of humans (including men and women of reason and science) remain blind to the existence and power of grace despite its ubiquitous presence. Marilynne Robinson intuits that much when she writes concerning the later plays of Shakespeare that he views grace as "an intimation of a great reality of another order."[6] Grace is the symbol humans use for the experience of presence; it is neither a concept nor an object.

Few contemporary authors evoke *parousia,* the all-pervasive presence of transcendent mystery and the grace that accompanies it, better than does Thomas Pynchon. That may seem an odd thing to say about an author often considered cynical, ribald, and brimming over with postmodern irony. Pynchon never withdraws from the emptiness, nastiness, and horror of the common world that both attracts and repels human beings. His stories even play with them. However, his play is very serious and, like the anthropologist Gregory Bateson, the reader finds in Pynchon's novels the belief that grace is all around us, in the form of the presence of some ineffable nonphysical reality, and attainable through integrating the reasons of the heart with those of the rational mind.[7] Or as Simone Weil would put it, we just need to genuinely pay genuine attention, on all levels, to the people, things, and spaces surrounding us.

Critics consider Thomas Pynchon one of America's best authors. *V.* won the Faulkner Award for best first novel in 1963. *Gravity's Rainbow* shared the National Book Award in 1974. As Tom Robbins wrote, "Mark Twain opined that the difference between the perfect word and the one that is merely adequate is the difference between lightening and a lightning bug . . .Thomas Pynchon has got both hands on the thunderbolt machine."[8] The literature on Pynchon is vast and there are multiple interpretations of his purposes, motives, symbols, views, and metaphors. Each view of Pynchon has something to offer. However, each of these interpretations is incomplete in a way that has important implications for politics. Because the one thing on which all readers of Pynchon appear to agree is that he is a thoroughly political writer, it may be important to examine an aspect of Pynchon's work that appears to be neglected—his connection of order with a grace available to any who are open to it. Grace, he might agree with Simone Weil, is the "descending movement" that envelops human existence best experienced by those who accept the paradox of consciousness because they are open to it. Belief in some God is irrelevant. Belief in an ineffable and unknowable Beyond and an attitude of awe and wonder in its contemplation is essential. For then grace is every-where.

GRACE AND PRETERITION

Without this understanding of grace as inclusive and ubiquitous, all hu-man beings are Pynchon's preterites—passed over—damned to a world that, at least in *Mason & Dixon*, Pynchon seems to abhor. Scholars have recognized iconoclastic spirituality as an essential aspect of Pynchon's work for almost thirty years.[9] T.C. Boyle summarized the central idea when he wrote that *Mason & Dixon* investigates "the order of the uni-verse, clockwork deity and all, and yet at the same time to reflect the inadequacy of reason alone to explain the mystery that surrounds us."[10] Yet many of the critics who perceive the spiritual in Pynchon's novels believe that spirituality is a "thing" that can be handled and discussed as one might discuss any physical object. We argue that our interpretation of grace more clearly unites and brings into focus the other elements scholars find in Pynchon's sprawling oeuvre: entropy, preterition, criti-cism of modernity, paranoia, and subjunctivity (possibility). Further, we suggest that in addition to exploding the myth of America as a city upon a hill and the bastion of all political good and virtue, Pynchon offers the possibility of a humbler politics of national identity that fosters citizen participation.

Pynchon is radical in his vision of order and disorder. He constantly confronts readers with the paradox of consciousness—the awareness of oneself as both subjects with intentions toward objects and as predicates within a larger reality or story struggling with the anxiety of existence, their sense of powerlessness over time and space, and of being cut off from the community of being. Many scholars can see a drama of being but miss Pynchon's characterization of the middle as an experience of potentiality where existent and nonexistent reality meet and bleed over into one another. In their view Pynchon paints life as a fruitless search for meaning. They see some who are saved and some who are passed over, but they miss the fact that Pynchon sees life as an "adventure of decision on the edge of freedom and necessity."[11] If there is preterition, it is a preterition by choice. Individuals are "passed over" because they almost invariably ignore the irruption of transcendence and grace into their world. In humanity's quest for certainty, they use dogma and ritual to replace possibility with reified *truth*. They build walls against a part of the Real.

Pynchon's work is rich with all aspects of human emotion and experi-ence. As Pynchon puts it in *Mason & Dixon*, "all history must converge to Opera in the Italian Style."[12] Eighteenth- and nineteenth-century Italian opera (especially Italian comic opera) broke with an older operatic form to include a full range of voice types (SATB), the experiences of the commoner as well as the nobility or the mythological gods, comic as well as dramatic characters and moments, and a playful, almost carnival, atmosphere. That atmosphere pervades all of Pynchon's novels. In other words, at least implicitly, the atmosphere Pynchon creates attempts to blend many aspects of human life to form a composition on a multiple plane.

The image of Italian opera might help sharpen the focus on Pynchon's work, casting him as engaged in puzzling about the perennial questions in the only way that seems to be available in the contemporary world—mythopoesis. Pynchon offers readers a vision of humans at play, trying to act out their part in a drama of being whose plot is unknown. *Mason & Dixon* skillfully symbolizes the almost incommunicable experience of life in the *metaxy* in which sometimes individuals are "the Slate" and sometimes "the Chalk."[13] His plots offer the possibility of both participation and of oblivion through alienation or folly. Pynchon may be showing his readers the points at which a falling out of participation through alienation or folly reaches civilizational proportions. This experience of civilization-wide folly provides the background for the novel as myth flowing out of the Pynchon's own experience of alienation and the possibility of grace. In doing so he comes full force to meet the heart of America's founding myth—the idea that America is exceptional because it is a city upon a hill.

As Eric Voegelin argued, historiogenesis (speculation on societal origins resulting in a founding myth) is "one of the great constants in the search for order."[14] David Schell saw that when he wrote that Pynchon deconstructs "the myth of cohesive and 'allegorical' readings of foundational narratives in order to foreground the presence of alternative and submerged narratives of foundational space."[15] That constant plays a starring role in America's vision of order. Presidents and pundits throughout American history have accepted the image of the United States as a city upon the hill and promoted it as a self-evident and unassailable Truth—the anchor of America's founding. For Pynchon the phrase is a magic incantation, without foundation, used to ward off the anxiety of existence, the response to the mystery of existence out of nothing.[16]

GRACE, THE ANXIETY OF EXISTENCE, AND A CITY UPON A HILL

One summer morning Kai asked: "Do you ever think about what happens to you when you die?" Thomas Pynchon engages the question of death in each of his works, however it takes center stage in *Mason & Dixon*. It also lies at the heart of the very human experience of anxiety and, thus, of preterition. It is an inherent aspect of the search for order.

Certainly, this question was important to the Puritan Independents who settled New England, for it became the core of the order they developed. Scholars make much of Pynchon's Puritan heritage and its doctrine of preterition under which all are depraved, only suffering brings atonement, and only a few elect are assured of salvation—a doctrine his forebear modified enough to be considered heretical.[17] Just as important as New England's Covenant of Grace, however, is the Social Covenant derived from it, without which there is no foundation for the myth of America as a city upon a hill. *Mason & Dixon* destroys the Covenant of Grace, replacing it with a world full of grace open to all, and makes the ideas of American exceptionalism and special favor in God's eyes appear ridiculous. He recognizes America was never a city upon a hill and is merely a nation like any other.

The late eminent New England historian Perry Miller called the Puritan movement to America an "errand into the wilderness."[18] Unlike the Pilgrims who arrived and founded the Plymouth Colony in 1620, the generation of 1630's Great Migration did not leave England because society was intolerant of its religious beliefs. By the time these Puritans emigrated, Cromwell and his New Model Army had won. The Puritans of the Great Migration left because they thought Cromwell was too tolerant, not too intolerant.[19] Nor did they believe God had commissioned emigration. Their errand was an "act of will"[20] designed to establish a perfect Biblical polity and demonstrate to Cromwell how he should govern England. The goal was "to improve our lives to do more service to the Lord, to increase the body of Christ, and to preserve our posterity from the corruptions of this evil world so that they in turn shall work out their salvation under the purity and power of Biblical ordinances."[21] This vision was not exactly the view of most others who came to America. Those who participated in the Great Migration stood solidly rooted in Augustinian piety from which they took the doctrine of predestination, and their worldview was medieval in its sense of reciprocal relations amongst members of a community. The system was federal in that the civil and the ecclesiastical components of society, while separate, reinforced one another to create the "pure Biblical polity" that Winthrop believed was set forth in the New Testament.[22]

As Winthrop stated in *A Modell of Christian Charity* (1630), they were entering a Covenant with God. The Covenant of Grace bound both parties. In it the members of the Puritan community vowed service to God and God, in return, bound Himself to look with favor on the Massachusetts Bay plantation if faithful service continued. At the individual level, "If a man can believe he has done his part; God then must needs redeem him and glorify him."[23] Testimony of direct spiritual experience in front of the minister and congregation sealed election. Only the elect were full members of the congregation eligible to vote and take communion; however, even the preterite were bound to the Covenant of Grace, for they had participated in adopting it. By doctrine, some were saved (the elect); others were damned, "passed over." The elect, only about 20 percent of the population, knew they were elect because they had experienced God directly.[24] Everyone else, although required to attend services and pay for the support of the minister, could only hope that sometime before their death they also would have the direct experience that would guarantee salvation.

Socially, all were bound to the covenant, and differences in wealth and class were an inherent part of God's will. However, Winthrop also listed a series of obligations of solidarity based on the idea that "every man might have need of others," such as a rule against usury, a commandment to do unto others as you would have them do unto you, and an admonition to feed the poor. They were to "follow the counsel of Micah, *to do justly, to love mercy, to walk humbly with our God.*" If they kept both the Covenant of Grace and the Social Covenant, then God would favor the community, and other communities would want to emulate theirs. Therefore, "we must consider that we shall be as a city upon a hill. The eyes of all people are upon us."[25] Everyone, they believed, waited to see whether the Biblical polity, united and totally committed to biblical principles in all aspects of life, would succeed. If it did succeed, other nations and colonies would follow its model. Material prosperity was a sign of God's approval of the mission, not of an individual.

Plagued from the beginning by internal dissension, the mission was never a success, at least not in its original sense. By the time Mason and Dixon arrived in Philadelphia to plot the disputed boundary line between Maryland and Pennsylvania, it was obvious no community in England or America took the Biblical polity as its model and that things were not going quite as planned in Massachusetts. Puritan leaders attempted to reinforce the sense of community through exiling "heretics" and "election" sermons given when new governors were elected or during times of stress. Originally the purpose of these sermons was to reinforce the *Modell's* plan. However, as early as the 1640s election sermons increasingly took the tone of jeremiads, lamentations on the state of society and calls for repentance and reform. Major tensions revolved around the doctrines of preterition and grace. Why, many asked, should either the elect or the preterite continue to be virtuous when nothing they did could affect what happened to them after death?

Thus, the election sermons given to the second generation focused on lists of sins (decay of godliness, heresy, swearing, speculation and price gouging, etc.). Increase Mather accused the colony of lack of civic spirit and allowing family government to decay. Most importantly, Mather was concerned that members of the community had no "disposition to reform."[26] Synods of this generation responded by delimiting increasingly long lists of sins and defining more institutionalized dogma. This dogmatic turn led to a split within puritanism in 1640 that made any one model impossible.[27] Further, even the English Independent movement wrote the General Court in 1645 suggesting that banishing "heretics" was a blot on the Independent religious movement.

For this second generation of Puritan Independents, Miller argues, developing an identity was difficult. It was plain no one was taking their polity as a model, most importantly, even those of the same religious persuasion in England. The eyes of the world were not upon them. What was to become of the concept that this society was a city upon a hill when no one was looking? And how were they to convince the generations to come that they should remain faithful to the covenant and avoid sin when Puritan doctrine stated that only a select few would be saved? Ministers developed the Halfway Covenant and successive ameliorations. The weakening of the doctrine of predestination provided a better supprt for a mercantile society in which the Social Covenant had lost most of its meaning. Puritans of the second and third generation faced identity issues. Thus, instead of America following them, Puritan New England began to become American.

In 1740 with the ascent of Jonathan Edwards and the Great Awakening, the vision of a city upon a hill became a political rather than a Christian conceptualization as economic prosperity put the focus on material things. Wealth became the sign of individual rather that societal election. Puritan New England had never believed in democracy. Its freedom was to do "what was good, just, and honest."[28] It certainly never believed in freedom of expression, conscience, or religion. However, Edwards overthrew the covenant and taught God's freedom from any obligation to humanity. Grace was irresistible and human beings had no natural ability.

At a time when election had become synonymous with wealth, Edwards "hammered it home to the average person that they had to speak up or else they were lost."[29] His sermons opened salvation to all who demanded it. The Great Awakening opened the gulf that still exists in America between intellectuals appalled by the evangelical movement and the average person. Edwards' movement also changed the idea of leadership. The leader must bring listeners "by active participation into an experience that was no longer private and privileged but social and communal."[30] No longer should the people select the most virtuous and honest to the magistracy. Rather, a leader's primary qualification was management skill. At that point, both Perry Miller and Eric Voegelin agree the image of a city upon a hill became a tenet of national rather than religious election.

PYNCHON AND THE ANXIETY OF EXISTENCE

In Pynchon's hands, Mason and Dixon's quest for meaning becomes intricately interwoven into their voyages and adventures. The hacking out of the Mason-Dixon Line was a mythic adventure—America's origin story, complete with the pre-founding idea of a city upon a hill. There is much to startle and amaze the reader of *Mason & Dixon*. *Mana*, as both the sacred and the extraordinarily powerful, is the backdrop for the action. Mythological creatures and actions abound in *Mason & Dixon*—levitating bathtubs, a prescient horse, a talking dog, a giant glowing Indian, a werebeaver, visits from the dead, strange experiences in the fog, Dixon's visit to a concave world inside the earth, a *Krees* that seems somehow to transfer itself from Mason's dream to his bed, and Jenkin's listening ear. Legendary and historical figures such as Benjamin Franklin, Jacques de Vaucanson, George Washington, Nevil Maskelyne, Chief Nemacolin of the Delaware Nation, Thomas Cresap, the Penn's and the Calvert's, William Emerson, James Bradley, Clive of India and the East India Company play their parts.[31] Pynchon uses these actions and figures to challenge and expand the reader's thinking about the values and the age they represent. Sometimes Pynchon adds a bawdy story or bits of doggerel or song. The depictions of these individuals and events always are entertaining. But these fantastic figures and absurd scenarios are part of the mythopoet's craft. Pynchon uses them to highlight the problems of a misplaced search for a ground of existence. Readers often find Pynchon's novels laugh-out-loud funny. However, underlying his novels always is a mood of gravity, an almost overwhelming compassion for the human condition, and sadness at human blindness and folly.

Pynchon's mythopoesis involves a "particular kind of knowing, in which intuition is fundamental."[32] His subject is what Kundera considers the task of the novel—reflection on man as such.[33] Investigating what it means to be human, the novelist focuses on existential issues and no longer is obligated to provide a "plausible" real world.[34] Like Vaucanson's duck, unbound by historical period or national ties, the novel moves beyond time and place to the universally human. Although most of Pynchon's stories rely on the American experience, their core (like that of every myth) is the human response to the anxiety of existence and the questions that anxiety generates. *Mason & Dixon* is an extended meditation on the drama of human existence and the human search for meaning. The novel's focus is the search for what it means to be human in a reality whose flaw is not the absence of meaning but its surfeit, not the absence of grace but our anxiety over what it requires. All that meaning demands that the reader respond. As Uncle Ives puts it, every reader of novels "must be reckoned a soul in peril."[35] Meaning demands acknowledgment. Acknowledgment demands action.

Always in a Pynchon novel, but most especially in *Mason & Dixon*, time and space help symbolize the experience of living in the *metaxy*. Time and space symbolize the tensional poles of existence/nonexistence—lasting and passing, beginning and beyond, life and death, remembrance and resistance. The attack on the *Seahorse* by the French ship *l'Grand* as the pair sail for Capetown and the eleven days "lost" when the British moved from the Julian to the Gregorian calendar in 1751 are especially important. Both reappear frequently during the book.

The cardinal moment of the book is the unexpected attack on the ship charged originally with carrying Mason and Dixon to Cape Town to observe the Transit of Venus. It occupies four brief pages, yet long afterward, one asks the other whether everything since hasn't felt "not a Dream, yet . . ." and the other breaks in with "Aye. As if we're Lodgers inside someone else's Fate, whilst belonging quite someplace else." [36] The *Seahorse* is barely out into the English Channel when the French *l'Grand's* sails appear. The captain immediately sends them below to make themselves useful. As Rev'd Cherrycoke remembers it, "Death was making itself sensible in new ways." [37] In the face of imminent death, the thin line separating the tensional poles of existence jumped out at all involved. As the Rev'd describes it, "Broadsides again and again, . . . the Thumps of reloading, the cries of the injur'd and dying, nausea, Speechlessness, Sweat pouring." And afterward "we stood afraid to breathe, because of what might be next." [38] In the imminence of death, Mason and Dixon experience the ultimate existential angst and the full force of human life in the *metaxy*.

They will never be the same. Neither had "fail'd the other." [39] They do not cease their work as scientists and their practice of surveying the surface of the globe to make it an object of human exploitation. They are still thoroughly modern men, formed by the Enlightenment. Their science is based on the model of mathematical physics and its offspring is a stupendous outpouring of technological marvels and techniques. Still they have "turned." From then on, they ask more questions. Their epiphany does not send them to religious dogma for answers. But they are less able to dismiss the seemingly miraculous when it appears and the experience on the *Seahorse* changes how they deal with each other and with those whom they meet. They have experienced presence as they will again and again throughout their story.

That same experience of the folding in of time and space occurs with the so-called eleven lost days. The jump from September 3 to September 14 required by adoption of the Gregorian calendar in 1752 caused great discontent in Britain and was still a controversial topic years later. In *Mason & Dixon*, people he meets frequently ask Charles Mason where those days went and who stole them. He invents increasingly bizarre stories to explain what happened, including one in which a band of pigmies colonizes the eleven days. However, it seems the real point is not the answers, but the question. Mason imagines a conversation between astronomer James Bradley and Lord Macclesfield in which Bradley asks whether the other would refuse those eleven extra days, if he could get them? In another attempt at explanation, Mason tells Dixon of his dream-like experience within those eleven days. It was as if he had fallen into a "Whirlpool in Time" empty but for the "mute effects" of the absent population's lives.[40] It was as if "this Metropolis of British Reason" was the home of "all that Reason would deny."[41] This is the irruption of presence into his world of scientific method.

The anxiety of existence, the feeling of powerlessness in the face of time and space, the need to *know* permeate all of Mason's fantastical explanations of the lost days. The eleven days is an historical fact—a line drawn in time—that put Britain on the same calendar as continental Europe. But how did people experience the change? As one more mysterious occurrence would it not have increased the natural human unrest over the meaning of the passage of time? Would it not have felt like precious minutes of life had been stolen and that they were being pushed more quickly into the unknown and unknowable?

The questions of existence and essence, the uncertainty and looseness of existence, the apparent "plot" of time and space to rob human beings of knowledge and certainty, haunt everything that Mason and Dixon do. At the Cape they realize that life there brought almost everyone to "consider the Primary Questions more or less undiluted."[42] Their job in Cape Town is to observe and record the transit of Venus. They are the agents and symbols of modernity's myths of rationality, economics, and the scientific method. Yet, wherever they are Mason and Dixon continually ask: "Why am I here?" What is my purpose? This is more than the wish to know the political or scientific reasons for their projects; it is every human being's most basic existential question. Mason pursues Fang, the LED (learned English dog), to ask for answers. He asks Dixon why there still cannot be "Oracles . . . Gate-ways to Futurity?"[43] In *Mason & Dixon* every character is the wanderer seeking answers to the questions of existence and essence. Characters, both the quick and the dead, are obsessed with the tension between life/death, lasting/passing, beginning/beyond. Rev. Cherrycoke asks "What machine is it that bears us along so relentless?"[44] The spirits of Rebekkah (Charles Mason's dead wife), the hanged man, and the Raby ghost hover at the boundary both mocking and comforting readers with their real presence.

Mason and Dixon's job between 1763 and 1767 was to create "order" by drawing a surveyor's line to settle land disputes among the Penn and Calvert families' competing claims to what is now Maryland, Pennsylvania, and Delaware. However, their work appears to produce mostly disorder and they come to wonder what it is they are doing. As Rev'd Cherrycoke indicated, the measuring of the visto—the drawing of an accurate line—required bravery and excellent science. Yet, ultimately, it was "meaningless—just a line.[45] They become concerned that Captain Zhang may be correct in maintaining that straight lines, such as the visto, are unnatural, offend the dragon, and are conduits for Sha (bad energy or evil).[46] They do not even really know for whom they are working. Jeremiah Dixon will ask that question one day. Mason's reply? "I rather thought, one day, you would be the one to tell me."[47] Are they independent scientists or front men for the powerful (both known and unknown)? Are the Penns in charge? The East India Company? The Royal Society? The government? Some hidden conspiracy? Living on the border of the visible and invisible worlds exacts a toll. It seems to affect Dixon the most. He finds himself "attacked by Vertigo" if he looks through his surveying eyepiece for too long.[48] They are lost emotionally and psychologically and cannot feel some solid ground. They epitomize the anxiety of existence and the search for some ground of meaning.

In *Mason & Dixon* the obvious grounds of existence are science, technology, and capitalism. But science, technology, and capitalism provide them no comfort. Neither does religion. Charles Mason (Anglican) and Jeremiah Dixon (lapsed Quaker) are tied to a vision of science and reason that, in Pynchon's view, stunts what is best in them, destroys their ability to imagine possibilities, and dooms them to unhappiness because they cannot give in to what they "see" and "know" through experience. As Fang, the talking dog, told Mason, in the Age of Reason the idea of a talking dog was as absurd as any mythical beast. Everything must have a rational explanation.[49] The real is decidedly physical, and Mason believes it is possible to quantify creation.[50] If instrumental reason and Newtonian physics are the ground of being, all other experiences must be explained away. The tremendous energy of the human intellect, psyche, and body must be bent only on the pursuit of profit and *knowledge*, despite what their lived experience tells them. In *Mason & Dixon* the price of progress has been the death of the spirit.[51]

One very explicit theme in *Mason and Dixon* is that the power to define boundaries, to draw lines on maps, is the power to determine reality and to define the reasonable, the rational. The drawing of straight lines and the definitions of reality imposed by them close off a truer understanding of reality and truncate and deform reason. Truncated, deformed reason leads to irrationality and willful blindness. Truth becomes unified and ossified and counter-narratives are viewed as unreasonable, superstitious, and unreal. Opinion no longer relies on the evidence of human experiences in the physical world. The stories told are of shrunken selves condemned to be free and alone in the world. These stories heighten, not reduce, the anxiety of existence. They lead to building second realities to fend off the "frictions" inevitable when facing reality with a shrunken, or contracted, self.[52] The heavens may declare the glory of God. The skies may proclaim the work of His hands, but the really important stuff is the spectacle of stupendous energy expended in gigantic enterprises. The life of the spirit, if it is real at all and not just some adjunct of a subconscious struggling to emerge, is sublimated into immanentized manifestations, earthbound and institutionalized, devoid of real spiritual substance. Now every society with sufficient hubris can proclaim itself a city upon a hill.

All through *Mason and Dixon* the protagonists are pulled by two worlds. The first is modernity and its dream of human development and progress through power. The visto hacked out of the wilderness is the visible symbol of modernity's nightmare of man alone and its unleashing of titanic human energies, as is America itself, as the visible manifestation of the possibility of making the cosmos into an object of conquest. Throughout the book, there has been a counter-pull from the Beyond that has been gently but powerfully transforming the lensmen. There have been moments when the Platonic turning of the soul to the Good was touchable. Listening to Jenkin's Ear, Mason believes "in its suggestion of Transition between Two Worlds, the space offers an invitation to look into his Soul for a moment."[53] Mason and Dixon visit the site of the 1841 massacre of Native Americans in Lancaster, Pennsylvania, and are sickened by it. They run away in disgust, even though they realize there are consequences to every act and evil must be faced rather than ignored.[54] During their stay in South Africa they observe that after the Transit of Venus, the atmosphere of the entire Cape changed for four months. However, the response to presence then subsided and all "return to their old Theatrics."[55]

HIDDEN IN PLAIN VIEW

Yet Mason and Dixon have been slowly turned around by the daily exposure to the primary experience of the cosmos. By the end, both Mason and Dixon have come to the inarticulate understanding that the cosmos is alive and breathed upon by something beyond itself. They experience presence—a presence that is alive with implications for the search for order—a presence beyond any truth offered by history, law, or individual remembrance. They become aware that history is neither lists of dates nor the memories of participants. Those who study history must be a "quidnunc, spy and Taproom Wit." Otherwise, they forget that history is not a "Chain of single Links." Rather, it is a "great disorderly Tangle of Lines, long and short, weak and strong, vanishing into the Mnemonick Deep."[56]

Truth may be contingent and fragmentary, but it does represent the inrush of something transcendent into the human world. If one is open to a comprehending reality, there will be moments of revelation to reflect upon and incorporate into life. There will be Platonic "turnings" of the Soul, like those described by Jeremiah Dixon. He told Mason that Quakers sit quietly to feel presence, "the Working of the Spirit within. . . .

Howbeit, 'tis all Desire,--and Desire, but Embodiment in the World, of what Quakers have understood as Grace."[57] There will be moments of grace in which experience is alight with presence. And, Pynchon suggests, the odd thing is that openness to the mysterious ground of existence will allow a person to view the all-pervasive and surrounding transcendent in others.

Giving up what weighs one down allows the freedom to act, instead of just admiring the actions of others, for instance Jeremiah Dixon's bravery in freeing a slave coffle in Baltimore. This was not the kind of bravery they had shown when their ship was attacked by the French, nor the bravery they demonstrated on the Warrior Path. In neither instance had they made a choice. They did what they had to do. However, in Maryland they did have a choice and Dixon chose to act, and Mason not to do "what each of us wishes he might have the unthinking Grace to do. . . . To act for all those of us who have so fail'd."[58] Presence offers the antithesis of a city upon a hill; it requires recognition and remediation of moral lapses.

Pynchon does more than merely take the spiritual seriously. Illuminating his novels is an experience that argues that meaning is impossible without acceptance of nonexistent reality—of the constant and ubiquitous presence of transcendence, whatever it might be. In *Mason & Dixon* grace is the ground of human existence, if human beings only will realize and acknowledge it. Housebound during the Cape's rainy season, Charles Mason sits in a chair willing grace to arrive, hoping to experience Christ. However, he cannot sit still and keeps interrupting Dixon to talk about his "progress."[59] In Pynchon, the world not only is full of the possibility of gods; it exists within transcendence. The universe is an ineffable mystery that generates awe and wonder.

In *Mason & Dixon* nature is being dominated, sawn, chopped and in general reduced to an instrumentalist cosmos. At the same time, however, nature reveals the spiritual reality behind, underneath, or permeating its apparent "natural" inertness. Dogs have human speech, lightning bolts utter, birds sing portents. A torpedo (electric eel) communicates. None of it should happen in the Age of Reason. Yet it is Mason who writes about the electric eel he saw, and "at the heart of the Eectrik Fire, beyond color, beyond even Shape" there was an opening into something that "welcom'd my Spirit."[60] That is why the visto is a scar. What has happened is comparable to the "bleeding trees" of Ovid and the talking horses of Achilles. The eight-yard wide visto that marks the line is an invisible wall designed to make disappear the tensional poles of reality, keep out nonexistent reality and reduce mystery to certainty. Whether consciously or unconsciously it demarcates reality and spells the doom of the nonexistent real.

Throughout *Mason & Dixon* the reader watches as mystery and ineffability are replaced with science and religion. There are missionaries of all sorts roaming the new world and numberless religious sects. But neither science nor religion responds well to the mystery of life in the *metaxy*. Rather, except for the Rev'd Cherrycoke, most characters in *Mason & Dixon* see religion as another way to build a wall and reduce the uncertainty of existence to certainty, just as the New England Puritans kept adjusting their dogma to stave off doubt about election. Pynchon's Jesuits believe that no soul should be allowed into heaven without passing through the society's "Toll Gates." In another place, they see arms makers accounted as men of "unquestion'd" piety.[61] Transcendence too must be "owned"—immanentized, bottled and sold to produce massive certainty. The Great Awakening's genuine meaning was that a direct relationship with Christ became the right of everyone. And it cost nothing in terms of sacrifice or action.[62] Here Pynchon, like Perry Miller and Eric Voegelin, perceives the Great Awakening as a turning point for the American mind by its refracting of social thinking away from the moral/ethical and to the practical and of Winthrop's vision for the Great Migration (a city upon a hill) from a symbol of religious commitment to a patriotic catchphrase.

History, Rev'd Cherrycoke tells one listener to his tale is "the Dance of our Hunt for Christ" and how far we have succeeded in meeting Him.[63] But the odd thing in *Mason & Dixon* is the sense that the more human beings try to track down transcendence and make it certain, the more transcendence resists human efforts. As William Emerson tells Jeremiah Dixon and the Jesuit, Maire, neither religion nor science has met transcendence, and neither would recognize it if they saw it on the street. Thus, Emerson says, both chase an "ever departing Deity."[64] With its loss, the hope fades that America would be a Third Testament.[65]

That fading hope can be seen when Peter Redzinger leaves his farm and family one day to go traveling with Christ. He returns heartbroken because Christ "went away" telling Peter that, although it will be very difficult, he must live in the expectation of Christ's return. When Peter asks how he can continue without Christ's physical presence, Christ demands to know what He has been teaching Peter during their travels together. Still Peter feels bereft because he thought he could count on Christ and believes he must have displeased Him.[66] What Peter cannot seem to understand is that transcendence is all around him. In moments of the inrush of transcendence and the outreach of the questing psyche human beings experience grace. It is real. It is free. It is mysterious. It is a source of order. However, as the Lutheran theologian Bonhoeffer maintained, grace is incredibly difficult. It can be neither owned nor assumed and religion does not guarantee it. The tragedy of human life is that most individuals can only accept transcendence when it has been immanentized in a bodily Christ or a talking dog. However, immanentizing transcendence, in Pynchon's view, has had very unfortunate consequences. Transcendence, once viewed as a thing, becomes just one more way of exerting power, refusing mystery, and building borders and walls.

GRACE AND POLITICAL LIFE

It is obvious even to the most casual reader of Thomas Pynchon's novels that he views government in modernity the same way he describes Benjamin Franklin—as a powerful magician. Mason and Dixon drew their line after the Covenant of Grace has been weakened again and again. By this time the Puritan emigrants' dream has dissolved into the pursuit of commercial prosperity.

Pynchon suggests these myths do not accurately reflect the human experience of the gods, of what it means to be human, of the universe, and of society. Each of these myths when examined through the lens of Pynchon's microscope is found wanting in some essential. Most frequently, he returns to American exceptionalism. Politics becomes one more attempt to provide massive certainty. The anxiety of existence must be staved off at all costs, even at the cost of lies. "Ev'ryone lies, . . . each appropriate to his place in the Chain."[67] All government is founded on power,[68] and the secret of governing in modernity is that human life is meaningless.[69] Slavery in many forms is ubiquitous; yet after seeing slavery throughout their travels, Mason and Dixon accounted America as the one place slavery should not have existed.

Further, the purpose of power is to eliminate possibility in the name of simple ideas that preserve the position of the powerful. In the process of eliminating the subjunctive, only the physical world and its neverending despair remain. The search for power also continually reduces belief in the potential for wonder and the miraculous.[70] Power finds uncertainty disconcerting and dangerous. Just as unenclosed spaces always made Jeremiah Dixon "uneasy,"[71] governments, too, require the certainty of virtual (and sometimes physical) walls and lines. For, the future belongs to walls and right angles. Human beings no longer have faith in or consent to any sort of authority and so power takes authority's place. In the future walls will confer and symbolize power.[72] Where physical walls are impossible, ideological walls will do.

Governments become so adept at closing off possibility that closure becomes part of everyday life—no longer noticed by either citizens or rulers. Ideologies become truths and what rational person would question Truth? Mystery is scary, so human beings seek to banish it and governments, even those considered the freest, are only too happy to oblige. Interior psychic walls require neither consent nor force to defend. They are accepted as part of the backdrop of citizens' lives. Everyone comes to assume that reason is no more than the rational calculation of advantage and that government is only about power. Everyone learns from childhood to agree that transcendence is found only in religion and that science is the only source of the real. Everyone agrees that the job of political science is to defend classical liberalism because it provides the certainty of righteousness that human beings require to withstand the anxiety of existence.

None of that, however, satisfies the mythopoets. For them there is more than physical facts and there is no escaping the anxiety of existence. Whether Christian or not, the mythopoets would understand these lines from *Mason & Dixon*: "The final pure Christ is pure uncertainty."[73] In the contemporary world, only mythopoesis seems able to confront disorder and the anxiety of existence—it alone remains capable of uttering the academically and scientifically incorrect word (like the word "soul"). Mythopoesis responds to human unrest with inherited truths; it reaches to the depths of the human psyche to (obviously using Aaron Wildavsky out of context) speak truth to power.

However, mythopoesis can only speak this truth in the language of film, art, dance, myth, and poetry. Direct speech no longer seems able to breach the walls. As Patel argues in *Negative Liberties*, his book about Thomas Pynchon and Toni Morrison, certain novelists do a better job of engaging and reimagining the dominant social paradigm of American liberalism than do many philosophers.[74] Such novelists "dramatize the fact that the story of individualism that has arisen from Emersonian liberalism in the United States has become a form of Bad History, a coercive narrative that serves to impose the will of a dominant culture."[75] Or as Zhang puts it in *Mason & Dixon,* nothing produces bad history better than drawing lines, especially lines that create arbitrary distinctions among human beings. Such distinctions, Zhang believes, always lead to war.[76] Thus, the work of authors that aim directly at countering official social and cultural narratives, humanity's myths about itself, may be the best catalysts for change, humanity's best guardians against the worldwide hubris of exceptionalism.

And that fact should be of concern to those who study politics. One of the most important unstated implications of Pynchon's body of work is that the discipline needs to be more open to arguments based on transcendence. Acceptance of presence—acknowledgment that grace is grace—fosters political and social possibilities in ways walled-off truths never can. A politics open to grace opens the door to the subjunctive—to possibility in politics—and demands acknowledgment and fulfillment of obligations of solidarity. That subjunctive may offer a route to a viable means of integrating authority without limiting human thought and conscience. A politics or a political science that remains rooted in the Enlightenment's conception of the individual, of science, and of politics cannot have much to say to the disorder of the current age.

In this way the current political world resembles Charles Mason and Jeremiah Dixon. Mason and Dixon are scientists. To them there is a rational explanation for everything. And that rational explanation must be empirical. Yet both consistently reject their empirical experiences of anything unexplainable through reason defined as rational calculation of means and ends. Their scientific method is their claim to purity and validity—the wall on which they rest their credibility. However, their experiences will not stop speaking to them, assaulting them with claims that their scientific truth is partial and that their walling off of reality is artificial—until Dixon at last feels compelled to act. There is one moment in *Mason & Dixon* in which Jeremiah Dixon makes a stand for order and acts on a moment of grace. After years of watching slavery in England, the Cape, and America, he frees a coffle of slaves in Baltimore and almost is killed for it. This, Pynchon seems to tell us, is the crowning moment of his life. Both Mason and Dixon certainly see it for that. Most often, however, they ignore the grace that appears right in front of them.

Pynchon takes the question and the mystery of human existence as the ground for order in a complex messy world that is shrouded in mystery, but demands decision. Humans want flourishing lives, lives that have meaning. That requires order. But it is very difficult to find any source of order in the contemporary world. What should be patently obvious to anyone who looks is the disorder that accompanies announcement of final answers. All claims to Truth have proven problematic. Contemporary societies do not want to hear that. They give their mythopoets Pulitzers, National Book Awards, MacArthur Foundation grants, Mann Booker Awards, Nebula Awards, and Nobel Prizes. However, society at large will acknowledge no link between the insights of the mythopoets and the real world around them. They are the most visible reminders of the idea that human beings are participants in a drama of being, that they run around searching for meaning that really is right in front of them but that almost always goes unrecognized. Like the Mason-Dixon Line, human beings want to make everything fit into nice, neat boxes and categories— to force reality into shapes and sizes humans can handle. Humanity builds walls to make their own reality because they cannot handle the fact of a comprehensive reality. No line is more scientific, or more arbitrary, than that of a surveyor. The walls humans build cloud their sight and render them incapable of receiving the very gift they most desire. And, thus, the search for order is endlessly short-circuited. The Mason-Dixon Line is a metaphor for all the walls humanity builds in the name of "humanizing" reality. And in "humanizing" reality humanity loses reality and dehumanizes its world.

What does one see when they move back and try to gain some "reflective distance" concerning the study of both empirical political science and political philosophy? We see that politics, as Jonathon Edwards suggested, is an exercise in effective management. Look through the introductory textbooks. What do they discuss? Taxonomies, institutional types, ideologies, structures, functions. There is little concern demonstrated for the stuff of people living together.[77] The word politics comes from the Greek *politēs*, "citizen", who would live in a polis (city, community). But the essence of political life is the shared evocation of experience, not only at its founding but also as the society changes and evolves.

Contemporary politics is solely the pursuit of self-interest and is not subject to the rules of real life. Can societies hold together using merely power and prudence as the definitions of wisdom? Contemporary classical liberalism of all varieties seems to have lost its ability to participate in the deep knowing of the lover of the beautiful that Socrates accords to both philosophers and poets in *Statesman*. It may be time to move at least a little way beyond that wall—even if it means writing and speaking genuinely about the ubiquitous presence of mystery. However, accepting presence and the paradox of consciousness challenges modernity's understanding of reason as instrumental. What sort of reason does acceptance of presence demand? The authors included in this book seem to think politics also requires a wisdom that goes beyond prudent calculation of means and ends. That is the subject of the next chapter.

NOTES

1. Eric Voegelin, "The Beginning and the Beyond: A Meditation on Truth," in the *Collected Works of Eric Voegelin, Vol.28, What Is History? And Other Late Unpublished Writings*, ed. Thomas A. Hollweck and Paul Caringella (Baton Rouge: Louisiana State University Press, 1990), 221.

2. Eric Voegelin, *Order and History, Vol. 5: In Search of Order* (Baton Rouge: Louisiana State University Press, 1955), 30.

3. We use the term "numinous" in the same way as does Rudolph Otto, *The Idea of the Holy: An Inquiry into the Non-Rational Factor in the Idea of the Divine and Its Relation to the Rational* (1923). It is a sense of awe and wonder.

4. Dietrich Bonhoeffer, *The Cost of Discipleship* (New York: MacMillan Publishing Company, 1963), ch. 1.

5. Gregory Bateson, "Style, Grace, and Information in Primitive Art," in *Steps to an Ecology of the Mind* (Chicago: University of Chicago Press, 1972), 128.

6. Mailynne Robinson, "Grace," in *The Givenness of Things* (Farrar, Straus & Giroux, 2015), 34.

7. Bateson., 129.

8. Tom Robbins, *Wild Ducks Flying Backwards* (New York: Bantam, 2005), 118.

9. Bernard Duyfhuizen, "Review: Taking Stock: 26 Years since "*V.*" (Over 26 Books on Pynchon." *NOVEL: A Forum on Fiction*, 23 (Autumn, 1989):77, accessed July 4, 2007, DOI: 10.2307/1345580.

10. T.C. Boyle, "The Great Divide," *The New York Times Book Review* (May 18, 1997): p NA. Academic OneFile. Thomson Gale. Radford University Library.

11. Eric Voegelin, *Order and History, Volume I: Israel and Revelation* (Baton Rouge: Louisiana State University Press, 1956), 1.

12. Thomas Pynchon, *Mason & Dixon* (New York: Henry Holt and Company, 1997), 706.

13. Ibid., 442.

14. Ibid., 56.

15. David Schell, "Engaging Foundational Narratives in Morrison's *Paradise* and Pynchon's *Mason & Dixon, College Literature: A Journal of Critical Literary Studies*. 41.3

(Summer, 2014): 73, E-ISSN: 1542-4286, accessed August 23, 2018, https://lib-proxy.radford.edu/login?url=http://search.ebscohost.com/login.aspx?direct=true&db=edsglr&AN=edsgcl.377529930&site=eds-live&scope=site.

16. Eric Voegelin, "Anxiety and Reason" in *The Collected Works of Eric Voegelin, Vol. 28: What Is History? and Other Late Unpublished Writings*, ed. Thomas Hollweck and Paul Caringella (Baton Rouge: University of Louisiana Press, 1990), 71.

17. William Pynchon (1590-1662) wrote *The Meritorious Price of Our Redemption*, the first book burned in America, in 1650. In it he argued that Christ atoned for humanity's sins through obedience to God's will, not suffering.

18. Perry Miller, *Errand into the Wilderness* (Belknap Press of Harvard University Press, 1956).

19. Ibid., 4.

20. Id.

21. Ibid., 5-6.

22. Ibid., 5.

23. Perry Miller, *The New England Mind in the Seventeenth Century* (Cambridge: Belknap Press of Harvard University Press, 1939), 377.

24. Miller, *Errand*, 5.

25. John Winthrop, *A Modell of Christian Charity* (1630), Collections of the Massachusetts Historical Society(Boston, 1838), 3rd series 7:31-48. Hanover Historical Texts Collection. Scanned by Monica Banas, August 1996. https://history.hanover.edu/texts/winthmod.html.

26. Miller, *Errand*, 7-8 quoting Increase Mather's *A Brief History of the Warr With the Indians.* Mather considered the was God's judgement for the people's sins.

27. Ibid., 13.

28. Ibid., 88-89.

29. Ibid., 98.

30. Ibid., 163.

31. Jacques de Vaucanson was an eighteenth-century inventor; Rev. Dr. Nevil Maskelyne became the Astronomer Royal in 1765 during the time Mason and Dixon did their work; Nemacolin was the chief of the Delaware Nation who helped Thomas Cresap widen a Native American path across the Alleghanies; Thomas Cresap served Lord Baltimore in the land dispute between Maryland and Pennsylvania; the Penn's and the Calvert's long fought over the boundary between Pennsylvania, Maryland, and Delaware. It was this dispute that Mason and Dixon were called in to settle; William Emerson was a mathematician with whom Jeremiah Dixon trained; James Bradley became Astronomer Royal in 1742; Clive of India, Major-General Robert Clive, helped establish the domination of the East India Company in India; the East India Company held a royal charter to trade with India and East and Southeast Asia. Ultimately it dominated politically and economically huge sections of these land masses.

32. Milan Kundera, trans. Linda Asher, *The Curtain* (New York: HarperCollins, 2005), 8.

33. Ibid., 7.

34. Ibid., 72-73.

35. 34 Pynchon, *Mason & Dixon*, 351.

36. Ibid., 75.

37. Ibid., 38.

38. Id.

39. Ibid., 42.

40. Ibid., 556.

41. Ibid., 559.

42. Ibid., 68-69.

43. Ibid., 12.

44. Ibid., 361.

45. Ibid., 8.

46. Ibid., 54.

47. Ibid., 347.

48. Ibid., 731.

49. Ibid., 22.

50. Ibid., 721.

51. Eric Voegelin, "The New Science of Politics," in *The Collected Works of Eric Voegelin, Vol. 5: Modernity Without Restraint,* ed. Manfred Henningsen, trans. Virginia Ann Schildhauer (Columbia: University of Missouri Press, 2000), 195.

52. Eric Voegelin, "Anxiety and Reason," 112.

53. Pynchon, *Mason & Dixon,* 175-177.

54. Ibid., 346-347.

55. Ibid., 99.

56. Ibid., 349.

57. Ibid., 101.

58. Ibid., 698.

59. Ibid., 101.

60. Ibid., 433–434.

61. Ibid., 481.

62. Ibid., 261.

63. Ibid., 75.

64. Ibid., 543.

65. Ibid., 353.

66. Ibid., 480.

67. Ibid., 194.

68. Ibid., 312.

69. Ibid., 226.

70. Ibid., 345.

71. Ibid., 241.

72. Ibid., 522.

73. Ibid., 511.

74. Cyrus R. K. Patel, *Negative Liberties* (Durham: Duke University Press, 2001), xv.

75. Ibid., 10-11.

76. Pynchon, *Mason & Dixon,* 615.

77. See, for example, James Danziger, *Understanding the Political World* (New York: Longman, 2001); Ellen Grigsby, *Analyzing Politics* (Belmont, CA: Wadsworth, 2002); Herbert M. Levine, *Political Issues Debated* (Englewood Cliffs: Prentice Hall, 1992); Robert Dahl and Bruce Stinebrickner, *Modern Political Analysis* (Upper Saddle River, NJ: Prentice Hall, 2003); *Essentials of American Government: Continuity and Change,* ed. Karen O'Connor and Larry J. Sabato (Longman Publishing: 2009); and James Q. Wilson, *American Government: Brief Edition* (Wadsworth Publishing: 2008).

FOUR

Do You Believe in Magic?

Wise Imagination and the Myth of Instrumental Reason in George MacDonald's Phantastes *and Neil Gaiman's* Anansi Boys

Kai's question came out of nowhere one spring morning on the way to school. "Do you believe in magic?" That question was easy because the world is full of magic. As one author phrased it, "The world is full of magic things, patiently waiting for our wits to grow sharper."[1] Magic shimmers around the edges of life in anything that astonishes one or awakens in them a sense of awe and wonder and in any thing or experience that pulls human beings out of their own worlds and personal concerns. In many ways, magic is the awareness of possibility.

However, magic is a double-edged sword. Magic, the unexpected, the nurturer of possibility, the driver of awe and wonder, can produce a longing for something beyond the self and exert a pull toward It-Reality and the "one story." Magic can be the possibility to improve as individuals and as political communities through realization that everyone is part of one mysterious story in the *metaxy*. Conversely, when ignored or misused, magic can lead to folly and alienation from self, pulling the self away from the call of It-Reality and into the belief one can dominate life and the world through their own power. It alienates those who pursue it from both themselves and others. Bad magic focuses solely on instrumental reason; it seeks the means to pursue selfish and often ill-considered ends. It is the product of rage, self-pity, pride, isolation, and self-interest. This is the magic that brought ruin to Adrian Leverkühn in Thomas Mann's *Dr. Faustus*, Cosmo in *Phantastes*, and almost to Fat Charlie, Spider, and Anodos in the two works considered in this chapter.

61

Genuine magic is not sleight of hand. Nor is it the sort of thing practiced by wizards in fantasy. The magic of sharpened wits is far more practical and serious than that. It seeks to evaluate ends as well as means. Magic requires an extremely rational mind and the ability to pay attention to both people and the world. Without the ability to pay attention, one misses the moments when magic flashes through the physical world. Attention is the tool of sharpened wit and sharpened wit focused on *diké* is noetic reason. Just as acknowledging transcendence does not require belief in God, as such scholars Hughes, Ranieri, and Voegelin point out, neither does noetic reason. It does require the wise of imagination of those who experience life in the *metaxy*.

MAGIC AND WISE IMAGINATION

This chapter's focus is on the type of imaginative reason needed to live with the acknowledgment of the Beyond's presence in the world and how to use one's mind to move past viewing life as merely the satisfaction of passions and desires and toward living in intentional pursuit of the Good and with wise imagination—imagination whose end is harmony.[2] If one thinks of reason as a dynamic continuum imbedded in the *metaxy*, then the passions (or the beginning, or life) would be one endpoint and the spirit (or some ineffable beyond, or death) would be the other endpoint. That image might make it is easier to understand the classic (noetic) sense of reason. Noetic reason is what helps human beings navigate life in the *metaxy*, in-between the two endpoints of the continuum, and achieve a balanced, healthy consciousness through a constant interaction of both ends of the continuum—the passions and the *Agathon* (Good, True, Just). It does not require belief in a personal God. Noetic reason is the use of intellect in pursuit of the *Agathon*. It is wise imagination.

We chose two authors for this chapter who both explore noetic reason despite being an odd couple. Over 100 years separate their births. George MacDonald sought to thaw hearts hardened by belief in doctrinaire positivist rationalism and an equally doctrinaire religious vision that eliminated any sense of joyful reception of the good news of the gospel message. Viewed as doctrinally unsound for his openness to everyone and emphasis on God as a loving father, MacDonald lost his only pastorate and spent the rest of his life preaching in family homes and as an essayist, lecturer, and novelist. To him, joy arose from love of all aspects of the world and from celebration of the world in a thoughtful and temperate manner. He believed the world "is infinitely deep," and everything that exists contains elements of God.[3] To MacDonald, imagination was not a license to make up whatever one wanted, for human beings live in the imagination of God. Rather, imagination was "following and finding out the work that God maketh. Her part is to understand God ere she attempts to utter man."[4] Wise imagination was a work of the intellect, a work of reason in the classic sense that encompassed all the realms of reality. For, "in very truth, a wise imagination, which is the presence of the spirit of God, is the best guide that man or woman can have."[5] In MacDonald's view, wise imagination is an aspect of the intellect as it searches for the transcendent. Wise imagination looks for the magic in the world which drives those who possess it to a balance of consciousness.

The other half of this chapter's odd couple, Neil Gaiman, is a winner of multiple awards for his writing (including a Newberry Medal, a Hugo award, and a Carnegie Medal). To him, "all have an obligation to daydream . . . an obligation to imagine."[6] These days Gaiman is the pied piper rock star of fantasy, myth, fairy tale, and fantasy horror. Vastly popular as an author, speaker, and audio performer, he seems to roam the world proselytizing for the imagination. Always Gaiman is a force for empathy, human decency, connections, and wise imagination. And always he asks his readers and listeners to rethink familiar concepts and beliefs. Unlike MacDonald, Gaiman is a puzzler more interested in telling a roaring good story than in setting forth beliefs about gods or a God.

As different as George MacDonald and Neil Gaiman are, there exist commonalities in their works. They write stories within stories often about a coming-of-age hero (sometimes an anti-hero as in Gaiman's *American Gods* or MacDonald's *Lilith*) on a portal quest their characters feel called upon to engage, but experience great uncertainty as to why. Both see the imaginative as a gateway to the ethical; they are moralists. Wisdom requires hard work and sacrifice, so their protagonists must overcome obstacles. Possibility, a subjunctivity much like Pynchon's, pervades their works, a subjunctivity that accompanies presence. In both MacDonald and Gaiman, life is lived in the *metaxy*, in the borderlands between that physical reality where individuals make choices and intend to do one thing or another and some ineffable, but equally genuine, reality they cannot see, hear, or touch, let alone control. Further their works often oppose their society's dominant culture and values.[7]

Finally, Gaiman and MacDonald share a common understanding of reason as Plato and Aristotle perceived it—as a way of life in which individuals use reason to mediate between passion and the Good. *Nous* is the symbol of the specifically human attribute that allows individuals to participate in World Order (*nous*) or World Soul (Divine *nous*)—some essence or thing that transcends physical reality and produces the universe's order and harmony. In *Gorgias*, for example, Socrates tells Callicles that "wise men claim that partnership and friendship, orderliness, self-control, and justice hold together heaven and earth, gods and men, and that is why we call this universe a world order, my friend, and not a world disorder."[8] For Plato and Aristotle, a flourishing human life is not possible without reliance on *Nous*. Aristotle called the human being "mature" who relies on noetic reason. Plato thought more in terms of such an individual having a musical (mathematical or balanced and harmonious) soul.

A strong thread of the classic sense of reason, of wise imagination, runs through the works of both George MacDonald and Neil Gaiman. At the heart of *Phantastes* and *Anansi Boys* readers find that the purpose of imagination is harmony and that the backbone of imagination is reason in its classic sense. They call their readers to pay attention to the world, experience the confusion, terror, and wonder of that world, take joy in that world, and then to turn that joy into loving action within it. As the three-time Newberry Award winner, Avi, put it, "in a world where the truth is often hidden, fantasy reveals reality."[9] That itself is a kind of magic. Both Gaiman and MacDonald have made this same point in their non-fiction essays.[10] They are writers of intellect and magic. Thus, readers can find in their works the use of mythopoesis to develop the classic sense of reason as essential to building individual and communal order, and ultimately to balancing the authority of the state and the importance of community. The orderly person exercises noetic reason and the result is a city that attempts to attune itself to the order of the universe.

The quest for the inner harmony that noetic reason requires is the engine pushing both Fat Charlie (*Anansi Boys*) and Anodos (*Phantastes*). They begin their stories capable of noble thoughts, but not noble deeds. Ultimately, Anodos and Fat Charlie/Spider will perform a truly selfless deed and demonstrate that they can become *spoudaios*, mature souls. This is not a one-time and forever achievement, but a constant quest. For Aristotle virtue is habit, not action, as human beings live in awareness of the tension of existence. Noetic reason "does not end history."[11] Noetic reason does throw light on existence, thus providing "a new luminosity" capable of taming the tendency toward the disorder that human passions sometimes generate. It attempts to foster harmony and wholeness by illuminating the consequences of disorder and the possibility for an order that can heal disorder and division in individuals and societies.

In choosing noetic reason human beings acknowledge they are not wholly autonomous and do not carry the meaning and origin of life within themselves. They acknowledge living in the *metaxy*. For MacDonald and Gaiman the essence of order is justice, and justice manifests itself through love. In *Phantastes* genuine love is demonstrated through self-sacrifice and witness. Therefore, deeds are more important than either intentions or words. Finally, a close reading of *Phantastes* and of *Anansi Boys* reveals that for MacDonald and for Gaiman, mythopoesis, in the sense described in chapter one of this book, is essential to any search for order because mythopoesis allows humanity to see parts of reality that escape description through equations, concepts, and categories. The heart of politics is a search for an order that allows citizens to find fulfillment, not only in their personal lives, but also in their communal lives. George

MacDonald and Neil Gaiman alert their readers to the fact that order requires *opsis* (insight) into Reality and that insight depends upon reason, just not reason as modernity understands it. They understand the eternal and powerful pull of longing for love, longing for meaning and purpose, longing for stories, and longing for harmony in the human heart and to satisfy that longing they will scour all the realms of reality.

An essential aspect of the classic experience of reason is the ability to pay attention. MacDonald scholars have written a great deal concerning the importance placed in MacDonald's fantasies on meeting the world as does the child. The classic understanding of reason focused on the ability to pay attention to the world—something at which the young child excels.[12] In *Phantastes* learning to pay attention lies at the heart of Anodos' growth during his time in Faerie. This emphasis on meeting the world as does the child also exists in *Anansi Boys*. However, as MacDonald, and later Chesterton,[13] wrote, childlike is not the same as childish. Children are acutely aware of the world and people around them and study them with almost scholarly zeal. The childish pay attention to nothing and no one. In other words, children tend to focus on a thing as it is; adults focus on abstractions and use them to build concepts and categories. Children see "things like life rather than words like evolution."[14] Anodos and Fat Charlie/Spider get into trouble every time they fail to pay attention and are most successful when they pay the closest attention and understand themselves as part of a story taking place in the *metaxy*. When individuals truly pay attention to something or someone, they become part of a bigger story. They are no longer the only and most important story. They learn moderation and proportion. And they realize that no human can have total control over the story.

ANODOS: "ALAS HOW EASILY THINGS GO WRONG"[15]

In *Phantastes* MacDonald's message is how humanity can awaken from its sleep and pursue order through noetic reasoning. Anodos, the story's hero, begins his journey hampered by hubris and an inability to pay attention. He, thus, is incapable of noetic reason. He is a well-educated and thoughtful young man. Thus, he believes himself perfectly capable of controlling the world so that it will serve his interests. He is wrong. His reason is purely instrumental and seeks only the best means of achieving his desires. Anodos' hubris and inability to pay attention continually warp his judgment and he pays dearly for his bad decisions.

On the evening of his twenty-first birthday he enters his father's library, locked since his father's death, and opens the desk. In it, he finds a secret compartment. When he unlocks the compartment, he sees the form of a tiny woman who comes out into the library and offers him one wish. Anodos wishes for Fairy Land to be real. The next morning when he awakes, he finds that the decorative leaves and flowers on his furniture and rug now are real and a real stream begins in his room and runs into a forest. Anodos follows the stream and begins a twenty-one-day journey through Fairy Land that will change his understanding of himself. Through his many adventures, Anodos will learn that noble intentions must be backed with noble deeds, that love wears many faces (not all of which are as beautiful as they seem), and that justice is the path of true order. He will awaken to the recognition that both existent and nonexistent things compose reality. Above all, he learns that justice, love, reason, order, and beauty rest on participation in a story that is much larger than one's self and that he cannot achieve without the help of empowering love.

Anodos begins his journal through Faerie as a headstrong young man confident in his own powers and greedy to see all the wonders of Fairy Land. During most of the story he refuses good advice and continually gets himself into troubles from which he must be rescued, usually by a woman, although sometimes by a knight in rusty armor seeking his own redemption. From his first moments in Fairy Land Anodos' choices highlight just how easily things can go wrong when one refuses to pay attention and rely on noetic reason. Walking through the forest, he meets a young girl who repeats to herself again and again that she must stay away from the Ash and the Alder and trust only the Oak and the Beech. Soon after he finds a cottage. The woman inside, the girl's mother, repeats the warning. In Fairy Land, one must be very careful whom one trusts. She warns him that the Ash and the Alder are greedy monsters consuming all they meet. It is better to be careful and travel by day and remain indoors at night.

However, Anodos decides to set off at evening in order to see as much of Fairy Land as he can. He *longs* for something, but he does not know what that something is. After watching some frolicking flower fairies, he enters the woods and hears the Thistles say: "He has begun a story without a beginning and will never have an end."[16] He has begun a story in the middle—in the *metaxy*—without a known beginning or end. Almost as soon as he enters the forest the folly of exploring Fairy Land by night becomes apparent. Anodos senses the presence of evil. The dreaded Ash and Alder trees stalk the night. Anodos sees the shadow of a huge hand, panics, and runs. Ultimately, he can run no farther and lies down in the shadow of the hand that has been pursuing him. Just as the Ash is about to consume him, however, he is rescued by the Beech. She tells him that the Ash and the Alder love no one. The Ash constantly attempts to fill the emptiness at its core. The Alder's beauty comes from the desire to gain love so that she can revel in her own loveliness through the adoration of others. The Beech warns Anodos that such love is self-destructive because it enlarges the hole at the Alder's center that eventually will consume her. Anodos spends the night in the Beech's arms. In the morning, she gives him a girdle of her leaves to protect him from the Ash—one he soon loses to the Alder.

This is a pattern that will be repeated many times in the story. Longing is everywhere in Fairie. The Beech longs to be human. The Ash and Alder seek to heal the holes at their centers. A childish Anodos, confident of his own powers, will ignore advice and think of love in selfish and possessive terms in his attempts to satisfy his longing for some mysterious something. Often, he has the same hole in his center as the Ash and the Alder. The reader sees it in his rescue of the white lady who had been trapped in alabaster until released by Anodos' singing. It is responsible for his rash and blind pursuit of the Alder mistaking her empty beauty for that of the white lady. Empty longing, without thought, makes him doubt the reality of Fairy Land in the farmer's cottage, enter the ogre's cottage, and open the cupboard that releases his shadow—a shadow the ogre tells him that everyone has "ranging up and down looking for him."[17] That shadow preaches to humanity the negation of wonder and the pull of instrumental reason guided purely by the passions. It is these shadows that destroy magic in the world once human beings decide they are the "sole creator of truth."[18] Both episodes demonstrate how difficult it is to achieve and maintain a foothold on reality—on the experience of *metaxy*.

At first disgusted by the shadow's presence, Anodos begins to feel comfortable with it, for the shadow "does away with all appearances and shows me things in the true colour and form . . . I will not see beauty where there is none. I will dare to behold things as they are. And if I live in a waste instead of a paradise, I will live knowing where I live."[19] Always easily manipulated, Anodos chooses darkness and nihilism until he meets a young woman carrying a globe from which issues sweet vibrating sounds. Possessed by a longing to hold it, Anodos grabs it and will not let go, even though the maiden still holds it as well. Ultimately, the globe shatters and Anodos becomes ashamed. Once more he loathes the shadow's presence. Disgusted with himself, Anodos begins to fight against his shadow. However, without noetic reason, he does not possess the weapons to do so successfully.

The pattern repeats itself in the Fairy Palace where he spends much time in the library reading. Longing, at least in Anodos' eyes, pervades every story. Further, he believes that every story is about him, especially the story of Cosmo. However, Anodos misunderstands the moral of the story. A university student, Cosmo buys an ancient mirror. Using dark magic Cosmo enchants out of that mirror the form of a beautiful, but tragic, woman. He longs to possess her and confuses that feeling with genuine love. Ultimately, he will die in the performance of a noble deed to save her from the mirror's spell. However, Cosmo acted on an idea of love as appreciation of a beautiful body, that is, from passion rather than *agape*. Anodos does not know yet that the "ideal" is a dangerous and alluring phantom. Nor does he understand that the Good is not a gift. Instead, it is something attainable only through great effort. MacDonald illustrates this point by dropping into the middle of Cosmo's story the words often attributed to Euripides: "Who knows if to live is to be dead and to be dead to live."[20] Throughout, MacDonald's message is simple: Life is a wasteland filled with meaningless diversions if it is only lived for oneself.

Anodos would indeed remember what he had read. Cosmo was the kind of man Anodos could have become. Cosmo is the self-sufficient (or "self-actualized") man who reaches a higher plane of existence by an exercise of his will-to-love and "proves" it by his sacrifice that saves the life of the beloved. This, he thinks, is a noble ideal and it is an ideal that Anodos strives to attain. However, it is an ideal that itself must die before Anodos really lives. Like Cosmo, Anodos remains a self who lives in a world of artifacts and people who are objects of conquest, exploitation and elimination—the essence of the heroic adventure of pitting all your heart, soul, and mind against danger and the threat of extinction for the prize of glory.

Misunderstanding the story's message, Anodos leaves the palace because, despite the "do not touch" warnings on the statues, he throws his arm about the statue he recognizes as the white lady. She flees again with him in pursuit. Always he follows some "irresistible attraction" or "a gush of wonderment and longing flowed over my soul like the tide of a great sea, or is "led by irresistible desire."[21] Without noetic reason to guide him his longing leads to pride, hubris, and the vain belief after a fight with giants that he is the equal of the most glorious knights. Because of that hubris a knight, who really is his own selfishness, pride and conceit, imprisons him in a tower—the tower of his ego. It appears that the knight is his shadow. Anodos will follow his longing, but without determining which longings to follow and which to ignore or the best way in which to follow his longing for love.

After days in the tower, a woman's singing arouses in him recognition of his own narcissism. He does what should have been obvious but was obscured by his lack of genuine vision. There was no lock on the door but his own conceit and pride. He opens the door and sees a woman, the same one whose globe he had destroyed. Her song was simple; its implications are a bit startling. She reiterates the message he has been given before, the same message found in the Border Trilogy and *Mason & Dixon*.

> Immortals mortals
> Mortals immortals
> Live the other's death
> The other's life die.

Freed from the tower, Anodos finally sees and understands his folly in letting his passions control his actions. He awakens to the fact that true honor comes from service, takes off the armor, and his shadow disappears. Anodos has learned that "he who would be a hero, will barely be a man; that he that will be nothing but a doer of his work, is sure of his manhood."[22] Anodos is growing into noetic reason.

As he continues his travels, he finds a cottage occupied by an old woman who was spinning and singing. She had "the most wonderful [eyes], I thought, that I had ever beheld." They were at the same time very old and very young.[23] The woman sings him a very long and mournful song that begins: "Alas, how easily things go wrong!" The cottage has four doors to the outside: the door of weeping, the door of sighs, the door of death, and the door of timelessness. Anodos tries all four returning to the cottage after experiencing what was behind each door. The door that most offers him insight into himself is the door of sighs. Once through the door, he stands in a lordly hall occupied by the white lady—the very woman he has been longing for and searching for. Then a powerful knight enters covered in shining steel. The woman flies into his arms. It is the knight of the soiled armor Anodos has met during the adventure with the Ash. His armor is now polished free of rust. The knight muses on a youth he had met in Fairy Land who he remembers, had saved his beloved from the cave and the Fairy Palace. "There was something noble in him, but it was a nobleness of thought, and not deed. He may yet perish of vile fear."[24] Anodos recognizes that youth as himself.

By her song the woman is forming the soul of Anodos by love, just as it had been formed by his own singing and the singing of others all along. Anodos still experiences longing, but it is longing of a different and better kind. The power of *Eros* impelled Anodos to seek the white lady for just a glimpse of her perfect female face and form. Now the image of the white lady changes and became blurred with the memory of the woman at the spindle. At one level love itself is going through a transformation from *eros* (physical desire), to *philia* (friendship), to *agape* (chosen love), to love of the Good itself. At another level it is Anodos himself who is undergoing a *periagoge*, a turning toward It-Reality. And this love toward the ineffable world-transcendent foundation of reality, when genuinely conscious in a human being, is reason itself. The young-old woman tells him: "Go, my son, and do something worth doing."[25] What that great good is, will seem to Anodos something like glory, the great prize of the epic heroes. In fact, that great good will be something far different. That something worth doing will require lifelong commitment to remembering what Fairy Land taught him—a commitment he is unsure he can fulfill.[26]

After a short time Anodos meets the rusty knight again in his clean and brilliant armor. Anodos agrees to become the knight's squire. As they travel, the knight rather matter-of-factly notes that although Fairy

Land is very beautiful, with many splendors, it also contains horrors, fiends, and weaklings. Thus, "All a man can do is to go to work with a cool brain and a strong will . . . and in the end he will get his work done." Anodos replies that in doing such work a person will not always "come off well." "Perhaps not," said the knight, "in the individual act; but the result of his lifetime will content him."[27] The more the knight speaks, the more Anodos recognizes him as a "true man" and the humbler he himself feels.[28]

They reach a large open space enclosed by yew trees. There is a throne at one end and three ranks of white-robed figures with swords stand on either side. The knight believes there must be something spiritually good about to happen, but Anodos has the strange feeling that here was something evil. Certainly the knight, who represents the virtue of courage, has developed, through much practice, that quality called by Carl Von Clausewitz, *Coup d'oeil*, or "strength of eye." He possesses the ability to quickly evaluate the nature of terrain, the rapidly changing disposition of forces, and the vision to "see" the non-material force of war at work, despite the "fog of war" which metaphorically blinds less favored men to the whirling maelstrom in which they find themselves.[29] But coup d'oeil is not *opsis,* and Anodos, through the fact of his soul being shaped by the power of love has finally found "true seeing." On the great throne sat a majestic figure who looked both proud and kind to the knight.

Anodos saw and understood more. He knew there was to be a human sacrifice. Borrowing a white garment from a young girl, Anodos moved to the front of the assembled masses and tore down the image on the throne. He had come to realize that not every story was about him and it was time to take "revenge on the self which had fooled me so long."[30] Through the gaping hole revealed when he tore down the image, rushed a great brute, whose throat Anodos gripped with all his will and force and purpose. He remembered no blow. He lost consciousness with his grip still around the beast's throat. Anodos then realized that he was dead and "right content."[31]

In death Anodos finally arrives at what he had been seeking all along in Fairy Land. As he thinks to himself: "The very fact that anything can die, implies the existence of something that cannot die."[32] Now he realizes that service is an essential aspect of life. He sees that his passions have been transformed and glow with light. Deep in his grave, Anodos, feels what has been driving him all along, the unexplainable pull of something beyond himself yet within himself. He knows that it is more important to give love than to be loved. Anodos is borne by a floating chariot over a great city and hears hopeless cries and mad shouts and mourns that he will not be able to minister to those who are suffering in it.[33] At this point, Anodos feels a terrible pang and once again becomes conscious of a bodily earthly life. Anodos finds himself at home in the open air, in the early morning, before sunrise. Lying in the summer air and looking about him, Anodos sees only his normal shadow cast by the sun.

Anodos has experienced (as too will Fat Charlie/Spider) participation in the nonexistent ground, which means participation in the timeless flow of existence at the "intersection of time and eternity." This experience awakens the "flow of presence" — an awareness of existence "that is, and is not, of time.[34] It follows that when individuals use the language of immanent and transcendent, external and internal, this world and the other world the words "do not denote objects or their properties." Instead individuals search for symbols that can evoke the experience of both tensional poles "becoming luminous" — an individual's brief recognition of all of reality.[35] For MacDonald, "reality is a story spoken in the creative language of God" and one of its figures, man, who is created in the image of God, himself becomes a storyteller.[36] The symbolism evoked by such storytellers expresses the fullness of life in the *metaxy*. In *Phantastes* the reader suffers the same pains as Anodos as the images of deep diving, of nature, of alienation and despair, of hope, faith, and love force him to engage in a process of *anamnesis* (remembering) that pulls out the reader's own experiences of longing, of living in the in-between, and of response to the pull of the beyond.

FAT CHARLIE FINDS HIS VOICE AND SPIDER (MOMENTARILY) LOSES HIS

Neil Gaiman has described *Anansi Boys* as a "magical-horror-thriller-ghost-romantic-comedy-family-epic."[37] It is all that and more. Part of the "more" is the understanding of reason as wise imagination that runs through many of Neil Gaiman's novels. Implied in these novels, and in *Sandman,* is the suggestion that reliance purely on instrumental reason will kill what Gaiman appears to value most—imagination, dreaming, possibility for change, wisdom, and concern for others. Instead, the importance of noetic reason and its role in the growth toward maturity and wisdom pervades his work. Noetic reason is the path to order. Characters like Grahame Coats in *Anansi Boys,* who often personify the worst aspects of the dominant culture and lack both wisdom and harmony, are forces for personal and social disorder.[38]

Anansi Boys is a play on the Anansi myths of Ghana's Ashanti people. Gaiman suggests that in the beginning all stories belonged to Tiger. However, Mawu, the sky god, decided to give all the stories and songs (for what are songs except stories set to music) to Anansi, the Spider god. In Gaiman's version, Mawu did this because in Tiger's stories "all the songs were dark."[39] They reeked of power and fear and blood. Mawu did not like those stories because songs last and songs and stories shape their hearers.[40] Anansi's stories, on the other hand, contained the full range of human characteristics and emotions. Further, the spider's stories made people laugh. Anansi may be a cunning trickster, greedy and full of lust. However, Anansi also can be "good-hearted, lucky, and even honest."[41] He is never mean-spirited. In his stories Anansi himself often is the butt of the joke.[42] He does not seek power, and his stories teach possibility and wisdom[43] —a wisdom one is never quite sure whether Anansi possesses himself. Anansi's stories teach human beings to use their minds, not their weapons, when confronting a problem.[44] Mawu also gave Anansi all the songs and stories because the spider wove together all the strands of life (body and spirit) so beautifully. That was important because without songs and stories that expressed who they were and how they should live in the world with others, humanity would not be able to "make sense of their worlds."[45] Tiger's stories were of cruelty. Anansi's stories were about joking around with folks who almost were your friends.

Fat Charlie Nancy (who is not and never has been 'fat') lives and works in London as a bookkeeper in the firm of Grahame Coats, a crooked talent representative. He is engaged to marry Rosie Noah, a nice woman who always wants to make the world a better place. He does not genuinely love her, but wants to marry her because she wants to do good and she is willing to go out with him. Rosie wants to marry Fat Charlie because her mother hates him; she does not really love him either. Fat Charlie is naïve and easily manipulated. Introverted and conventional, Fat Charlie does not ask questions and looks only at the surface of things. Fat Charlie is vague, almost blurry. Few remember meeting him; no one remembers his name or anything about him five minutes after meeting him, even if they still are in his company. Further, even though excellent with numbers, he is unable to pay real attention to either the world around him or the implications of the numbers he crunches daily. He begins the story as one of those people the narrator says sees impossible things, responds with "funny old world, isn't it?" and without a second thought continues their day. Fat Charlie lives in the "real" world, and reality to him is purely physical. He possesses some childish characteristics, but there is nothing childlike about him.

A former neighbor, Mrs. Higgler, calls Fat Charlie to tell him that his father has died, prompting him to get on a plane and head to a place he had hoped never to visit again, Florida. Now, as sad as they are, interesting things can occur at funerals. People begin to tell stories and often the bereaved learn things about the dead that they never knew. Fat Charlie does not know his father is the god Anansi until Mrs. Higgler tells him after the funeral. To Fat Charlie, his father was an embarrassment with his practical jokes, green fedora, lemon-yellow gloves, sand-dancing, singing, and belief in mermaids.

Nor does Fat Charlie know he has a brother. As a young boy living in Florida with his parents, Charlie, accidentally broke a gazing ball in another neighbor's (Mrs. Louella Dunwiddy) yard. Mrs. Dunwiddy, tired of Charlie's mischief, split off from Fat Charlie "all the tricksiness" and all the magic and put them into a new person—Spider.[46] Then she sent Spider away, forbidding him from coming to Florida ever again. Charlie has never known of his existence. At first Spider appears to be the opposite of his brother. Spider is charming and good company. People remember him. He is vivid. He is carefree and just wants to enjoy life, not a problem when you are the brother "with all the god stuff."[47] He loves and is loved by women. However, Spider is just as unable to pay attention to anything or anyone around him as is Charlie.

Although not mean-spirited, Spider is careless, thoughtless, and self-centered. Where Fat Charlie is too concerned about making a mistake and becoming embarrassed, Spider is never concerned about the consequences of his actions for either himself or others. He constantly seeks diversion, not realizing that his diversions bring him no genuine joy. Fat Charlie fumbles with words; Spider can "push" reality a little with his. Fat Charlie, who has a terrific voice, is so self-effacing he cannot sing in front of other people. Spider has a song: "No boredom." When Spider becomes bored, he just goes someplace else. Where Fat Charlie hates to be in the spotlight, Spider loves being the center of attention.[48] Having no loyalty to anyone or anything, every relationship is contingent to Spider. Spider lives in-between the real world and the world of the gods but participates in neither because he accepts no responsibility for anything.

Neither brother is a harmonious whole. Both are immature and lack any sort of wisdom. Everything changes when Fat Charlie returns to Florida for his father's "funeral."[49] After the funeral, Mrs. Higgler, a family friend, tells Fat Charlie that if he ever wants to talk to his brother he should "tell a spider."[50] In jest, Charlie does just that and, unbeknownst to himself, sets in motion a complicated plot in the theater of the *metaxy.* Charlie must engage in his own portal quest to the caves at the end, or beginning (depending on where one begins), of the world. He and Spider learn, like Anodos, that the road to wisdom involves hard work and suffering, that love, loyalty, and family are important (even if you consider your father the most embarrassing person in the world), that confidence in one's song is essential, and that climbing the ladder of love is the essence of a flourishing life. They figure out the happiest person is the one who most lives in harmony with the order of the cosmos. In the process, Spider's song becomes "Rosie" and Fat Charlie's becomes "Sing."

All this sounds far removed from Anodos' journey into Fairy Land. How do trickery, love of a good joke, and a quick wit have any connection to the quest for the wisdom of Aristotle's mature man or Plato's musical soul? However, two bridges connect Anodos' story and that of Fat Charlie Nancy. One is the longing for harmony (Plato's musical soul) and love. The other bridge is song. In Faerie, Anodos both learns to sing and is transformed by songs. The ageless woman's song advises Anodos to become a "well of love" if he wishes to keep his "spirit pure"[51] and reminds him "how easily things go wrong." The woman whose song allows him to free himself from the imprisonment of his ego tells Anodos to leave his self-imposed desert of pride and "come into the house, so high and wide" the one home of all people.[52]

In *Anansi Boys*, Fat Charlie must find his singing and speaking voices in order to grow up, tell his story, and learn genuine love. To accomplish those goals, Charlie needs to "lighten up," worry a bit less about making mistakes, and begin to be comfortable with himself (and his heritage). After all, it is never easy to be the son of a god. But every person, Gaiman writes, "has a song" that they themselves compose. Those who cannot sing their song "live their songs instead."[53] To live in harmony with themselves and others, each must find and claim their song the same way the character Daisy claims her song of "Evildoers beware!"[54] Even though they have no goal of ascent to heaven, Spider, Rosie, Charlie, and Daisy must climb the ladder of love and accept life as an experience in the *metaxy* in order to achieve the wisdom necessary to fulfill their longings for harmony and maturity. They must accept that "myth places" do exist, some of which "are overlaid on the world; others exist beneath the world."[55] These myth places hold the oldest stories in their mountains and caves and have existed far longer than people.[56]

Spider answers Fat Charlie's message by arriving at Charlie's doorstep. Spider's sudden appearance in London turns Fat Charlie's world upside down. His spare room somehow becomes a tropical resort once Spider occupies it. When Spider leaves, it again is just a "box room." Discovering that their father has died, Spider insists on an evening of "wine, women, and song" in order to drown their sorrows. Uncomfortable from the evening's start to its finish, Fat Charlie gets drunk. Then, jealous of Spider's domination of the evening, he decides to participate in the "song" part of the adventure—karaoke. He knows he can sing, but he "wanted to be able to sing without embarrassment, somewhere there were never any people around to hear."[57] He stands up on the stage, opens his mouth, and promptly passes out. The next day Fat Charlie wakes up with a terrible headache and a woman named Daisy beside him. She is one of the women Fat Charlie and Spider met the night before. After helping Spider bring Charlie home, she decided that staying the night in Charlie's apartment was easier than heading home. Almost immediately Mrs. Noah, Charlie's unhappy and shrewish future mother-in-law, arrives just as a half-dressed Daisy appears in the doorway. Mrs. Noah immediately decides Fat Charlie has betrayed her daughter.

Meanwhile, trying to be helpful, Spider has taken the hungover Fat Charlie's place at work. Spider manipulates reality just enough that everyone thinks he is Fat Charlie. Everything is fine until Spider gets bored, rummages through Grahame Coats' private files, finds evidence of embezzlement, and hints to Coats that he knows about what is happening to Coats' clients' money. As soon as Spider, still disguised as Fat Charlie, heads off to meet Rosie for a lunch date, Coats uses his own and Fat Charlie's computers to frame Fat Charlie for the crime. At lunch Spider decides he wants to sleep with Rosie and seduces her. In twenty-four hours, Spider brings just as much embarrassment and chaos to Fat Charlie's life as had his father. Charlie wants Spider gone—and fast.

So Fat Charlie heads back to Florida to ask the old women for help. Mrs. Dunwiddy and Mrs. Higgler, and their two friends Mrs. Nolls and Mrs. Bustamonte, tell him he must ask the inhabitants of "the other world" for assistance. Already having banished Spider once, Mrs. Dunwiddy cannot do it again. The women form a circle, the chanting begins, and Fat Charlie finds himself in a mysterious place full of caves and mountains. Blurry half-human, half-animal figures inhabit the caves. Fat Charlie asks the Lion, the Elephant, the Python, the Hyena, the Monkey, the Crocodile, and the Tiger for help in getting rid of Spider. All these figures from the Ashanti stories bear grudges against Anansi and refuse to help him send away Spider.

The request especially angers Tiger who feels that Anansi stole the stories from him and that children need to be taught to fear and be cruel.[58] Hyena does tell Charlie to find an empty cave if he wants help. Monkey warns him not to enter the empty one he finds because "Nobody" is in it. In the cave there appears to be nothing, but just at the furthest edge Fat Charlie "saw one thing with his eyes, and he saw something else with his mind, and in the gulf between the two things madness waited."[59] It was something part female and part bird. She wishes "Anansi's bloodline" in return for making Spider go away. Mrs. Dunwiddy has warned Fat Charlie not to make any bargains unless he gets something of equal value in return. Fat Charlie remembers the warning and demands something of equal value. Bird woman gives him a feather and the bargain is struck. Desperate to rid himself of Spider without hurting him, Charlie does not understand that the bargain will mean both his and Spider's deaths.

Fat Charlie returns to the physical world and London where Rosie and Spider have fallen in love and Grahame Coats has called the police to investigate Fat Charlie and murdered a client named Maeve Livingstone who had become suspicious of his management of her accounts. Using a fake passport, he has absconded to the island of St. Andrews. Coats has been preparing his eventual escape there for years. He is happy with himself for murdering the client and getting away with it. He also wonders whether and how soon he will get to kill again. The policewoman in charge of the investigation, of course, turns out to be Daisy.

At the same time, Spider, believing he was having lunch with Rosie, tells her the truth about who he is. Only this Daisy is the Bird Woman in disguise. Narrowly averting her attack and chased by thousands of crows, he heads back to Charlie's flat where he and Fat Charlie have a fight. The police arrive, led by Daisy, and arrest Fat Charlie for fraud. Rosie arrives, and on learning the truth about who Spider is slaps him and leaves. Hundreds of Flamingos attack Spider's tropical retreat and crows try to get at Fat Charlie as he walks in the prison yard.

Spider visits Fat Charlie and Spider in jail and promises to "fix things." Fat Charlie is released because examination of Coats' accounts demonstrates that the embezzlements pre-dated Fat Charlie's employment at the agency. He tells Daisy about the hidden door to Grahame Coats' walk-in-safe where police find the client's body. After a nightmarish plane flight to Florida, Fat Charlie consults with the dying Mrs. Dunwiddy and heads to St. Andrews to retrieve the feather from Mrs. Higgler. He wants to return it to the Bird Woman so that she will leave him and Spider alone. Daisy too heads for St. Andrews in pursuit of Coats despite the fact there is no extradition treaty with the island. That is what happens when one's song is "Evildoers beware!" Mrs. Noah and Rosie arrive in St. Andrews as passengers on a cruise ship. And last of all, Maeve Livingstone's ghost arrives after a brief stopover in Florida where she goes dancing with Anansi.

The set-up seems like the plot of a slapstick comedy and, in some ways, it is. This is one of Neil Gaiman's funniest books. However, nothing is more obvious in this story than that the time has arrived for Fat Charlie and Spider to grow up. Both already have suffered—Charlie from the loss of Rosie to Spider with whom she has fallen in love, police suspicion, a dream he has of Spider in trouble and Spider from losing Rosie and the attacks by the birds. They are beginning to "get it" as Anansi tells Fat Charlie later in the book. Spider has given himself to Bird Woman in order to "fix things." She has pulled out his tongue (Anansi's favorite tool for playing jokes and settling problems) and staked him out for Tiger to kill. It is nothing personal, she tells him. She just has an obligation to "another" to fulfill.

Both Charlie and Spider are way out of their comfort zones. Spider believes he was a "wholly better person" when he saw himself in Rosie's eyes. He misses her terribly. Generally, Spider left town when confronted with problems or difficult situations. Now Spider has "second thoughts" about decisions, when he usually did not have "first thoughts," let alone second ones.[60] Fat Charlie has been jolted out of his drift through life by the dying Mrs. Dunwiddy's explanation of Spider's origins, her demand that he "look the world in the eye," and the results of his selfish desire to be rid of Spider.[61] He finally realized that there "was reality and there was *reality*, and that some things were more real than others."[62] Reality *was* more than the physical world and living in a drone-like rut. He was human and there was more to being human than he had suspected.

Both brothers (with some help from Maeve Livingstone's ghost) respond with imagination and wisdom and their responses rescue Daisy,

Rosie, and Mrs. Noah from being collateral damage in a never-ending war between Anansi and Tiger. Grahame Coats is totally consumed by Tiger. Spider and Fat Charlie must come together as Anansi if wisdom is to triumph over blood and claw. Spider thinks his way out of the cave in which he was imprisoned and finds a way to call forth an army of spiders to protect him from Tiger. Fat Charlie sings *Under the Boardwalk* in front of a hotel dining crowd to free Daisy and himself from Grahame Coats' abduction attempt; then assembles an impromptu magic circle, complete with substitute ingredients, in the belief that it is all "a matter of confidence . . . the important thing isn't the detail. It's the magical atmosphere."[63] Entering the other reality may be a matter of confidence and atmosphere, but one has to believe in its reality first. The circle works, sending Fat Charlie first to his father who gives him his beloved fedora and the advice that stories and songs "don't mean a damn unless there's people listenin' to them."[64] Old myths do not die. Some people will cling to them. Bits and pieces of them will find their way into the new myths. But no myth works unless people are willing to listen.

Charlie, who has retrieved the feather from Mrs. Higgler, puts it in the fedora and sets off to the caves at the beginning of time. He exchanges the feather for Spider's tongue, and he imagines the world "as a web . . . connecting him to everyone he knew."[65] Following Spider's strand, he finds his brother and realizes they are two halves of the same whole and that each, like a severed starfish, had grown into a whole person.[66] The two of them return to the caves. Confronting them, they saw "each of the hundreds of totem figures from before the dawn of time."[67] There Charlie begins to sing "the world." He sings of "the truths beneath the way things are" and "appropriate ends and just conclusions."[68] He sings a wish for long life and happiness for Mrs. Noah. "He sang of his life, all their lives as a web a fly had blundered into, and with his song, he wrapped the fly, made certain it would not escape, and he repaired the web with new strands."[69] All the totems but Tiger join in with stomping and clapping, much like C.S. Lewis' great dance at the end of *Perelandra*. And Charlie knew he would spend the rest of his life singing.

Then comes the happy ending with Mrs. Noah and Rosie saved and Grahame Coats dead and Maeve Livingstone willing to pass over to her beloved husband, Morris, and with Tiger confined to his cave (at least for a time) with the ghost of Grahame Coats in the guise of a stoat. Spider and Charlie have found meaning and purpose—Charlie (no more "Fat Charlie") with Daisy, a son, and a singing career, and Spider with Rosie who works hard helping people and a restaurant. Mrs. Noah remains Mrs. Noah, but their attitude toward her is better.

Once again sacrifice and pain are part of the road to a wise imagination, individual harmony, and growth. Spider and Charlie have found meaning, purpose, harmony, and love. They no longer drift through life. Charlie, walking the beach with his son, finally can see and speak with his father's mermaid. He has found a sense (and a source) of awe and wonder in the world. Spider has found joy in Rosie, supporting her vision of a better world through kindness and goodness, and (of all things) cooking. They pay attention to the world and its people. They know that each person is a strand of story (or song) and that every story is connected because the web includes those they have not met. Words are important and creative and full of possibility for both good and evil. They are good magic in the right hands. Life is not confined solely to physical reality. Another reality, or realities, also exist. To re-create their lives Spider and Charlie must participate in both their human and their "god" sides.

PHANTASTES, ANANSI BOYS AND THE QUEST FOR COMMUNAL ORDER

However, as Gaiman's narrator in *Anansi Boys* tells its readers, Tiger can only be shut out for a time. Tiger always returns and human beings again and again will have to stop his story from becoming the only story. An inability to pay attention, a meaningless quest for happiness that brings no happiness, and a lack of harmony and wisdom characterize contemporary Lockean liberal political systems. They make impossible any genuine reconciliation of authority and community. People in Western liberal societies all are Cosmo, Spider before Rosie, and Anodos at the start of his journey—isolated, self-sufficient, narcissistic, and wedded to the belief that there is only one story line built on the myths of reality, reason, preterition, and absence of grace that dominate Western modernity. Most individuals living in the contemporary West are stuck in a quicksand composed of bad myths and bad magic. Those myths give them their song: "Don't Tread on Me"—and the mistaken belief that only in isolation will they be safe.

Anansi Boys and *Phantastes* challenge every one of those myths. These books suggest that none of us are anything special, that life is lived in the experience of *metaxy*, that human beings are co-creators of what they see, that the wise are those who accept the order of the cosmos, that grace and magic pervade the world, and that life is lived best when lived in association with others. These authors prefer Anansi's stories to Tiger's. Tiger is alone and lives only for himself. Anansi lives in relationships with others, and Anansi's stories are about how to use the human mind to balance the individual with the community. Anansi is a trickster and his example is not always the best, but the stories about Anansi require human thought and wise imagination. They pull the listener beyond the individual to the communal.

Human beings possess reason to assist them in meeting the same anxiety of existence that afflicted Mason and Dixon. Everything depends on the version of reason human beings choose to assuage that anxiety. Do they accept the mystery, messiness, and challenge of life in the *metaxy*— in the in-between of life and death, the mortal and the immortal spiritual, confusion and knowledge, the beginning and the beyond? Do they choose to evaluate whether what they want is just or exhibits noetic reason? Or, do they choose instrumental reason and spend their lives calculating desired goals and searching for the most efficient means of achieving them with no heed of either others or any ethical or moral code? Instrumental reason always revolves around "me." Noetic reason continually searches for justice and the Good.

The answer is not some new religious or political fundamentalism. As Anodos and Fat Charlie discover, human beings never will possess "truth," always the search must continue, because human beings always will be questioners. There will never be a point at which humankind can cry "Eureka, we've got it" and cease asking questions about life, the world, and everything, as Douglas Adams put it in *The Hitchhiker's Guide to the Galaxy*. The answer is not "42"; it is not one or another religious belief; it is not capitalism or socialism or communism or Lockean liberalism, or nationalism. Humanity has put its faith in each of these at one time or another and, ultimately, has found each wanting.[70]

Although it may not be possible for contemporary Western cultures to adopt noetic reason as their standard and criterion for action, it is time to move beyond the myth of purely instrumental reason. Instrumental reason fosters prudence, not wisdom. Moving beyond the myth of instrumental reason that brings only Tiger's stories to fruition is not a pipe dream or a chimera. The meaning of reason has changed throughout human history. Plato and Aristotle bequeathed humanity noetic reason. The scholastics separated faith and reason. After the new discoveries made by science and the rediscovery of Lucretius' work, people moved to instrumental reason. However, instrumental reason, taken to its logical conclusion, has resulted in the disorder and disarray of polarization and tribalism. It is time to once again rethink reason and work to foster wisdom rather than prudence. Machiavelli sold Western civilization a myth—the myth of prudence. Hobbes sold humankind a version of Tiger's story. Those myths have now been adopted not only by political rulers, but by whole populaces. In today's world, those myths no longer fit human experience. Noetic reason at least should be a starting point for developing a new human experience of reason—one that can produce a healthier political order than does contemporary Western liberalism, an order that seeks a just balance between the individual, the community, and overall political authority.

One of the many figures Gaiman acknowledges as an influence on his writing is Lou Reed, the late singer and songwriter for Velvet Underground. In *The View from the Cheap Seats*, Gaiman writes that Reed told him "there's a lot of magic in everything, and then some loss to even

things out."[71] The universe, the world, and all that are endlessly complicated, mysterious, fascinating and worthy of exploration—especially the
search for meaning and order. However, human beings must learn to pay
attention, seek wisdom and clear-sightedness, be open to the world's
magic, and find their voice. They must remember that what authors do is
give people "dreams and magic and journeys into minds and lives that
they have never lived."[72] They open doors for possibility and change.
Phantastes and *Anansi Boys* suggests that human beings weave the songs
and stories by which they live. There are boundaries, but there also is
room for possibility. If they want different stories, stories that include all
of reality and find a tentative answer to the problem of authority and
community, then people need to start weaving them, for it is the clear-
sightedness promoted by noetic reason that allows an individual to experience magic.

NOTES

1. Eden Phillpotts, *A Shadow Passes* (Cecil Palmer & Hayward, London, 1918), 19.

2. George MacDonald, "The Imagination: Its Function and Its Culture," in *The Heart of George MacDonald*, ed. Rolland Hein (Wheaton, IL: Harold Shaw Publishers, 1994).

3. J. Philip Newell. *Listening to the Heartbeat of God: A Celtic Spirituality* (Paulist Press, 1997), 65.

4. MacDonald, "The Imagination: Its Function and Its Culture," 418–419.

5. Ibid., 420.

6. Neil Gaiman, "Why Our Future Depends on Libraries, Reading and Daydream-ing: The Reading Agency Lecture, 2013" in *The View from the Cheap Seats* (William Morrow: *An imprint of* HarperCollins *Publishers,* 2016).

7. See, for example, Ruth Jenkins, "Imagining the Abject in Kingsley, MacDonald, and Carroll: Disrupting Dominant Values and Cultural Identity in Children's Litera-ture," *The Lion and the Unicorn* 35, no. 1 (January 2011): 67–87, accessed April 1, 2014, DOI: 10.1353/uni.2011.0003.

8. Plato. *Gorgias*, trans. Donald J. Zeyl (Indianapolis, IN: Hackett Publishing Com-pany, 1987), 508a.

9. Catherine Kurkjian, Nancy Livingston, Terrell Young, and Avi, "Worlds of Fan-tasy," *The Reading Teacher* 59, no. 5 (February 2006): 496, accessed March 4, 2014, doi:10.1598/RT.59.5.10.

10. See George MacDonald, *A Dish of Orts* (CreateSpace, 2012) and Neil Gaiman, *The View from the Cheap Seats* (New York: William Morrow-*An Imprint of* HarperCollins *Publishers*, 2016).

11. Eric Voegelin, "Reason: The Classic Experience," in *The Collected Works of Eric Voegelin, Vol. 12: Published Essays, 1966-1985*, ed. Ellis Sandoz (Baton Rouge: Louisiana State University Press, 1990), 265.

12. There is an essential and important distinction between saying that a young child pays attention to the world around her and saying that she pays attention to the world as it is seen by adults.

13. Chesteron, G. K. *Everlasting Man* (Watchmaker Press, 2013).

14. Ibid., 158.

15. MacDonald, *Phantastes: A Fairie Romance* (Mineola, New York: Dover Publica-tions, Inc., 2005), 143.

16. Ibid., 23.

17. Ibid., 62.

18. Eric Voegelin, *Order and History, Volume V: In Search of Order* (Baton Rouge: Louisiana State University Press, 1987), 53. Abbreviated as *OH V*.

19. MacDonald, *Phantastes*, 67.

20. See Matthew 16:25–26.

21. MacDonald, *Phantastes*, 81.

22. Ibid., 183.

23. Ibid., 141.

24. Ibid., 152.

25. Ibid., 158.

26. Ibid., 204.

27. Ibid., 189.

28. Ibid., 193.

29. Carl von Clausewitz, *On War* (Princeton: Princeton University Press, 1976), 102.

30. MacDonald, *Phantastes*, 196.

31. Ibid., 198.

32. Ibid., 200.

33. Ibid., 201–202.

34. Eric Voegelin, *OH V*, 30.

35. Eric Voegelin. "The Beginning & The Beyond: A Meditation on Truth" in *The Collected Works of Eric Voegelin, Vol 28: What Is History? And Other Late Unpublished Writings*, ed. Thomas A. Hollweck and Paul Caringella (Baton Rouge: Louisiana State University Press, 1990), 185.

36. Id.

37. Neil Gaiman. Interview with Chris Bolton. August 2005. www.Powells.com, cited in Hank Wagner, Christopher Golden, and Stephen R. Bissette, *Prince of Stories: The Many Worlds of Neil Gaiman* (New York: St. Martin's Griffen, 2008), 336.

38. The body of scholarly work on Neil Gaiman is enormous. Most of it focuses on his *Sandman* series. However, *American Gods* also have attracted much scholarly interest. The works we found most helpful in thinking about *Anansi Boys* are Ruth Jenkins, "Imagining the Abject in Kingsley, MacDonald, and Carroll: Disrupting Dominant Values and Cultural Identity in Children's Literature." *The Lion and the Unicorn* 35, no. 1 (January 2011): 67–87, accessed April 1, 2014, DOI:10.1353/uni.2011.0003; Stephen Rauch. *Neil Gaiman's "The Sandman" and Joseph Campbell: In Search of the* Modern *Myth* (Holicong, PA: Wildside Press, 2003); Daniel Baker, "Within the Door: Portal Fantasy in Gaiman and Miéville," *Journal of the Fantastic in the Arts* 27, no. 3 (2016): 470–493, accessed October 22, 2018, https://lib-proxy.radford.edu/login?url=http://search.ebscohost.com/login.aspx?direct=true&db=hlh&AN=124769634&site=eds-live&scope=site; Rut Blomqvist, "The Road of Our Senses: Search for Personal Meaning and the Limitations of Myth in Neil Gaiman's *American Gods*," *Mythlore* 30, no. ¾ (Spring/Summer 2016): 5–26, accessed October 22, 2012, https://lib-proxy.radford.edu/login?url=http://search.ebscohost.com/login.aspx?direct=true&db=edsglr&AN=edsgcl.288689245&site=eds-live&scope=site; Paula Brown, "Stardust as Allegorical *Bildungsroman*: An Apology for Platonic Idealism" *Extrapolation* 51, no. 2 (2010): 216-234, accessed October 22, 2018, https://lib-proxy.radford.edu/login?url=http://search.ebscohost.com/login.aspx?direct=true&db=edsglr&AN=edsgcl.243526092&site=eds-live&scope=site; Sandor Klapcsik, "The Double-Edged Nature of Neil Gaiman's Perspectives and Liminal Fantasies." *Journal of the Fantastic in the Arts* 20, no. 2 (2009): 193–209, accessed October 22, 2018. https://lib-proxy.radford.edu/login?url=http://search.ebscohost.com/login.aspx?direct=true&db=hlh&AN=48657467&site=eds-live&scope=site; Derek Lee, "The Politics of Fairyland: Neil Gaiman and the Enchantments of Anti-Bildungsroman." *Critique: Studies in Contemporary Fiction*. Online journal http.tandfonline.com/loi/ocrt 57, no. 5 (2016): 552–564, DOI: 10.1080.00111619.2016.1138444; Tara Prescott. *Neil Gaiman in the 21 st Century* (Jefferson, NC: McFarland and Company, Inc., 2015); and Anthony Burdge, Jessica Burke, and Kristen Larsen, ed. *The Mythological Dimensions of Neil Gaiman* (Createspace, 2013).

39. Neil Gaiman, *Anansi Boys*, 290.

40. Id.

41. Ibid., 181.

42. Ibid., 184.

43. Ibid., 290.

44. Id.

45. Ibid., 42.

46. Ibid., 269.

47. Ibid., 38.

48. Ibid., 54.

49. In this telling of Anansi's story, he is merely resting and will return in a generation or so to check on how things are going with his grandchildren.

50. Ibid., 40.

51. MacDonald, *Phantastes*, 154.

52. Gaiman, *Anansi Boys*, 182.

53. Ibid. 189.

54. Id.

55. Ibid., 83.

56. Ibid., 173.

57. Ibid., 70.

58. Ibid., 167–168.

59. Ibid., 174.

60. Ibid., 201.

61. Ibid., 268.

62. Ibid., 209.

63. Ibid., 333.

64. Ibid., 336.

65. Ibid., 350.

66. Ibid., 357.

67. Ibid., 366.

68. Ibid., 368.

69. Ibid., 370.

70. Eric Voegelin. "In Search of the Ground" in *The Collected Works of Eric Voegelin,
Vol. 11: Published Essays 1953-1965*, ed. Ellis Sandoz (Columbia: University of Missouri
Press, 2000): 224–251.

71. Neil Gaiman, "Lou Reed in Memorium: 'The Soundtrack to My Life'" in Neil
Gaiman, *The View from the Cheap Seats* (William Morrow, *an imprint of* HarperCollins
Publishers, 2016), 400.

72. Gaiman, "A Speech to Professionals Contemplating Alternative Employment,
Given at PROCON, April 1997," 250.

FIVE

Do You Believe in Dragons?

Blindness, Opsis, *and the Myth of the Administrative State in* Waiting for the Barbarians *and* Blindness

What does choosing Anansi's stories rather than Tiger's require? That choice requires wise imagination rooted in common experience of life in the *metaxy*. It also requires a clear-sightedness in the creation of a common story to guide vision without claiming infallible and ultimate truth. The ability to discern requires not only noetic reason, but also clear sight and the ability to think past the dragons lurking along the path. Kai asked about the existence of dragons when he was seven or eight. His favorite books involved them. At that point he already knew there was no scientific evidence for their existence. However, he also knew that dragons were part of almost every culture's stories from time immemorial. In some cultures, they were benign. In others they were greedy, cunning, acquisitive, and rapacious. In still other cultures they were merely intelligent and self-interested creatures that paid very little attention to humans.

Dragons loom in the background of human history as a conundrum. Someday paleontology may find some physical evidence of their existence or conclude dragon was the name humans gave to the ancestors of Komodo dragons or the remnants of flying dinosaurs. Maybe not. However, real or not, they left an imprint on human thought and humanity's understanding of the world in which it lived. Some medieval maps showed areas marked "There, be dragons." Those areas generally were in the deepest and most remote part of the woods. And, you know, there always were dragons in those woods. First, the dragons everyone carries around inside themselves—all the demons that haunt human psyches.

And then, as anyone who watches horror films will understand, there are the dragons unleashed by the dark, the mysterious, the outlaw, and the unknown. Modernity's dragons include the search for unlimited power and fame, blind acceptance of technical rationality and superiority without a guiding vision rooted in noetic reason, lack of theoretical clarity regardless of the validity of a vision, and ideological fundamentalism found in many religious and political creeds.

Most human beings have a dragon or two lurking in their mental or physical closet. Among them are hopelessness, economic and social insecurity, mental illness, racism, nativism, selfishness, loneliness, PTSD, fear of the future. Yet, most would rather not think about them. Sufferers may turn to isolation, addiction, outbursts of rage, or endless and mindless diversion to fight their dragons. The rest of humanity chooses blindness under the faulty assumption that if they do not see something, it does not exist. Even worse, many succumb to the chimera that there is nothing they can do to battle those dragons.

In modernity the myth of the Neutral Administrative State, or in the case of very large states, empire—the idea that policy administration is best left in the hands of trained and neutral professionals—fosters such dragons as careerism, self-interest, and an attempt to maintain and expand personal or agency power. Fighting those dragons requires *opsis*, the ability not only to do more than look and observe, but also to get past external appearances and into the heart—to see as Anodos did when he looked at the "Priest" and understood him to be evil, or as Anodos did after experiencing his "death," and as Charlie did when he sang his world into existence. Close reading of the two texts examined in this chapter suggests that the magistrate in *Waiting for the Barbarians*, although he conducts an important interior dialogue over conscience, never reaches *opsis*. In *Blindness*, however, the ophthalmologist's wife does, indeed she appears to possess it even before the story's events occur. Her fight is to maintain that clear-sightedness in the face of guilt and horror.

The United States' participation in Vietnam is a case study in the blindness that can accompany the administrative state. A belief in process, production, and logistics helped to blind the United States to the reality of an enemy who recognized the genuine life or death reality of its struggle. Other examples of administrative blindness include the claims of defendants of Nuremberg that they were just following orders. What was true of the Nuremberg defenses also is true of those in the contemporary world who blindly cling to the dictates of any institutionalized ideological faith. This chapter re-examines the culture of technical rationality and its institutionalization in the neutral administrative state. The problem is that intelligent and ethical members of complex formal organizations lack noetic reason and, like Cosmo and, for a long time, Anodos, Spider, and Fat Charlie, miss important cues. Thus, they are unable to recognize and effectively counter evil. Only those with *opsis*, clear-sightedness will even notice that evil is occurring or has been done. Unfortunately, in the contemporary world, vast numbers of human beings remain blind. They are blind people "who can see but do not see."[1] They fall prey to the myth of a neutral administrative state under which personnel base all decisions on technical rationality and there is a sharp distinction between the political and the administrative. Because they do not see, they sometimes unwittingly, sometimes through lack of courage, or sometimes through the peer pressure of an organization's culture foster genuine evil.

What then is *opsis*? *Opsis,* according to Plato, is vision, clear-sightedness, the eyes of the soul. It is the companion of the rational person and of rational action as discussed in the previous chapter on noetic reason. Like noetic reason, it does not require formal belief in any god. For Voegelin, *opsis* is the "experience of the Beyond and its *parousia* (presence) in the soul of man."[2] *Opsis* is that moment when human beings catch a glimpse of both It-Reality and Thing-Reality in their interconnectedness, a remembrance that "The Beyond is not a thing beyond the things but the experienced presence" of It-Reality "in all things."[3] *Opsis* is a brief glimpse of the sum of things. Heidegger might see it as a glimpse of unconcealment, of Being, that humans try to preserve through language. Florensky describes it as a moment of *ikonostasis*—a moment which shows human beings the boundary between the visible and invisible worlds and illuminates the ground of existence. *Opsis* opens up the mystery of human realization that "the spiritual world of the invisible is not some infinitely far off kingdom, instead it everywhere surrounds us as an ocean."[4] Without it, prisoners of their passions, human beings see no further than themselves and are not capable of genuinely rational choices. At that point they become easy prey for whatever dragon pursues them.

THE MYTH OF THE NEUTRAL ADMINISTRATIVE STATE

In 1932, candidate for president Franklin Delano Roosevelt gave a speech at the Commonwealth Club in San Francisco. The heart of his speech was these words: "Our task now is not discovery or exploitation of natural resources, or necessarily producing more goods. It is . . . administering resources and plants already in hand . . . the day of enlightened administration has come."[5] Underscoring the importance of such administrative decisions, eighty-seven years later the venture capitalist, investor, and businessman Roger McNamee wrote in *Time Magazine* that "Every decision that management makes can matter in the lives of real people. Management is responsible for every action."[6] The myth of the neutral administrative state is that well-trained, professional competence will lead to effective, just, and ethical decisions. Put bluntly, it cannot because there is no "neutral" in most formal organizations, and especially in the Administrate State. Organizations exhibit a blindness caused by the combination of the underlying foundational assumptions and the actions of some of those who compose it. That blindness sometimes leads to poor ethical choices and sometimes to murder and evil.

Technical rationality gained its reputation for efficiency and justice because it was fairer and more efficient than what it replaced—the graft, incompetence, and nepotism of administration by members of political party machines or, in Europe, by estates (classes or orders). It relied on procedures rather than individuals. Max Weber's was one of the first voices to call for professional administration. In "Politics as a Vocation" and "Bureaucracy," Weber outlined what he meant and the ethical system that underlay it.[7] He began by analyzing the two views of ethics most often cited in his era—ontology and deontology.

Ontological and Deontological remain the most commonly found forms of ethics today. Some argue for virtue ethics, but the approach has not gained as large an audience as have ontology and deontology. John Stuart Mill bears the banner for the ontological approach. In his view ethical disputes should be decided based on producing the greatest good for the greatest number of individuals. His is not the vulgar ontology of Jeremy Bentham. For Mill, both the quantity *and* the quality of the good produced need to be considered. Those who favor deontology tend to look to Immanuel Kant who argues for duty-based ethics. His categorical imperative states that one should only make choices that they would will to be universal laws.

Weber did not believe in the deontological view's commitment to absolute ends. Neither, however, did he believe that the end always justified the means. His ethic was based on responsibility. As he said in his first lecture in Freiburg, "In the last analysis, the processes of economic development are struggles for power. Our ultimate yardstick of values is 'reasons of state'."[8] Reasons of state, however, meant more in his view than that the state is always right. Although Weber's focus was on consequences, on the ends, his goal was to reach some compromise that did as little damage as possible to all involved. He called this an ethic of responsibility.

On a trip to the United States, Weber saw machine politics in action and recognized it as the wave of the future. Modern politics, he thought, required professionals to manage organizations and activities, and this process was among those pushing toward an administrative culture based on cohorts of professionals geared to rational efficiency. For him, democracy had no intrinsic worth, but was superior to other forms of government only because it held the potential for more efficient leadership.[9] Following Schiller, he saw the world as "disenchanted." That disenchantment meant that society did not do what was morally good, but what was expedient in producing wealth and good social order. Weber's legacy was thoroughly modern definitions of the state as "a human community that (successfully) claims the *monopoly of the legitimate use of physical force* within a given territory" and of politics "striving to influence the distribution of power, either among states or among groups within a state."[10] He also left the world the central idea of administration—neutral competency.

In Weber's view, the neutral administrator pursued a course of training, operated according to set rules of procedure, usually was appointed by someone higher up in the administration based on task-related education and/or experience, received set compensation, and received social esteem commensurate with their rank. Often, the possibility of life tenure accompanied appointment. This form of social organization, Weber maintained, would be very difficult to destroy as increasingly "the specialized knowledge of the expert became the foundation for the power position of the officeholder."[11] He considered political officials with high moral standards—those who accepted Kant's deontological ethics—to be politically irresponsible.[12] For "no ethics in the world can dodge the fact that in numerous instances the attainment of good ends is bound to the fact that one must be willing to pay the price of using dubious means or at least dangerous ones."[13] That was the political/administrative dichotomy. An administrator would gather and present the facts, but the political branches would have to make the decision. He saw an ethics of responsibility as the only course open to the "*mature* man." This individual would not follow the principle that whatever could be done, should be done. At some point the mature person "is aware of a responsibility for the consequences of his conduct and really feels such responsibility with heart and soul."[14] At that point, if conscience demanded, the administrator would step down.

The problem is that the development of technical rationality followed a different path than that outlined by Max Weber. The Brownlow Committee Report (1939) and the 1980 report of the National Academy of Sciences both viewed neutral competence and technical rationality as the norm and as the ideal for public administration. However, neutral competence is far from prevalent in mass democracies. Weber's vision of ethical responsibility, of finding solutions to problems that did the least possible damage to all involved, faded and neutral competence became an excuse for blindness and ethical failure. Spicer attempts in his work to deal with the problematic that is the dragon lurking behind the concept "Neutral Administrative State." The mask of neutral competence leads to an inability to "see" people as they genuinely live and, a blindness to such institutional or long-term societal biases as racism or gender inequality.[15]

Ontological ethics rules the day. Deontological ethics, virtue ethics, and even Weber's responsibility ethics are not considered. The end will always justify the means, especially in Western liberal societies where

Hume's vision of the useful rational person (the individual of "discretion, caution, enterprise, industry, assiduity, frugality, economy, goodness, prudence, discernment, constancy, perseverance, . . .") is ubiquitous.[16] Society dismisses many of its citizens as incapable of Humean virtue. Further, it dismisses the thoughtful, the questioners, as standing "like a schoolman's ass, irresolute between equal motives."[17] The myth of the Neutral Administrative State believes itself the site of those who "can do." Thus, the myth can lead, as Adams and Balfour argue, to administrative evil—even with the best of intentions, all the best qualities of Humean man, and the most professional of experts. Adams and Balfour maintain that a culture of technical rationality leads to "ordinary people, within their normal professional and administrative roles" engaging "in acts of evil without being aware that they are doing anything wrong."[18] These scholars define evil as human action that causes "needless" suffering and death to other human beings.[19] They see a continuum of evil with events such as small white lies at one end and the Holocaust at the other.

Administrative evil differs from other kinds of wrongdoing in that it is difficult to recognize.[20] In fact, evil is not a term that social scientists want to use in this disenchanted age. Some scholars have criticized Adams' and Balfour's work as unscientific for this reason.[21] Administrative evil is difficult to assign in organizations that diffuse "individual responsibility" and require the "compartmentalized accomplishment of role expectations in order to perform work on a daily basis."[22] Finally, technical rationality has increased the possibility of moral inversions (branding some moral evil as a positive good) because law and practice have narrowed the policy-making process. It now is easier to do evil without actually understanding it as an outcome of one's individual contribution to final policy development and implementation or by becoming convinced that one's actions "serve the greater good."[23]

Technical rationality, as a culture with social, economic, and political implications, revolves around a "scientific-analytical mind-set" and a belief that technological progress is always positive. Moreover, a commitment to social and political Individualism can make it difficult for those living in societies strongly influenced by classical liberalism to recognize the institutional dynamics found in organizations. Administrative evil often proceeds through a number of small choices made over time that begin to tilt ethical considerations. At some point the accumulation of those small choices reaches a critical mass and supports administrative evil,[24] as for example, in the cases of Abu Ghraib, the Challenger disaster, the Dalkon Shield, Enron, and Blackwater.[25] These evils arose when organizational cultures existed in which individuals, although competently doing their jobs and committed to technical rationality, failed to see the ethical implications of their work or did not see it as in their self-interest to point out those implications. More importantly, the organizational culture punished those who did point out potential or real problems. In some ways the Neutral Administrative State is a scapegoat for human failings; in other ways it is blind to those failings and is itself at least partially culpable.

Rather than offering an antidote, contemporary political science may have contributed to this lack of insight. A past president of both the American Political Science Association and the International Political Science Association, Theodore Lowi, describes himself as a "student of the pathologies of the body politic."[26] He views technical rationality as one of those pathologies. Technical rationality and political science's emphasis on quantification and rational choice theory produces, he argued, large amounts of information. None of the information produced was false. However, quoting Ricci, Lowi adds: "None of it was especially true."[27] Beginning in the 1950s, political science ran to such quantification in a rush to prove that it was just as scientific as the hard sciences. It forgot it was a different sort of science—one based on the Oxford English Dictionary's definition: "knowledge acquired by study."[28] Lowi suggests a return to Aristotle's view of science as careful observation and *comparison* between objects as they are and as they ought to be. The belief that quantification is the only way to make fair political decisions leads, he argues, to a "political science of pathologies tending toward authoritarianism" both in the United States and internationally.[29] People, actions, and behaviors become no more than countable units.

Under these circumstances *opsis*, as described by Plato and Camus is almost impossible. If one does not "see" people, they may not treat them well or even fairly. The myth of technical rationality guiding the Neutral Administrative State leads to an inability to recognize and acknowledge the reality of what many groups and individuals experience. Who wants to know the story of the homeless or the criminal? Who wants to look at, let alone make eye contact with, others on the metro or walking down the street? Even mere eye contact seems to generate a link, a connection, and connection means some responsibility. In a world increasingly fearful of obligations of solidarity, even looking is disastrous. Think about all the people sitting with others in restaurants, each person at the table engrossed in their cell phone. They barely look at one another. They rarely speak to one another. In the increasingly rationalized and institutionalized societies fostered by the classical liberal model, *opsis* is frightening and, thus, few individuals try to tame the dragons that haunt the human condition.

Modernity's focus is on the intra-mundane. It argues for a strictly human-based virtue and view of the world and for a purely human good. Like Protagoras, modernity believes that humanity is the measure of all things. However, without reference to some more general standard of good, too narrow a focus on the particular in human life leads to blindness and murder. The persistence of technical rationality's tendency to wittingly or unwittingly do evil demonstrates the point. In the end "the blind are always at war."[30] Plato's quest is not outside the human realm as such critics as Martha Nussbaum argue. Humans need to "see," if only in order to recognize that seeing is essential to the practice of common human decency. Thought, sometimes even Platonic deep-diving, is a requirement of all speaking and acting that goes beyond the purely animal, beyond a pragmatic reason that weighs the cause and effect, goals and capabilities. Openness, receptivity, and *opsis* are inherent parts of human life in a human world and without them human decency cannot exist. What scholars must look for in literature, and in political philosophy, may be found in Iris Murdoch's view that good art motivates human beings to "true vision"[31] that comes from studying how people live. No serous artist, George Steiner wrote, "has ever doubted . . . that his work bears on good and evil, on the enhancement and diminution of the sum of humanity in man and the city."[32] Neutral administrative states are not in a good opening position to follow Steiner's maxim.

The Age of Reason made human reason, defined as calculating means to achieve goals, the ultimate ground of existence and the measure of all action. Noetic reason requires both measuring means against ends and measuring ends against some ultimate good, even if Max Weber considers that a bad idea. In the contemporary world, such language tends to prompt images of religious intolerance, oppression, and warfare. The problem, however, is that when human beings prohibit, even through peer pressure, or render impossible the development of symbols evoking experience of the search for a ground of existence beyond the transitory material, they also make impossible the construction of a public order based on those experiences, that is, based on noetic reason. They have no assistance in facing their individual and communal dragons. That fact almost guarantees that they will be murderers in Camus' sense of the term—the failure to accept responsibility for evils that do not directly affect themselves. Recognition of that fact, although treated differently in each individual thinker, is one of the constants in twentieth-century political philosophy.

José Saramago and J. M. Coetzee are mythopoets who explore the meaning and implications of *opsis*. They view it as essential to humanity's ability to see others as human beings with the same sorrows, joys, and needs as they have or of developing any feeling of ethical responsibility for others. Saramago's and Coetzee's works may seem strange choices for a book about mythopoesis. No gods or goddesses appear or are mentioned. There is only the gaze of a Waterbuck and a dog of tears who carries faint echoes of Father Zossima's suggestion in *The Brothers Karamazov* that when humans suffer, God cries. Both stories are set squarely in the intra-mundane world where whatever can be done will be done. However, the extraordinary pervades both works. These works are guides to the qualities of personal, political, and natural order that evoke the presence of mystery and the unknown. Based on acceptance of both

Thing-Reality and It-Reality, *Blindness* and *Waiting for the Barbarians* will question the morality of decisions made by neutral administrators under the guise of protecting society and preserving public order—the essence of the myth. In so doing they answer the question of who possesses superior vision and place the responsibility for order firmly in the hands of the everyday person who possesses *opsis*. Humanity will be the "reward" of the clear-sighted suffering servant, not the figure able to dominate through innate physical strength, technical rationality, or technology. The suffering servants are the figures most capable of rationally responding to the pull of both tensional poles of existence.

Coetzee's magistrate manifests modern reason just as much as does his opponent, Col. Joll. The magistrate rejects participation in the drama of being and becomes blind to everyone and everything but his own shrunken self. Throughout *Waiting for the Barbarians,* the magistrate asserts his right "to be ignorant of the reality and truth of common experience," the feature Voegelin argues is the twentieth century's "most remarkable and characteristic institution of Western societies."[33] He is, in many ways, irrational. By contrast, Saramago's character, the ophthalmologist's wife exemplifies what Voegelin called reason in the classic sense and possesses *opsis*. She acts as though the essence of human existence is "partnership in being."[34] Throughout, she puts the common good ahead of her own self-interest. As rational calculations of self-interest her choices appear insane. No "rational" person relying on instrumental reason, would disregard self-interest and, following conscience and love, choose to follow her husband into internment. Nor would such a "rational" person accept responsibility for the lives of a group that the ophthalmologist's wife did not know or take sin on herself to save strangers by killing the head of the hoodlum gang terrorizing those interned by the government.

Ultimately, however, Saramago suggests (and Coetzee might agree) that she is far more rational than the magistrate. Without ever talking about God, religious dogma, or any form of God, she acts in faith, hope, and love. She possesses "that openness of the soul in existence that is an orienting center in the life of man."[35] She participates in mystery, sees beyond her own self-interest, and accepts the reality of grace. Unlike the magistrate, the ophthalmologist's wife possesses the *opsis* required for Camus' common decency. Thus, these novels can teach the contemporary world a great deal about a capacity for clear-sightedness that Plato and Aristotle considered essential to fighting personal and political dragons. In today's world, however, people tend to view that clear-sightedness as naïve and totally out of place in the study of politics.

OPSIS AND RESPONSIBILITY

Blindness takes place in a city not far removed from contemporary times. The book begins as a man is sitting at a traffic light. Suddenly he begins to shriek, "I am blind!" All he can see is white. Someone drives him home, and then steals his car. Suddenly the car thief too is struck blind. The first blind man's wife takes him to the eye doctor. She will go blind, as will the ophthalmologist, and the rest of the occupants of the doctor's waiting room.

At first the government seeks to isolate the outbreak and quickly gathers together the blind citizens. The ophthalmologist's wife, who pretends to be blind in order to stay with her husband, also goes into internment. The government quarantines them in a former insane asylum. There they meet a young prostitute called the "girl with dark glasses," a "boy with a squint" who has been separated from his mother, and an "old man with an eye patch," all of whom were members of the group in the ophthalmologist's waiting room. [36]

There is no thought of things as they ought to be. There is no compassion, no help for the car thief dying of gangrene or the unidentified woman with cancer. The state has abandoned the blind completely except for inadequate and random food deliveries. The military guards the asylum gates and threatens to kill anyone from inside who comes too close. There is only the anonymous tape recording played every day in the hospital citing important reasons of state for their quarantine and assuring them that the law was the same for all and would not allow "preferential treatment," even for the sick and dying. [37]

Nothing seems able to stop the spread of the mysterious malady. More and more inmates arrive at the asylum, which truly becomes a hell. The inmates suffer from hunger, filth, stench, and extortion by a group of violent inmates. The gang confiscates all the food and demands first anything the others have of value and then sexual favors from the women as payment for rations. Step by step the blind inmates are led into a horrific maelstrom of degradation, violence, and utter hopelessness.

The descriptions in *Blindness* of moral corruption and the subsequent loss of rationality becomes a fable of civilizational decline. The pull of lasting things is replaced by the pull of passing things (the passions) and the result is a short-circuiting of the soul that deprives almost every character of the source of reason and hence of "seeing." Again and again there is the talk of organizing, but citizens find no capacity for that and no organization ever occurs outside the small group led by the ophthalmologist's wife. When human beings reach the level of animals, Saramago seems to say, they lose contact with the ground of existence, flee from others into themselves and from community into isolation. There is no ability to separate good from evil or justice from injustice. The citizens are more blind than a person born completely without eyes. Moral conscience is one of the first victims. Conscience "is something that exists and has always existed."[38] However, in the contemporary world, conscience can be dwarfed by narcissism, isolation, and reliance solely on instrumental reason. Now human beings put their consciences "in the color of blood and the salt of tears, and if that were not enough, we made our eyes into a kind of mirror turned inwards, with the result that they often show without reserve what we are verbally trying to deny."[39] Again, what can be done trumps what should be done.

There is no Beyond and no sense of the paradox of consciousness and its accompanying presence. Only the animal part remains, and reason becomes indistinguishable from unreason. Then the symptoms of not seeing—pride, wealth, power, and selfishness—are taken as the norm for human nature. The soul (*psyche*) is reduced to a collection of bio-psychological impulses which blocks its role as the sensorium of joint participation with transcendent reality in the *metaxy*. Therefore, to rely on an image from Heraclitus, *opsis* becomes atrophied and loses its ability to see clearly. Those without *opsis* are sleepwalkers. But the eyes remain part of reality and do not lose their function as windows into the soul. As the ophthalmologist puts it, "I've spent my life looking into people's eyes, it is the only part of the body where a soul might still exist, and if those eyes are lost"[40] so is the soul. The ophthalmologist has realized that losing the soul means losing love, judgment, and justice. The blindness experienced by the city's inhabitants merely is a symptom of the loss of those human qualities.

What is this strange phenomenon that prevents the characters from seeing? Is this a disease of the body or of the soul? The narrator asks "who can say that this white blindness is not some spiritual malaise . . . ?" If so, "then the spirits of the blind casualties have never been as free as they are now, released from their bodies, and therefore free to do whatever they like, above all, to do evil, which as everyone knows, has always been the easiest thing to do."[41] Blindness, the absence of noetic reason, and *opsis*, lead to evil. It allows humanity's various dragons free range.

From passages like this the reader receives hints that this blindness has something to do with *opsis*, the eye of the soul, or of the mind if you prefer, with the ability of the human to "see" good and evil, justice and injustice. This blindness results in chaos because there is no vision or spiritual substance to bind humans together. Someone even has covered the eyes of the statues in the city's central church. *Blindness* is a tale of spiritual disease brought on by the shrinking of the self (both individual and social) to only one part of what it means to be human in the Platonic sense. Saramago asks the reader to understand that human order is a precious island in a sea of dragons that threaten to overwhelm it and that *opsis* and valor must be constantly raised as bulwarks against it.

Finally, the inmates act against the gang, cause the asylum to burn down, and are free. The flight from the building is chaotic and deadly.

The soldiers are gone. Those who manage to get out find nothing but silence. The disease finally has reached the police, army, and government. The entire town has gone blind. The ophthalmologist's wife leads her husband, the first blind man and his wife, the boy with the squint, the girl with dark glasses, and the old man with an eye patch into a city in anarchy. People smell food and follow each other down the stairs to a storeroom where they die because they cannot find their way out. People die in the streets without friends or compassion. Corpses remain unburied—food sources for animal scavengers. After leaving her band in order to find them food, the ophthalmologist's wife becomes temporarily lost on the way back to where she left them and breaks into tears. Suddenly she is comforted by a dog she comes to call "the dog of tears." The dog will follow her wherever she goes.

Only the doctor's wife has retained something that allows her to see for her little band of blind beggars. The only thing special about the ophthalmologist's wife is her continuing vision of faith, hope, and love and her willingness to serve, even to the point of being willing to publicly assume the guilt of murder for killing the leader of the criminal gang. She possesses a genuine sense of ethical responsibility. The "dog of tears" who finds her in the city also possesses those characteristics. The wife continually reminds the others of some vision of what it means to be human. After the asylum burns down, the woman helps not only for her husband, but also for others because "today is my responsibility."[42] She leads the small band back into the city to her and her husband's apartment. She asks them to take care of their "necessities" out on the balcony so that the apartment can be kept orderly. The order she seeks is not that of a good housewife, but of staking out the difference between living a human life or a feral animal's life. She wants them to remember they had led an animal's life during their confinement going "down all the steps of indignity . . . until we reached total degradation." That could happen in the apartment just as easily as in the insane asylum. Further, she reminds them they knew the difference between good and evil before they went blind. They know that right and wrong "are simply different ways of understanding our relationship with the others,"[43] ways of understanding that everyone participates in the same story.

The ophthalmologist's wife wants them to understand the horror of the sighted person "in a world in which everyone else is blind." She is not special, "I am simply the one who was born to see this horror."[44] Her husband responds that if he ever regains his sight he will look carefully at eyes as "if I were looking into their souls." The old man with the black eye patch does not like the word "soul." The doctor replies: "Or their minds, the name does not matter." Mind, soul, whatever—the name does not matter agrees the girl with dark glasses: "Inside us there is something that has no name, that something is what we are."[45] *Opsis* allows human beings to see and act upon that something.

What is that something inside every human being that is the "something that we are?" It is only at this point that Saramago's little group of pilgrims in the realm of white blindness become aware that they are participants in some kind of story and that "All stories are like those about the creation of the universe, no one was there, no one witnessed anything, yet everyone knows what happened."[46] The writers of Genesis likewise were not there at the beginning. However, they were conscious of participating in a story and of the necessity of wrestling the symbols of their experience of the paradox of consciousness out of that story. The little squad in *Blindness* in some way becomes conscious of its participation in the story told by transcendent reality. Consciousness demands a responsive relation to every other countenance.[47] They had begun their journey as faces. Now they were countenances revealing some truth of human existence in the *metaxy*.

As mysteriously and suddenly as the onslaught began, the strange white halo begins to disappear, and sight returns to the city's inhabitants. In the tragedies of Aeschylus, wisdom comes through suffering, which binds the tragic heroes to their fate. The doctor's wife had painfully discovered the paradox of leadership that utters the harsh command that who would be the greatest must be the least. She, and everyone else in the city, seeks only to return to normal life. However, the citizens of this city now perceive the "normal" in a slightly different way—a way that suggests greater clear-sightedness.

In a sequel published during the summer of 2006 (*Seeing*), Saramago picks up the story four years later. Another catastrophe has struck the city, this time a political one. At the parliamentary election "more than 70% of the total votes cast were blank."[48] The government's immediate response is to suspect an anti-democratic plot. No good citizen would cast a blank ballot. The government withdraws from the city and blockades it. Life in the city goes on as usual. When someone attempts to rob a bank, he is apprehended by the citizens, taken to the fire station for a strong "talking to," and released. Common decency seems to reign. People seem to have realized their role as actors in a common story.

However, the government perceives that very common decency as undermining its authority. Just as it could not be Agamemnon's fault that he took Achilles' prize, it cannot be the government's fault that so many cast blank ballots. There must be some conspiracy. Saramago's prose turns to satire at this point. His descriptions of cabinet meetings are eerie. What is apparent is that the government, although it considers every one of its actions strictly rational and appropriate, is moving blindly toward dictatorship. Particularly interesting is the government's use of spies among the citizens. The spies hear parts of conversations and based on that bring in random citizens for a "questioning" that borders on torture. The government, as metaphysically blind now as it was physically blind four years prior, sees the tactic as upholding democracy. In addition, it turns out there was an unspoken agreement in the government (and among the citizens) never to mention the occurrence of white blindness. In fact, the word "blindness" itself appeared to be stricken from the vocabulary.

Then the inevitable happens and the first character to go blind in *Blindness* writes a letter to the government denouncing the doctor's wife. She must be the source of all the blank ballots because she never went blind. The reader learns this first blind man has divorced his wife because in order to save the others by providing them with food, she went with the ophthalmologist's wife and the other women in the ward when the tormentors demanded them. She had been raped and she was wrong because she had "allowed" it to happen. She had, he believed, degraded and demeaned both him and her. He could not live with such depravity.

It is interesting to contrast his response with that of the ophthalmologist's wife to a situation that occurred in the asylum in *Blindness*. One night the "girl with dark glasses" gets into bed with the eye doctor and has sex with him in front of his wife, while they both think she is asleep. The wife's response, which echoes the narrator's comment that the best human traits are "generosity and compassion,"[49] is immediate and unconditional forgiveness.

In contrast, throughout both books the first blind man, who divorces his "sullied" wife and accuses the ophthalmologist's wife of causing the failure to vote, is spiritually blind. In the end government snipers kill both the ophthalmologist's wife and the "dog of tears." Blindness reigns masked as a rational response to a threat to society. Administrative evil hides behind "reasons of state." Ultimately in the real world, the result of extreme reliance on technical rationality, overreliance on the administrative/political dichotomy, and lack of *opsis* is the failure to see one another. In Saramago's work, human beings need constant reminders of what it means to be human if they are to successfully fight dragons. The ophthalmologist's wife is such a reminder.

BLINDNESS AND THE ROAD TO NOWHERE

On the other hand, the magistrate in J. M. Coetzee's *Waiting for the Barbarians* misses the meaning of all the reminders sent him concerning what it means to be human. *Waiting for the Barbarians* takes place at an unnamed oasis on the border of an unnamed empire at the point where the world of the empire ends and that of the "barbarians" begins. The Empire feels that the barbarians pose some threat and so sends Col. Joll of the Third Bureau, wearing odd dark glasses no one in the hinterlands of the empire has ever seen before, on a mission to pacify the area. The book opens with a conversation with the novel's protagonist, the magistrate of the frontier farming community protected by a fort, and Col. Joll. Joll's philosophy is

summed up in the aphorism "Pain is truth; all else is subject to doubt."[50]
His method of dealing with captured barbarians is simply an extension of
this axiom. The magistrate, on the other hand, is a seemingly compas-
sionate man who has treated the barbarians with some justice.

The plot of *Waiting for the Barbarians* is simple. Col. Joll of the Third
Bureau of the Civil Guard arrives at the oasis in order to put down what
appears to be a nonexistent barbarian rebellion. He and his companions
do not know the indigenous people; they do not know the terrain. They
are blind to everything but their job as guardians of the empire. At first
the magistrate is polite and deferential. The magistrate of the colonial
oasis does not want to become "embroiled" in the Third Bureau's operation against the "barbarians."[51] He sympathizes with the plight of the
indigenous peoples, but is not willing to upset his tidy little life. However, he cannot help himself and increasingly opposes Col. Joll's activities,
which include torture and humiliation of captives—most of them poor
fisher people. The magistrate takes in a barbarian girl who has been
tortured and partially blinded, almost lovingly nurses her back to health,
and later returns her to her people. This act damns him in Col Joll's eyes.
The magistrate is incarcerated, interrogated, and tortured. However,
Joll's blindness leads to a disastrous military operation, all the troops pull
out of the fort on the oasis, and the magistrate once again takes up the
administration of his duties.

The key is that doleful adjective "almost." All through the book the
reader has a feeling of an immense and inalterable emptiness. It is not just
the remoteness of the imperial outpost, because there are many things to
do. It is not just the encroaching desert or the remote mountains that are
home to the barbarians. The emptiness is a strange negative force that is
streaming through the gaps in human order, and both Col. Joll and the
magistrate represent those breaches. The emptiness comes from the inability to see into Joll's eyes and read his soul and from the magistrate's
incapacity to make a genuine connection to any other human being, even
one he has convinced himself he loves.

Col. Joll cannot bear the thought that anyone could read his thoughts
or emotions. He must always present a mask and never become a countenance. The magistrate is always desperate to touch the women around
him, especially the barbarian woman, whom he bathes and massages.
Nothing, neither people nor things, can be real until they are touched
and, in some way, made his own. And although, many people and things
are touched by both men, none are seen or understood. Both are symbols
of the magistrate's thought that "There has been something staring me in
the face and still I do not see it . . . I leave . . . feeling stupid, like a man
who has lost his way long ago but presses on a road that may lead
nowhere."[52] Possession is very different from love, empathy, and understanding.

The fact that this story takes place at an outpost on the borderland between the empire and a vast wilderness is no accident. This is a story of the *metaxy*. Indeed, the magistrate finds himself in many middles and many stories. He is in-between the story of the empire and story of the other (the girl), in-between youth and old age, in-between the Third Bureau and the barbarians, and in the middle of whom he thinks he is and what he experiences himself as being. He experiences life in the middle between blindness and seeing.

The magistrate perceives himself as an actor in some sort of drama of meaning but does not know with certainty who he is. Yet no human being is totally ignorant because their participation in being is not blind. It is illuminated by consciousness.[53] However, suppose that an individual becomes blind because they are not illuminated by consciousness. Suppose a man or woman fits Heraclitus' description of the individual who lives outside the common world of reason. Suppose the world of common reason has come to consider technical rationality as the only true form of consciousness. The magistrate wants only his quiet life collecting taxes, pursuing his little hobbies, and "administering commercial lands."[54] He views himself merely as the Empire's neutral administrative arm steeped in technical rationality. He conducts his work efficiently and fairly, mostly leaving the fishing folk and the barbarians to take care of themselves. His one hope is that when he dies three lines about him "would appear in the Imperial gazette."[55] The magistrate is neither thoughtful nor insightful. And he cannot see what stares him in the face once the contingent from the Third Bureau of the Civil Guard arrives. Despite his sense of common decency and his effective administration he will become a participant in administrative evil.

Although, the magistrate makes some progress in understanding the empire which employs him and in finding and following his conscience, he remains without *opsis* and learns very little. The barbarian girl he could never understand is more clear-sighted than he is. She understands the magistrate and his self-centered vision of her, even as he takes her back to her people. The magistrate's continual internal dialogue with himself has made him aware of others' existences and of his, at least minimal, responsibility toward them. However, he has not achieved *opsis*. It requires more. It requires empathy and connection. Like Cosmo in *Phantastes*, his final actions with regards to her and to the "barbarian" prisoners are the product of an ethical ideal rather than a genuine sense of common humanity.

The magistrate, at one point during a hunt, pauses on the brink of "seeing." He is watching his intended prey, a waterbuck, chewing his cud. The waterbuck turns and their eyes are locked together. Staring at the buck, he feels that there is "time for all things, time even to turn my gaze inward and see what it is that has robbed the hunt of its savor." During the moment that they gaze at one another "the stars are locked in a configuration in which events are not themselves but stand for other things. . . . I stand trying to shrug off this irritating and uncanny feeling" until the buck runs into the surrounding reeds.[56]

The magistrate seemed poised on the cusp of an experience of intra-cosmic mystery. A whole stream of meaning seems ready to flood the psyche of the old hunter. The magistrate has felt the wonder of the soul's search for truth breaking out in joyous amazement at discovering the mysterious world-transcendent ground of being that was rushing toward him at the same time in an act of metaleptic participation. However, the magistrate turns away from the experience and falls into a kind of paralysis.

He knows he has missed something more important than the buck. However, his sense of reality will let him go no further. Something is holding him back from responding to any experience he cannot hold onto physically. Yet he believes, at least intellectually, that all are born with "the memory of justice"[57] The justice in which he believes is not linked to any observable physical reality. Something has dulled the soul of the magistrate. This is a decent man who cares not only about the welfare of oasis's citizens, but also of the barbarians. He seeks only a peaceful life. What he is missing can be found in the central episode of the book, the return of the barbarian girl to her people.

The expedition to take her back to her people sets out from within the territory of "the Empire." the anonymous but brooding presence that looms over the entire adventure. It is not a community based on *homonoia* or a common spiritual substance. Rather, it is built around its wealth and great military power. The empire seems duty bound to use these assets somehow and because it has no purpose other than itself, the empire is constantly afraid. No one ventures far beyond the settlement. Who knows what might happen to them "out there?"

Still, the magistrate is pulled by something and becomes determined to take the girl home, perhaps asking her to make the choice to stay or come back with him. The reader is never sure. So, a little band (the magistrate, the girl, and two soldiers) leave the oasis settlement, with its bondage to blindness, and pass over the border to the freedom of the desert. Perhaps the mountain realm of the barbarians is really the promised land of full consciousness. Their path moves through large stretches of salt marsh and desert. More importantly, they are beyond the protection of the army in territory controlled by the barbarians far more than by the empire. Although they cannot see the barbarians, all members of the expedition know they are being watched.

During the journey the magistrate feels the tension of life in the *metaxy* and constantly is on the brink of insight. But he never understands exactly what he is doing or why he is doing it. Thus, he can never truly respond to the pull of the transcendent beyond. He lacks *opsis* and, thus, his trek becomes an irrational and incomprehensible whim rather than the movement of reason in his soul. His inability to participate dulls his sight and his understanding. Just as he has done most of his life, he seduces himself into taking a wrong turn that merely leads him further into the labyrinth. The decision to ignore reality and choose ignorance can be costly.

The expedition meets the barbarians, who have been subtly guiding them on their travels. The confrontation is laconic and tense, carried out down the sights of barbarian rifles. Nothing much happens. At some level he loves the barbarian woman and wants her to stay. Several times he is on the brink of making a declaration. But he does not know what love is, only sexual pleasure, and so every time he pulls back from giving up total control over himself. Without some clear-sighted understanding of love, it is impossible to disobey the soul's command to "make us a captain" and so he can only respond to the pull of the empire. It is all he knows. The girl goes with her people; the magistrate returns with the soldiers.

With that non-decision the magistrate has missed his opportunity for sight and participation in the drama of being and is caught in the empire's web. For, with the loss of *opsis*, humanity's only weapon against plague according to Camus, common decency dies as well. It already has died in Joll who comes to order the interrogation of the magistrate for no rational reason, merely because Joll cannot understand him. Like the magistrate, Joll has lost any tie to a common humanity and a common ground of existence and knows only one thing about the creature called human. Thus, when the interrogators come to the magistrate's cell, they did not come to get a confession or force him to sign some piece of paper. "They do not even ask about the barbarians. They come to my cell to show me the meaning of humanity, and in the space of an hour they showed me a great deal."[58] The soldiers abuse and torture him for reasons of state. They did it because they could. This road must surely lead nowhere.

Slowly but surely the administrative-military machinery of the empire begins to eclipse reality and move into a position that blocks participation with the ground of existence and, therefore, of participation in reason. The only knowledge the Empire seeks is "how not to end. . . . By day it pursues its enemies. . . . By night it feeds on images of disaster: the sack of cities, the rape of populations, pyramids of bones, acres of desolation. A mad vision yet a virulent one."[59] Even in his captivity, the magistrate recognizes himself as part of that "mad vision."

The magistrate finally realizes that he was not simply the pleasant hedonist who was the opposite of Col. Joll. Like the Colonel, he has constructed his own second reality, one that imaginatively obliterated life as participation in the full paradox of consciousness. "I was the lie that Empire tells itself when times are easy, he the truth that Empire tells when harsh winds blow."[60] The magistrate recognizes that something more than technical competency and a sense of fairness is needed to be a person of conscience.

Waiting for the Barbarians ends with a shriek of despair. The magistrate does come to understand himself as the self-seduced participant in a second reality. He does partially overcome his blindness. He sees that from the beginning the barbarian girl "felt a miasma of deceit closing about her: envy, pity, cruelty all masquerading as desire. . . . She listened to me, then she listened to her heart, and rightly she acted in accord with her heart. If only she had found the words to tell me! 'This is not how you do it.'"[61] However, he still believes it was her job to tell him, not his job to seek and know. He is no closer to sight than before. He cannot really *see* her. The magistrate has grown enough to follow his conscience and try to stop the public torture of the prisoners Joll brings back. He has felt the utter emptiness of the empire as an object of meaning. Empires rise and fall, like Troy and Nineveh, while the meaning of history as it moves toward a mysterious eschatological moment is contained in the psyche of humans who, if they are clear-sighted, are pulled at from the Beyond and respond to that pull.

DRAGONS, BLINDNESS, AND ORDER

Col. Joll and the unnamed city in *Blindness* appear quite orderly when viewed superficially. Col. Joll has turned the chaos of the Magistrate's physical office into a place of calm and pristine cleanliness. He believes he has faithfully fulfilled his duties. The politicians of the unnamed city try to decide the most rational and efficient way to deal with the epidemic of blindness. However, they fail to see reality as anything more than their own construction, and, failing that, they are blind to the dragons they unleash—dragons of fear, hysteria, ethical failure, cruelty, and death. As technocrats they are blind to anything but the narrowest understanding of Weber's "reasons of state." They epitomize Voegelin's remark that "The right to be ignorant of the reality and truth of common experience has become, in the twentieth century, the most remarkable and characteristic institution of Western societies." The job comes first, just as Weber said it would for anyone who followed the vocation of politics. Reasons of state trump ethical considerations for many and its practitioners lose sight of their own and others' humanity. In effect, they are more blind than those experiencing Saramago's "resplendent" whiteness. Instead of agents of order, they are agents of disorder. So too is the magistrate who acts blindly and without reflection, first according to the principle of neutral competence and later according to a vague ethical principle of human decency. Thus, the magistrate, never gets beyond commitment to noble deeds displayed by Cosmo in *Phantastes* and never understands what he is about and why he should be about it.

For Saramago and Coetzee, there is a universal humanity. This is the truth perceived in the mystic experience of the ancient Greek philosophers and in the irruptions of divine flux in the founders of the world religions. It is the focal point of Saramago's and Coetzee's work. But that universal humanity as the equality of all souls is rather a pointer to eschatological fulfillment than a hard reality that breaks through historical and geographic barriers to the intra-mundane world.

This chapter has had the pall of darkness all around it. Often the darkness looks like light. The darkness that looks like light is existence played out in the half-shadows of second reality in which human beings are like Plato's tyrant who does awake what most people do only in dreams. This eerie world has the appearance of the bright ring of reality because it is based on ordinary human drives. Often these drives are exercised in the pursuit of old dreams—empire or the salvation of man from Hesiod's short list of evils (sickness, poverty, the need to work). These actions occur in a human world, but they lack any trace of noetic reason, *opsis*, love or compassion. The drives and the dreams ultimately are not done in "the light," because there is no source of incandescence. Put another way, the action in these novels takes place in an uncomprehending, unresponsive reality in which the luminosity provided by genuine human order is absent.

If there is one thing Saramago and Coetzee share, it is their belief that there is a light beyond blindness that those who are clear-sighted can understand. That light is the source of the order the reader glimpses in both *Blindness* and *Seeing*, an order outside of government that illustrates Plato's anthropological principle that the city is a person writ large. Saramago and Coetzee illuminate humanity in the present century. They show their readers humans devoting their lives to dominating and grinding out the lives of their fellow creatures in a macabre dream world in which groups and races are reduced to things to turn into corpses while humanity becomes blinder and blinder with each pull of the trigger, with each view of the victim in the telescopic kaleidoscope of death-dealing. They illustrate a world dominated by dragons. However, these novels suggest that *opsis* also is a part of the human experience and should be important in any search for personal and political order. Those who study politics and literature choose well when they focus on the particular in human experience, but they also might want to consider moving beyond a paradigm that focuses on only part of Aristotle to one that includes the wider Aristotelian and Platonic notion of human orientation to the Good. Without that interior dialogue, how will individuals recognize human virtue or understand "what is deepest" in human lives?

As Sheldon Wolin argues, focus on a human notion of the good means focus on interest rather than conscience.[62] Classical Liberalism from Locke to Hume to Smith to the Utilitarians revolves around replacing individual conscience with conformity to social conscience in order to reduce the existential anxiety classical liberalism produces. Under it, Wolin maintains, human beings know the consequences of actions, but are blind to the reasons behind those actions. They need validation and social conformity in order to feel secure.

Thus, in difficult ethical situations why should they not vest authority in society in order to feel more certain they are "right." Let society define who is a genuine member or not, who is "in" and who is "out." And if society defines a group as "out," then society will be blind to its existence. It is always easier to conform to the social conscience. To do so, however, is to lose sight of the altruism and generosity[63] that Saramago considers the two best human qualities, and exhibit only the qualities the ophthalmologist initially sees in humanity: "half indifference and half malice."[64] Willful blindness loses humanity on the magistrate's road to nowhere where dragons rule—always feeling as if there was some important insight or piece of information that could correct the path, but never quite glimpsing it. Blindness will never allow human beings to maintain a humane life in a human world. As *Waiting for the Barbarians* and *Blindness* demonstrate, blindness is the enemy of both order and community. And, blindness to others, especially to those who are too different from oneself, precludes the possibility of acting as a witness against both blind mistakes and active evil. *Opsis* demands much more. It mandates witness.

NOTES

1. José Saramago, *Blindness*, trans. Giovanni Pontiero (Harcourt, Brace & Company, 1997), 326.

2. Eric Voegelin, "The Beginning and the Beyond: A Meditation on Truth," in *The Collected Works of Eric Voegelin, Vol. 28: What Is History? And Other Late Unpublished Writings*, ed. Thomas A. Hollweck and Paul Caringella (Baton Rouge: Louisiana State University Press, 1990), 232.

3. Ibid., 30.

4. Pavel Florensky, *Ikonostasis* (St. Vladimir Seminary's Press, 2000),

5. Franklin Delano Roosevelt, "Campaign Address on Progressive Government at the Commonwealth Club in San Francisco, California, September 23, 1932. https://www.presidency.ucsb.edu/documents/campaign-address-progressive-government-the-commonwealth-club-san-francisco-california.

6. Roger McNamee, "How to Fix Social Media Before It's Too Late: An Early Investor on How Facebook Lost Its Way," *Time Magazine* vol. 193, no. 3 (2019), 21, accessed January 29, 2019. ISSN: 0040-781X.

7. H. H. Gerth and C. Wright Mills, *From Max Weber: Essays in Sociology* (New York: Oxford University Press, 1946), chapter VIII.

8. Gerth and Mills, 35.

9. Ibid., 38.

10. Ibid., 78.

11. Ibid., 235.

12. Ibid., 95.

13. Ibid., 121.

14. Ibid., 127.

15. Michael W. Spicer, "Neutrality, Adversary Argument, and Constitutionalism in Public Administration," *Administrative Theory and Praxis* vol 37 (2015): 188-202, accessed January 10, .2019, DOI: 10.1080/10841806.2015.1053363.

16. David Hume, *An Enquiry Concerning the Principles of Morals* (LaSalle, IL: Open Court Books, 1966), 78.

17. Ibid.,

18. Adam B. Guy and Danny L. Balfour, "The Problem of Administrative Evil in a Culture of Technical Rationality," *Public Integrity* vol. 13, no. 3 (Summer 2011), 275, accessed January 10, 2019. DOI: 10.2753/PIN1099-9922130307,

19. Ibid., 276.

20. Ibid., 277.

21. See, for example, Steven G. Koven, "Revisiting Administrative Evil: Is It Consistent with Principles of Administration? Does It Move the Discipline Forward?" *Public Integrity* vol. 14, no. 1 (Winter 2011–2012): 85-92, accessed January 10, 2019, DOI: 10.2753/PIN1099-9922140106.

22. Adams and Balfour, "The Problem of Administrative Evil . . . ," 277.

23. Id.

24. Ibid., 284.

25. See also, Gary B. Adams and Danny L. Balfour, "'Open Secrets': The Masked Dynamics of Ethical Failures and Administrative Evil," *Research in Social Problems and Public Policy* vol. 19 (2011): 403-419, accessed January 15, 2019, DOI: 10.1108/SO196-1152(2011)0000019025, and Guy B. Adams, "Reply to Professor Koven," *Public Integrity* vol. 14, no. 1 (Winter 2011–2012): 93-94, accessed January 10, 2019, DOI: 10.2753/PIN10-99-9922140107.

26. Theodore J. Lowi, "Where Do We Go from Here?" *International Political Science Review* vol 32, no. 2 (March 2011): 224, accessed January 10, 2019, DOI: 10.1177/0192512.111405787

27. Ibid., 226.

28. Id.

29. Ibid., 227.

30. *Blindness*, 193.

31. Iris Murdoch, "Literature and Philosophy," in *Existentialists and Mystics* (New York: Penguin Books, 1977), 14.

32. George Steiner, *Real Presences* (Chicago: University of Chicago Press, 1991), 144.

33. Voegelin, "The Eclipse of Reality," in *The Collected Works of Eric Voegelin, Vol. 28: What Is History? And Other Late Unpublished Writings*, ed. Thomas A. Hollweck and Paul Caringella (Baton Rouge: Louisiana State University Press, 1990), 155.

34. Voegelin, *Order and History Vol. V: In Search of Order* (Baton Rouge: Louisiana State University Press, 1987), 1–2.

35. Eric Voegelin, "In Search of the Ground," in *The Collected Works of Eric Voegelin, Vol. 11: Published Essays 1953–1965,* ed. Ellis Sandoz (Columbia and London, England: University of Missouri Press, 2000), 230.

36. Saramago does not use proper names for any character in this novel because "names are of no importance here" (59). He identifies characters only by role or some physical trait. The characteristics who most exemplify *opsis* tend to be those who are described in terms of others—the "first blind man's wife," the "ophthalmologist's wife."

37. Saramago, *Blindness*, 162.

38. Ibid., 17.

39. Id., 17.

40. Ibid., 134.

41. Ibid., 85.

42. Ibid., 252.

43. Ibid., 276.

44. Id.

45. Id.

46. Ibid., 265.

47. Ibid., 310.

48. José Saramago, *Seeing*, trans., Margaret Jull Costa (Harcourt, Inc., 2004), 16.

49. Saramago, *Blindness*, 16.

50. Ibid., 5.

51. J. M. Coetzee, *Waiting for the Barbarians* (New York: Penguin Books, 1980), 8.

52. Coetzee, 155–56.

53. Eric Voegelin, *Order and History, Vol. I: Israel and Revelation* (Baton Rouge: Louisiana State University Press, 1956).

54. Coetzee, *Waiting for the Barbarians*, 8.

55. Id.

56. Ibid., 39–40.

57. Ibid., 139.

58. Ibid., 115.

59. Ibid., 133–134.

60. Ibid., 135–136.

61. Id.

62. Sheldon Wolin, *Politics and Vision* (Princeton: Princeton University Press, 2004), chapter 9.

63. Saramago, *Blindness*, 16.

64. Ibid., 32.

SIX
Why Can't People Accept Each Other?

Community, Alterity, and Witness in The Book of Phoenix *and* Who Fears Death

The conversation went like this:

> Kai: "You know how some people don't like other people because of their race?"
> Grandparent: "Yes."
> Kai: "They should just get over it."

For Kai, a twenty-first-century child in the United States, the issue was race. However, the genuine issue involves everyone considered "Other," whether "Other" is race, religion, economic class, gender, sexual orientation, or ethnicity. At best the "Other" is a figure of sympathy whom the majority believes it can do little to help. At worst, "Other" equals abomination. This is a dilemma for both the idea of politics and of community. How can there be community without some form of *homonoia* or like-mindedness, without any unity of thought or purpose? What guise should like-mindedness assume? How can politics exist without some sense of community? Is a democratic political sphere possible without community?

In the contemporary West both community and the idea of the political often seem close to disintegration and disorder. A major source of the disorder is unwillingness by various groups to accept those individuals and groups they consider "Other." The failure to accept "Others" poses immense dangers for human rights and democracy, as well as dooming any possibility of balancing authority and community. As Martin Luther King Jr. said in his speech "Beyond Vietnam": "We are called to speak for the weak, the voiceless, for the victims of our nation and for those it calls "enemy," for no document from human hands can make these humans any less our brothers."[1] The myth of the unnatural "Other" also stands in marked contrast to the hints of possibility offered by the authors included in this book. It is not possible to experience the paradox of consciousness, acknowledge presence, use noetic reason, and be clear-sighted and remain blind to the one story of humanity. As Glenn Hughes maintains, any recovery of political philosophy "will have to appreciate that the human orientation to transcendence through stories of the Whole *must* be pluralistic and 'multicultural,' because while there is only one realm of transcendence, a drama of the Whole can be convincing to a person only if it succeeds in integrating the particulars of local experience and history into a comprehensive narrative."[2] Any viable political philosophy, any truthful story of the human life in the *metaxy* rests on a bedrock of concrete human experience. Ineffable mystery might be ubiquitous, but the sense of awe and wonder that mystery generates will evoke different symbols in different places, cultures, and times. The lesson of the novels canvassed in this book is that there are stories within stories and humanity needs to listen to them all.

However, getting "over it," or even "past it," is much easier said than done. In the contemporary world the situation of the "Other," the "Outsider," has deteriorated even in liberal democratic societies. In the first quarter of the twenty-first century Anti-Semitic, racist, ethnic, and religious attacks have increased in the United States, Great Britain, and Europe.[3] Reports from Asia indicate Anti-Rohingya violence reaching almost genocidal proportions. Human rights organizations fear for the Uighur in China. As of November 2018, there were more than five million registered refugees from the conflict in Syria. Few Western countries are willing to accept more than a handful. The United States has seen a marked increase in asylum seekers from gang violence targeting women and children in El Salvador, Guatemala, and Honduras. The American response is to separate the families of asylum seekers from their children and debate building a wall along the southern border of the United States.

Neonationalism, with its accompanying racial and ethnic hatreds, is on the increase in Europe and has risen above 10 percent in Sweden, Finland, Denmark, the Netherlands, Germany, France, the Czech Republic, Austria, Hungary, Italy, and Switzerland. A 2018 article and map published by *BBC News* demonstrates the trend. In Austria, the neonationalist Freedom Party took 26 percent of the vote in the most recent national election. That figure for Switzerland is 29 percent. It is 21 percent for the Danish People's Party, 17.4 percent for Italy's The League, 17.6 percent for Sweden's Sweden Democrats, and 13 percent for the French National Front.[4] Instead of "getting over it," contemporary humanity has moved consistently over the past twenty years toward self-segregation and neo-tribalism.[5] Racial, religious, and ethnic hatreds and violence are likely to increase as intra- and inter-state conflicts become more numerous and as global warming generates large numbers of climate refugees.

If human beings cannot learn to live with diversity, they will ignore noetic reason and never achieve the reflective distance from the self, a perspective learned from interacting with both physical reality and the reality of nonexistent things, that is required for *opsis*. They will never participate in life fully or be able to creatively and successfully address the world. As Miroslav Volf has pointed out, it really is not possible to "talk about human rights, economic justice, and ecology without addressing issues of identity and otherness."[6] Human beings cannot live the one tale or recognize, as McCarthy put it, that every person's journey is like every other. They do not see that "The world of our fathers resides within us. Ten thousand generations and more."[7] For McCarthy at least, all individual stories are one. The world human beings regard as objective facts really is a tale. "And all in it is a tale and each tale the sum of all lesser tales and yet these also are the selfsame tale. . . . So everything is necessary. . . . Nothing can be dispensed with. Nothing despised. Because the seams are hid from us. . . . They joinery. The way in which the world is made."[8] Humanity has no idea what is the correct idea or individual or group to leave out or to despise except as its members continually tell the tale. That tale will always be a mixed one. The crux of the problem today is that the notion of community suggests witness for all humanity. Committing to life in the *metaxy*, offering visions of community based on human dignity and all the multiple planes of life—requires witnesses, and witnesses come in all shapes, sizes, genders, and colors, even the shape of some hated "Other."

In the end it will be unlikely that the members of a tribe will be able to stand for one another, let alone anyone else. They will become Hobbes' view of the individual as aggressive, competitive, and completely self-interested. They will lose sight of all tales but their personal one and consider it superior and unique. There will be no joint participation in the world of human beings and some ineffable mysterious ground of being posited by the paradox of consciousness. Without joint participation, witness against injustice and violations of human rights is difficult or impossible. That would likely be the death blow both to functioning democracy and to any idea of re-establishing a distinctly political sphere. There will only be the individual and the void. It is witness that opens possibility for change and the creation of alternative lives. It is witness in public space, as Hannah Arendt maintains, that is the site of freedom and the political.

Part of the problem is that so many citizens today feel that they are the "Other," the "Outsider" who is not valued or respected by some other group or groups in society. Rural citizens in many countries believe that urban and intellectual elites do not respect their lifestyle, beliefs, and culture. Ethnic, racial, and religious groups feel the same way. Sexual orientation is another flashpoint for feelings of alterity.

Identity politics, as sociology professor Arlie Russell Hochschild argues, builds empathy walls that prevent human beings from seeing the "Other" as anything but alien and an obstacle.[9] The Tea Party adherents she interviewed believe that the elites and the strangers, the "Others," women, racial and ethnic minorities, immigrants, and refugees, are "line-cutters" in the competition for the American dream. The dream is to be better off than the generation that came before them, but they are not. Their movement seems to have stopped. Only the "line-cutters," whiners who "don't really work for what they get," seem to get ahead. Someone must be helping these "Others" and not them.[10] For them, identity politics is about protecting their share of honor and achievement from those who either are undeserving or who slander or compete with them.

If a cardinal aspect exists, some point on which all these feelings of being "Other," "Outsider," "Unnatural," or "Abomination" hinge, then it is emotion. In a classical liberal society that is the beginning of morality. At bottom, these men and women accept the classical liberal model of morality developed by David Hume who wrote that morality is based on tradition; tradition is based on custom; custom is based on sentiment; and sentiment is based on utility.[11] He erected his moral vision to give humankind peace of mind. It turned out to be a costly peace of mind. If citizens in Western societies continue to see morality and ethics as founded on sentiment, the "getting over it" Kai seeks will not occur.

This chapter examines the "problem" of the "Other" through the lens of Nnedi Okorafor's *The Book of Phoenix* and *Who Fears Death*. We argue that until human beings reach some rapprochement with those they consider "Other," they will inhabit cramped and sterile second realities—imaginary worlds of their own ideological creation. Those second realities are not likely to be humane, for "the world is not humane just because the human voice sounds in it, but only when it has become the object of discourse."[12] Speaking and listening in echo chambers, they live only for their own fulfillment and self-interest. This cramped world may still retain the institutions of a democracy, but those institutions will not function well. This cramped and polarized space will fail as a democracy at the level Eric Voegelin called existential representation and representation of/in Truth, that is, it will possess all the trappings of democracy but fail totally in living its ideal.

As many scholars of democracy have said, a functioning democracy requires talk; it requires the presentation of multiple ideas by multiple voices. Only that interchange of ideas can reconcile community and authority. However, the political goal of well-functioning democracy rests on so many levels of the idea of alterity that the political level may not be the most appropriate starting point. It is the consequence, not the source—a logical but problematic product of the maximization of self-interest. The other levels—interpersonal, social, and ethical—are the foundations on which the political rests, just as a balancing of authority and community rests on the paradox of consciousness to the mythopoets considered in chapters 2–5. Yet, at another level, the key to understanding Western liberal societies' poor response to alterity is Lockean liberalism's emphasis on emotion over noetic reason and its core belief that the anxiety of existence means one's wealth and status are constantly endangered by others. *The Book of Phoenix* and *Who Fears Death* challenge Lockean liberalism on this key point.

PHOENIX AND ONYESONWU: HEROINES AND ABOMINATIONS

Storytellers are a lot like magicians. They share the ability to mix illusion and reality in ways that make their listeners question which is which. They also sometimes share a difficulty in distinguishing between the two. In telling and retelling the story, reality and illusion argue, negotiate, compromise, and ultimately sacrifice their essential principles to a "reality" with which their creator can live. They create myth. In some ways the stories are lies. But, always remember, that myths are true lies designed to explain lives and worlds that seem to exist out of nothing and have no intelligible goal or reason—worlds that are complicated and tangled. All the political philosophy in the world will never get around the basic fact that reality is messy and that to clean up that mess human beings organize their individual and communal lives as they can. Human beings do create their realities, ones that seem true to them. The stories by which they order their lives, thus, have great power.

However, false stories may also achieve power, if the myths they support soothe the human sense of complacency and entitlement. Further, even the victims of false stories sometimes accept them as true rather than undertake the grueling task of witnessing against them and the agony that may accompany that task. The Great Book, the Book of Ani, was one of those powerful, but false, stories. Although filled with lies, it ruled life in "the Seven Rivers Kingdom that once was the Kingdom of Sudan"[13] for hundreds of years. No one seemed to know who wrote the story or where and how it originated. The false story brought a few people, the Nurus (people the color of the sun who were descendants of Arabs), ease, wealth, and a sense of superiority. It brought many others, the Okeke (once all of humanity but in the Great Book's version only those with dark skin) nothing but degradation, humiliation, slavery, and death. Ultimately, that false story brought rebellion and witness. However, the witness's road is never easy. As Martin Luther King wrote, "The calling to speak is often the vocation of agony."[14] It is difficult to move from *opsis* to action. It takes courage to accept that "vocation of agony." The protagonists in both these stories possessed that courage.

The Book of Phoenix and *Who Fears Death* are the stories of two women considered worthless and unnatural abominations and of the lengths to which they go for justice. In the process they "write" a true story, see it disfigured into a tale of fanatical oppression, and re-write it as it should have been. The work of the acclaimed Nigerian-American author Nnedi Okorafor who won the World Fantasy Award for *Who Fears Death,* these novels blend the technological with the spiritual to offer new ways of thinking about alterity. Human beings must, she believes, listen to each other's stories.[15]

Phoenix is a "biologically accelerated organism," a SpeciMen, designed as a nuclear weapon that, like the Phoenix for which she is named, arises anew from the ashes of destruction. At the age of two she looks forty and is six feet tall with wings that span thirty feet. She is but one of the products developed by Life Gen Technologies for the military-industrial complex. Few of the millions of people living around Life Gen's seven towers know or care about the existence of the SpeciMen developed, tortured, and exploited by the company in a post-climate change New York. And if they did know, they would not care because the majority of the tower's victims were abducted from Africa. Researchers and citizens saw her, and the other SpeciMen, as they had seen African slaves in the past. They believed that they needed "no leash" to hold her because "my leash was in my DNA."[16] The SpeciMen were subhuman and unnatural. They could not be a threat. Thus, all could be sanguine in their enjoyment of the towers' benefits.

Phoenix's story is heard for the first time 200 years after an apocalypse turned most of the world into a desert. An old Okeke man named Sunuteel leaves his wife for a few days to wander the desert. As he leaves, his wife tells him to bring her back a good story. During his trek he finds a cave containing piles of old computers. They are remnants of what he has been taught are the "Black Days, the Times of the Dark People, the Era of the Okeke."[17] Touching one of the computers, he is surprised when something is uploaded to his portable palm unit. The title of the transferred audio file is "The Book of Phoenix." The audio file he hears over the next few days frightens and amazes him. It is the story of how and why that apocalypse occurred.

Before the apocalypse technology ruled as a god. Human beings had ignored the warning that "we must rapidly begin the shift from a thing-oriented society to a person-oriented society. When machines and computers, profit motives and property rights are considered more important than people, the giant triplets of racism, extreme materialism, and militarism are incapable of being conquered."[18] Life Gen Technologies' seven towers might produce unnatural SpeciMen, but the products of the research generated billions of dollars in profits and such medical breakthroughs as cures for AIDs and for the New Malaria brought on by the rise in sea levels. However, "behind the good intentions and amazing science . . . was abomination. . . . The foundation of all the towers was always always corrupt, driven by greed."[19] Anything that could be done to manipulate the human body was done in the name of progress. Although there were peoples of many colors, all human beings were the Okeke. The term possessed no specific racial or ethnic meaning. However, relying on the beliefs of the old colonialism, most of the individuals taken from their homelands for experimentation were African. Life Gen searched for those who were different or who possessed special, usually spiritual, powers.

Her best friend, her lover, and her physical and spiritual guardian are among the abducted. The Nigerian engineering student, Mmuo, believed in the spiritual and could walk through any wall and door except the lobby floor and outer door of Tower 7. The Egyptian Saeed, who Phoenix comes to love, "dies" but always survives. He no longer could eat food; the scientists had manipulated his body in such a way that he only could eat rubble—sand, dirt, glass, metal, rock. The Mali-born winged man who calls himself "Seven" is an immortal guardian angel as a result of dying honorably in the highest competition of Algeria's secret Leopard Society. In death, he goes to the wilderness, the world of the spirits, where he remembers hearing "a song that called me to become one with God."[20] He returns to life as a winged man waiting to become the guardian of change. Phoenix, he says, is that change, for, "wherever you go, you bring revolution."[21] Seven tells her she is "SpeciMen" and that she is more than a bomb. Her light is "beacon . . . life . . . hope." Her fire makes her "reaper, death, and redemption."[22] And it is revolution that she wants and leads. She wants freedom and justice for the SpeciMen and the end of the complacent arrogance of those who allow human experimentation and continue the colonial tradition of exploiting those from supposedly primitive or backward societies.

An insatiable reader and lover of stories, Phoenix lives and undergoes experiments in Tower 7. Rising through the floor of the Tower is a huge tree surrounded by plants and flowers. The tree is called the Backbone, although no one knows why. It seems to have some sort of magic power that helps plants grow. The beautiful garden in Tower 7's lobby masks the horror within. At first, Phoenix is compliant. The researchers allow her to read anything she wants because they do not see her as a threat, and she sees no other possible life. They also burn every part of her to see how much heat she can tolerate. She knew "the smell" of her burning flesh."[23] She focuses on her books and tries to make the best of the experiments they perform on her.

She lives like that until she hears that Saeed, the man she loves, has committed suicide. Part of the story is true. One evening at dinner he asks Phoenix for her apple. Because drawing is his hobby, she gives it to him thinking that he will draw it. However, she is told that he eats the apple and dies. He does not. What really happens is that, after seeing images of genocide, he threw the apple at the Big Eye (the name SpeciMen called the ever-watchful guards and cameras that surround them). Guards "dragged" him to his room and beat him. Later the same night they returned, injected him with a lethal substance, and sent his body to Tower 4 in the Virgin Islands for organ harvesting. The next morning, he wakes up and escapes.

Without Saeed, Phoenix becomes desperate to escape. With Mmuo's help, she frees herself and the winged man "Seven." Her light and warmth generate luxuriant plant growth all around the Backbone whose root system grows so much it brings down Tower 7. Surrounded by guards, Phoenix is shot and tells Mmuo to escape. Then, as her body continues to heat, "radiance . . . pulsated" from her. She burns killing many of those trying to contain her. Seven days later Phoenix returns from the ashes and her wings emerge. Phoenix will burn several more times before she scorches the earth, always in self-defense. Mmuo and Saeed are there when she comes back the third time. She already has been successful in freeing the SpeciMen in Life Gen's Chicago Tower, the nexus of its operations. The three rebels plan a revolution designed to liberate the inhabitants of Life Gen's remaining towers, tower by tower, arguing that what occurs in the towers "will be the end of humanity if it is not stopped."[24] Humanity has gone too far in its pursuit of immortality. The end of longer life can never justify the means used by Life Gen.

Tower 5 in Las Vegas revolts on its own. Its former inmates call themselves the Ledussee and consider Phoenix their inspiration. The Ledussee leave a manifesto citing Nat Turner and warning "Let us see what happens now that we have freed ourselves. Let us see what you've created. We will spread terror and alarm amongst all of you."[25] Their words echo Fanon's arguments defending the use of violence by colonized peoples in *The Wretched of the Earth*. The residents of Life Gen's towers are the colonized and they no longer accept what the "normal" wish to do to them. Even the Anansi Droids 419, never very discriminating about whom they kill, that Nigerian engineers designed to protect oil pipelines are in revolt. The rebels view Phoenix as their leader. Phoenix's picture is everywhere, but Life Gen's propaganda machine emphasizes that because Phoenix is a woman, she poses no threat. Because she is African, it is all right to kill her on sight, and because "A winged human being was an abomination, not an angel," citizens should forget about her once she is captured or killed.[26] Every story refers to her only as an "it."

Phoenix, Mmuo, and Saeed next targeted Tower 4 in the US Virgin Islands. This tower was the source of most of Gen Life's income. It also was where Saeed found himself after the Big Eye tried to kill him. In finding his way out of the tower Saeed came across children who could not speak. These children lived very long lives, but always remained voiceless children. Their purpose was organ harvesting because their organs would grow back. As they prepared a plan for freeing the children, a Big Eye guard named Dartisse found them. He wanted the rebels' help to free the woman he loved. Her name was HeLa because she possessed immortal cells like those of Henrietta Lacks. Besides selling organs harvested from the children in this tower, Life Gen sold billions of dollars' worth of HeLa's blood to seven very rich men who knew a vial of it would make them immortal.

With Dartisse's help, Phoenix, Mmuo, and Saeed initially are successful in freeing the children. However, Big Eye guards kill both Dartisse and HeLa. Phoenix burns to make sure the guards cannot re-take HeLa. When Phoenix resurrects, she finds Mmuo, Saeed, and the children still on the island. All is peaceful. It seems as if Life Gen has forgotten them in the face of attacks by Anansi Droids and the Ledussee. So, Phoenix slips (bends time and space to instantaneously appear thousands of miles away and at whatever time she wished) to the tower in Los Angeles where Life Gen keeps her biological mother.

Life Gen promised her mother a university education, a house, and an annuity in exchange for being a surrogate mother. After Phoenix's birth, they gave her nothing and discarded her to Los Angeles afterward as "radioactive refuse."[27] Her mother was dying of cancer brought about by carrying and giving birth to Phoenix but recognized her daughter and told her "to give 'em hell."[28] Phoenix briefly returned to the island. However, she was so upset from visiting her mother that she flew off fearing that the heat she generated in her grief and anger would harm Mmuo, Saeed, and the children. When she returned from this flight, the Big Eye were there. They killed Mmuo and the children and captured Saeed. Phoenix also learned that an angry mob "killed" Seven and destroyed the Backbone in New York after he reminded them that their complacency and disinterest had played a major role in sparking the SpeciMen rebellion.

At this point Phoenix can handle no more agony. She slips back to what is left of the Backbone at the remains of Tower 7. She thinks of the story about Ani she has heard. In this story Ani saw that her lands were desert, so made oceans and rivers and lakes. Then she needed a rest. As she rested, humans sprang up. They believed themselves gods in competition with Ani. They wanted to be omnipotent and immortal and they manipulated and twisted the human and natural world to gain their goal. When Ani awoke, she was displeased and angered so she "pulled a sun to the land" to wipe it clean. Phoenix saw herself as that sun and the soldier of Ani. She would be the "reaper come to reap what was sown. Wherever those seven men lived. Let them die. Let everything die. Let that which had been written all be rewritten."[29] Phoenix scorched New York and then "blew across the earth" burning cities and turning the oceans to steam. Then Phoenix disappeared after naming herself "SpeciMen, Beacon, slave Rogue, fugitive, Rebel, Saeed's love, Mmuo's sister, Villain."[30]

Her story shook the old man Sunuteel to the core. Further, he knew her spirit was near him and he was afraid. He knew then that Ani had not destroyed the earth because only the dark people had violated the moral law. Phoenix had caused the apocalypse when she scorched the earth. Dark-skinned people were not the villains. When Phoenix used the word Okeke, she referred to all of humanity.

However, long training, patriarchy, and fear took over. He decided the book told the truth about women. They were emotional and could not control their anger or "irrational whims."[31] He remembered the teacher who had taught him the post-structuralist view that "once the author wrote the story, the author became irrelevant."[32] It was up to him, to Sunuteel, to decide what the story was. He would ignore the warning that Phoenix's voice gave him from his portable: "I know what you think" came her voice. "You can rewrite a story, but once it is written it lives. Think before you do; your story is written too and so is the map of the consequences."[33] Still he went home and wrote what became the Great Book, the Book of Ani. He did it by rewriting and changing Phoenix's story from one about the fall of humankind due to a pride and arrogance worthy of those who built the Tower of Babel to a story more in tune with the world of his time. He defined the Okeke as the dark-skinned ones destined to be the slaves of the Nuru, even though he was Okeke himself. He made a story that supported patriarchy, arrogance, entitlement, and racism. He wrote a story that eliminated the essence of Phoenix—the search for justice and freedom for all in a world full of the paradox of consciousness where, as Mmuo said, "the spirit world rules the physical." He ignored her warning that "human beings make terrible gods."[34] She no longer was the soldier of Ani, the sun that Ani pulled from the sky to make a new start. She did not exist at all. It would be up to Onyesonwu to change the story again.

Who Fears Death appeared five years before its prequel. It too is a story of rebellion. It too is a story of the search for justice by and for the despised. Onyesonwu, whose name means "who fears death," is Ewu. Generally, Ewu children were the product of violent rape. Born an unspecified amount of time after Sunuteel, who finds and rewrites Phoenix's story, she is a pariah in both Okeke and Nuru societies. As the product of violence, both Okeke and Nuru believe that Ewu are violent, dirty animals. Even her friends Binta and Diti sometimes forget their friendship and refer to her as an "ugly Ewu woman" who "is used to living like an animal in the desert."[35] She not only is an outsider because of her parentage, sandy hair and skin, and freckles. She also is a powerful and strong woman in a deeply patriarchal culture which will despise her even if she were Okeke because she does not "know her place." She is not the soft, pleasant, compliant woman who accepts her assigned role. As Ewu, that assigned role meant she should "serve the normal." Yet when she did serve the normal, she finds, they still hated her.[36] Besides her mother and stepfather, only Mwita, who also is Ewu, though not a product of rape, truly understands her and loves her. Even Mwita sometimes accepts "the old beliefs about the worth and fate of men and women."[37] In the face of these beliefs, Onye (a nickname given by her friends) rebels but must always fight for self-confidence. She teeters between demanding to be known and accepted for who she is and attempting to fit in with the other people of Jwahir, her town.

During one of her attempts to fit in, she undergoes the Eleventh Year Rite of female circumcision. At the ritual she meets and bonds with the three other girls undertaking it. They are the spoiled and beautiful Diti, the sexually abused Binta, and the independent, free-thinking Luyu. She also goes alu (slips into the wilderness) for the first time. The wilderness is the world of the spirits, forces, and deities and it is the framework on which the physical world stands.

For Onye there is an unpleasant side effect of the ritual. Her unknown father, the man who raped her mother, becomes aware of her and on multiple occasions tries to kill her. A powerful sorcerer, he sends a snake and a scorpion. Once he chokes her as she sleeps, even though he is many miles away. She believes the only way to stop his attacks is by undergoing training in sorcery and learning the Mystic Points. However, despite knowing that she possesses obvious mystical gifts, the local sorcerer, Aro, refuses to teach her because she is a woman and he fears female emotions.[38] After turning her down three times, Aro finally decides he must teach her after Onyesonwu's anger erupts when Aro summons a Masquerade to guard his gate against her. She defeats the Masquerade and, slipping into the wilderness, attacks and almost kills Aro.

It is only then that Aro accepts her as his apprentice. His rationale is that if he does not teach her, she will be a menace to herself and others. Before they begin, he asks her four important questions. When asked Onyesonwu replies that she will not interfere with others as long as they do not harm anyone; that she believes in a creative author of all things; that it is her responsibility to leave the world a better place; and that to give and to receive are the same because "one cannot exist without the other."[39] These are the answers Aro wants to hear because they indicate understanding of the importance of putting others ahead of self and of concern for the whole of life.

Onyesonwu is also Eshu, a shape-shifter, with a powerful ability to manipulate the Mystic Points. Aro teaches her that it is the task of the sorcerer to balance the physical (Uwa), the wilderness (Mmuo), the forces, deities and spirits (Alusi), and the Creator (Okike). Sorcerers use their skills and talents to work with the Mystic Points to ensure balance and harmony, the golden rule of bushcraft. As a shape-shifter, Onyesonwu can make small adjustments in the physical world. She possesses great energy. She sings beautifully, so she can communicate with other people and with the Alusi (wilderness spirits). She can enter and act in the wilderness, the home of spirits and souls. She can "go Alu" and travel as a wilderness spirit.

These are her tools, her bushcraft: shape-shifting, energy, singing, and the ability to enter the wilderness at will. She will use each of these tools to track down her father and the genocide's leader, a man committed to eliminating every Okeke as he claims the Great Book demands. He tells the people of his town, Durfa, that "When we've wiped them out *what next*? We make the Great Book proud! We make Ani proud. We build an empire that is the most good of good."[40] The Kingdom of the Seven Rivers must be purged and pure in order to attain greatness.

At first Onyesonwu does not know who either man is. However, she learns that the genocidal leader's name is Daib. She also learns that he is her father. He also is Mwita's first teacher. Daib hates Onyesonwu because she is not the boy he wanted to conceive when he raped Onyesonwu's mother. Daib wanted a son to train into a powerful sorcerer who would continue his evil cause. Like Phoenix, she comes to believe that if you want to kill a snake, you must "cut off its head."[41] To end the genocide, she must commit patricide. Further, after almost being raped on the journey west, Phoenix realizes that many people, believing all Ewu women were whores, "hadn't heard me until they feared me."[42] Threats and violence would be an inevitable until the Great Book was healed. If Phoenix were there, she would have noted the sad similarity between Daib's goals and the desire of the researchers working in Life Gen's towers for power and control far beyond the boundaries of the humane. There is no balance of consciousness in his words. There is nothing but pure tribalism and the need to feel superior.

Onyesonwu will come to understand that killing her father is the key to ending the genocide. She also knows that the Great Book is the root of the kingdom's hatred of the Okeke. It needs to be rewritten. When a storyteller comes to her village, she and Mwita go to hear her and learn of a prophecy. The prophecy tells of an Ewu man who will rewrite the book. Few have come to listen to the storyteller. The dominant response is "who wants to hear more bad news. . . . Nothing can be done about the problems there anyway."[43] Jwahir is just as complacent and arrogant as the Nuru in Daib's center of operations, Durfa, and as the inhabitants of the cities where Life Gen planted its towers. In anger one day she "shows" citizens in Jwahir's marketplace the attack on her mother. They do not want to know. So far, they have not been bothered by the Nuru and the town's leaders tell the people not to worry, the danger is far away. The townspeople turn on Onyesonwu and would have killed her. At that point the only option is for her to leave the town and take up the task of finding and killing her father. Mwita, her friends Diti, Luyu, and Binta and Diti's betrothed, Fanasi, choose to accompany her.

They travel west toward the cities of the seven rivers to undertake Onyesonwu's task. Over the course of their journey, Onyesonwu will have several spiritual experiences. When she goes on retreat with the women of the Red People, much happens to her. First, Onyesonwu immediately goes *alu*, into the wilderness. A *Kuponyungo*, a fire-spitter or phoenix, appears. It was "the brilliant color of every shade of fire."[44] Her mother, Najeeba, had told her stories about them when they lived in the desert. Kuponyungo, her mother told Onye, "like to befriend travelers."[45] The phoenix is her mother who tells Onyesonwu to change into a fire-spitter and follow her. Najeeba and Onye fly for a very long time to a green island.

After returning from the trip with her mother, Onye became very sick as "the wilderness and the physical world battled for prominence around her."[46] To help her, Ting, an apprentice sorcerer with the Red People, marks her with an ancient magical (Nsibidi) symbol that "speaks directly to the spirit." Ting marked her with the symbol of "the crossroads where all your selves will meet."[47] It is a symbol for enacting change. Both Onyesonwu and the world needed to change.

Suddenly Onye was "gone" again. Her teacher Aro had told her no one can touch the Creator, but at that moment the Creator touches her. She dies to herself and some powerful creative mystery reconstructs her. "Every part of me. . . . All was destroyed. I was dead, broken, scattered, and absorbed."[48] She was obliterated. Then, she felt herself being put back together in a new order that "made more sense."[49] She possessed a new balance and outlook. She had been "gone" from her body for a week. She felt so powerful that, seeing Daib's spirit there, she attacked him. He almost kills her. Onye becomes confused. Sometimes she believes she can defeat Daib; but part of her dwelled on how badly he had hurt her in the wilderness. Her friend, Luyu, pushes her onward. It is time to re-write the Great Book and destroy Daib.

Binta and Luyu will die for Onyesonwu. Diti and Fanasi will turn back after immediate danger threatens. What Onyesonwu encounters confirms what Aro told her: That there are so few sorcerers because no one becomes one by choice. "That's why we are plagued by death, pain, and rage."[50] In the end, with Luyu standing lookout, she and Mwita will face her father. Daib will kill Mwita; Onyesonwu will cripple Daib.

After disabling and almost killing Daib, Onye and Luyu reach the island that houses the Great Book and she "rewrites" it. However, she will write nothing. Much like Fat Charlie singing his world into existence, Onyesonwu will sing the song of the desert to the book and it will be healed. The killing stops. Everyone begins to change. Onyesonwu will not be there to see it. She understood Aro's warning that change always comes at a price. The price may or may not be Onyesonwu's life. A mob kills Luyu while she tries to buy Onyesonwu time to heal the book. After singing the book back to health, Onyesonwu is taken to prison and con-demned to stoning, the death she had foreseen for herself when she underwent her initiation as Aro's apprentice.

Maybe she accepts her fate and dies stoned to death in a hole in the ground. Maybe her body is burned, and her ashes buried by the man to whom she told her story in the jail cell and his twin sister. Maybe the final chapter where Sola again has his say, just as he did at the end of *The Book of Phoenix*, is a lie. Or maybe not. Maybe he tells a truth when he says that Onye's "fundamental nature was change and defiance," and that she does change shape into a Phoenix, spit fire at the guards who come to take her to be stoned, and fly off to the green island her mother showed her and that she saw in her dreams. Indeed, he says "she did die, for something must be written before it can be rewritten."[51] Maybe her return flight to the green island is ascendance into heaven. Maybe it is not. Sola, Aro, and her mother Najeeba, who now is Aro's apprentice wonder "if we will ever see her again. What will she become?"[52] What is certain is that in death, Onye "gave birth to us all. This place would never be the same. Slavery here was over."[53] Sorcerers would accept female apprentices. The Okeke were no longer a cursed people. Maybe she took on death as the price of the change that needed to come and then rose up as Phoenix.

WITNESS, TRIBALISM, AND REFLECTIVE DISTANCE

Phoenix's and Onyesonwu's stories change the world. Both are angry, very angry. Neither believes in the goddess Ani or in God. They do believe in an "author of all things" and this belief will help them to act as witnesses against genocide and injustice to the "Other" whoever that other might be. They stand against patriarchy, misogyny, arrogant entitlement, colonialism, greed, technology that uses human subjects without their consent, and racism. In doing so, the reader finds stories within stories centering on the paradox of consciousness, justice, freedom, the importance of balance, and death and resurrection. Ultimately, both will become assassins, "villains for the sake of justice,[54] not revenge. Phoenix's heat will ravage the earth and turn it into desert. Onyesonwu will cripple her father after Mwita dies fighting him. Her decision to use her power to join Mwita's sperm with her egg will kill every man in Durfa capable of fathering a child. Yet she also is a healer. The women of Durfa all are pregnant and possess new powers. During the journey to Durfa she undoes the damage to Diti's, Luyu's, and Binta's bodies by the Eleventh Year Ritual. In one of the Okeke towns close to Durfa she heals many people.

Phoenix and Onyesonwu, separated in time by at least 200 years, offer their listeners/readers border stories.[55] Their stories are full of the paradox of consciousness and the experience of life in the *metaxy*. They cross borders of literature, referencing both Western literature and African, especially Nigerian. These women move from life to death to resurrection more than once. They move from childhood to adulthood. They believe and participate in both physical and spiritual reality. They are aware of presence. They play with time and space. They are both human and "Other." They cross back and forth between the search for justice and the need to express a destructive righteous anger. They cause both destruction and rebirth. They are, as the deeper meaning[56] of Phoenix's name suggests, possibility. They understand that fulfilling possibility requires sacrifice.

Both Phoenix and Onyesonwu experience stories within stories and the power of stories, knowing that stories stop time. As Phoenix relates "I tell you a story in which are more stories. Universes within universes."[57] She warns that any storyteller "starts it in her own place, in her own moment, in her own point of view." While you listen "You and the storyteller share everything, even your existence."[58] They will both tell their own stories in their own way and allow the others within their stories to tell theirs as well. They want to listen to many stories.

Both are healers. Plants love Phoenix's light and she restores a wholeness to the Ghanaian town when she plants an alien seed that she found buried beneath the Backbone. Onyesonwu has given up her belief that only the crimes of the Nuru are to blame for the violence. As Mwita told her, "there is sickness on both sides."[59] She must try to kill her father, but only to stop the genocide and heal the Great Book. Both believe that everything is part of some whole and commit themselves to diversity within community. They look to all the things that are and affect human beings, both the physical and the spiritual. They are young, but as their stories progress, Phoenix and Onyesonwu begin to achieve reflective distance. Their stories offer possibility, alternative ways of thinking about and living with those human beings considered too unnatural, too "Other" for any response other than domination, patriarchy, oppression, colonialism, and genocide.[60] As Aro tells Onyesonwu, no one ever knows "exactly why we are, what we are, and so on. All you can do is follow your path all the way to the wilderness, and then you continue along because that's what must be."[61] By following their path, Phoenix's and Onyesonwu's passion for human dignity and justice can help balance authority and community.

DEMOCRATIC THEORY, ALTERITY, AND THE ANXIETY OF EXISTENCE

The Lockean liberal myth which has dominated the Western societies for hundreds of years has never been good at dealing with alterity. As it has changed and evolved over the years, this inability in its theory has become worse and increasingly undermines both the underpinnings of deliberative democracy and any notion of the peoples' business (those things that affect the polity as a whole), the very stuff that politics is about. As Michael Sandel points out, it "cannot address the erosion of self-government and community" inherent in it.[62] Classical liberalism, despite its commitment to human freedom of choice and dignity, seemed to find acceptable only one sort of life—the life dedicated to ceaseless economic activity to ward off uncertainty. Classical liberalism asked human beings to split themselves into an interior and an exterior self and to make the exterior self, the one shown the world, the most important. The classical liberal myth is full of what Charles Taylor called hyper-individualism, narcissism, and reliance on instrumental reason.[63] These are the very trends that form the basis of self-segregation and identity politics and undermine deliberative democracy.

The issues ubiquitous in the Lockean worldview pervade Sheldon Wolin's work in *Politics and Vision*. Wolin argues that liberalism is the product of both anxiety over the fact that human existence seems to come out of nothing, out of some unknown and unknowable mystery, and over protection of wealth and status. Both anxieties ultimately generate a need for validation through social conformity. If one conforms, others will see them as just like themselves and will designate them as part of the group. One will fit in, much as the young Onyesonwu attempted to do. The classical liberal mantra is "Man Alone." And the man, or woman, who stands alone is *homo economicus*, economic man. Taught from childhood the Humean moral values and the idea that they are destined to produce economic gain, Western children grow up to follow acceptable paths rooted in economic production and a sort of "group think." They wear the same jeans, listen to the same music and at the same time consider themselves unique. Complexity in the human personality, the search for insight into the human consciousness or for other modes of perception beyond the economic could entail feelings of guilt that would destroy the individual's self-respect and peace of mind by pulling them in different directions. There would be too many of existence's tensional pulls. Multiplicity is dangerous. Therefore, there must be some unification of the human personality, some way to provide that precious certainty. To Hume, ensuring peace of mind required people to give up an inner reality. There could be no reality unrelated to business and production.[64]

The path from Locke to the Utilitarians, Wolin maintains, is one of the "gradual erosion of a separate human sphere of political action."[65] Estranged from political action, society and economics become the focus of human life in a desperate attempt to stave off the inherent pain and anxiety of the human condition. In Wolin's reading, Locke, Hume, and Smith did not see progress as inevitable or view reason as the sole authority of knowledge. They were neither arrogant nor "naively optimistic" and so did not see human will as able to remold either humanity or society.[66] Politics "was significant only insofar as it impeded upon men's interests."[67] The function of "social and political arrangements" was to lower human anxiety levels by "securing property and status against all threats excepting those posed by the competitive chase itself."[68] In the process, liberalism attempted to turn political problems into administrative ones.[69] It also based morality on sentiment and utility.

As chapter 3 indicates at greater length, Eric Voegelin approaches the anxiety of existence differently. However, his assessment of liberalism is not dissimilar from Wolin's. For Voegelin, the anxiety of existence is a response to the mystery of existence out of nothing.[70] The questions surrounding why things exist and why are things the way they are means that human beings live surrounded by uncertainty. The looseness of existence appears to humanity as an apparent "plot" of time and space to rob it of knowledge and certainty. Human beings constantly fear "falling out of time" and into nothingness. They spend their lives in an endless search for either control or forgetting. For both Voegelin and Wolin, uncertainty is the key to deconstructing the classical liberal myth as formulated from Locke to John Stuart Mill.

It is this search for certainty in the face of the individual's lonely and insecure existence in time and space that links Wolin's and Voegelin's accounts of the anxiety of existence to tribalism new and old. Classical liberalism cannot deal with the "Other" because the "Other" presents one more huge and dynamic uncertainty in an already complicated existence where the most prevalent emotion is insecurity.

Various contemporary works on democratic theory view self-segregation in residential enclaves, identity politics, and overreliance on populism as detrimental to democratic ideals.[71] Depending on the strength of their attachment to Western civilization and Lockean liberalism, however, these works offer widely different remedies. Most of the insights offered, though laudable and thoughtful, are counterproductive because they do not go deep enough into the human fear of change and uncertainty. They also fail to address the bottom-line problems facing the classical liberal myth—isolation, competition for its own sake, conformity, and the lack of any space for politics commensurate with, and distinct from, the social and economic spheres.

Such innovative ideas as Sunstein's "architecture of serendipity"[72] or William E. Connolly's "agonistic democracy"[73] are tough sells unless citizens are willing to accept a normative position of inclusion. As Harpham argues, the field of ethics revolves around "the other."[74] Ethics is about inter-human relations. Hannah Arendt says much the same thing in her *Introduction* into *Politics*."[75] The question is this: What is the most appropriate ethical position for individuals or a political community to take vis-à-vis the Outsider. In what sort of ethic does possibility lie, not only for the inclusion of the other but also for balancing authority and community?

These ideas are important. However, the desire to preserve the classical liberal paradigm is ill-suited to ever successfully addressing alterity. Although the liberal vision talks about pluralism, it tends to foster conformity by making society the final arbiter of right and wrong and who is acceptable and who is not. Thus, each alterity remains perceived as a thorn in the side of community. Further, *The Book of Phoenix* and *Who Fears Death* suggest that although changes in discourse are important, something else must precede the nurturing of agonistic democracy, discourse ethics, or an "architecture of serendipity." It is frightening to even consider developing a new paradigm to meet the demands of the twenty-first century, but at some point, a beginning must be made if human rights and a just version of deliberative democracy are to exist. It is necessary to return to the ethical level and examine it first for ideas that reflect the paradox of consciousness, life in the *metaxy*, noetic reason, and *opsis*. Ethics and political theory must work together. Dietrich Bonhoeffer, Emmanuel Levinas, Jacques Derrida's late work, and Miroslav Volf have made important contributions. Sandel, too, maintains that America's present political situation demonstrates the need for "substantive moral discourse."[76] Each of their works is unique, but all point in the same direction. Eric Voegelin's work in the area of representation supports the sort of work undertaken by these philosophers and theologians. They offer starting points. The work of these thinkers contains their own contradictions and imperfections, but they offer a better starting point to re-examination of alterity than does most of contemporary Lockean liberal theory.

Voegelin argues that human beings can never go back; they can only move forward. There is no recovering universal commitment to "western civilization," or the original form of Locke's, Smith's, and Hume's classical liberalism, or the Greek understanding of friendship. Human beings must look to the "concrete historical situation of the age."[77] The historical situation of the day is much different than it was when Hobbes gave humanity the idea of "Man Alone" and Locke began writing that solitary, but social, individual into human political history. In the contemporary world human beings have moved from the historical perspective of solitary human beings facing the anxiety of existence by walking the same road to what might best be described as "Humanity Against Itself." Everyone wants what they want yet continues to believe that what a different group wants must be unnecessary or immoral. They constantly believe they must repel attackers from outside their status or belief system. This is apparent not only in the United States but also in other Western democracies.

Recognizing that each human being is both a self and an "other" and committing to the human dignity of all requires a return to the paradox of consciousness and its implications, especially the anxiety of existence and human responses to that anxiety. The mythopoets canvassed in this collection of essays have suggested that human beings experience life as a paradox of consciousness that requires joint participation of human beings with some transcendent ineffable mystery. Whatever the mysterious experience is, it pervades existence in the *metaxy* as human beings seek to adjust to the anxiety of existence (chapter 3). However, human beings must cultivate noetic reason (chapter 4) in order to become genuinely rational human beings living in the paradox of consciousness and its requirement of joint participation in the *metaxy*. Chapter 5 makes clear that the mythopoets encountered in this book believe that those capable of noetic reasoning also are those most likely to be clear-sighted (*opsis*). It also highlights the danger of blindness in reliance on a purely technical rationality. Running like a thread through these chapters is the idea of possibility.

As the story of Ani changed, so has the story of classical liberalism—so does any story. Now it is up to political philosophers to write a new story capable of integrating community and authority. That new story, while maintaining freedom of thought and action, must also be inclusive. Respect for all human beings requires witness and only a strong ethical base that emphasizes human humility, noetic reason, and *opsis* prepares human beings for that difficult task. Phoenix and Onyesonwu witnessed for others who had no voice. They demonstrated an unselfish love. Neither of them was perfect. Both were very young and made the mistakes of the young. Phoenix's final act was one of desperation and despair. Onyesonwu wavered between self-doubt and confidence. Sometimes their anger got the better of them. In the end, their grasp on clear-sightedness failed.

However, their energy and love for oppressed others in their societies demonstrate that sitting by is not a productive or positive option in the face of the vilification or ostracizing of the "Other." They were willing to accept guilt as Bonhoeffer put it, or dirty their hands as Arendt wrote. Nurturing the requirements of a functioning democracy requires witnesses capable of listening to many stories and committed to improving "their little corner of the world." The mythopoets discussed in this book tell today's citizens that positive ground in the search for an ethic of inclusion and a new democratic myth can be gained by accepting the paradox of consciousness with its accompanying experience of presence, reliance on noetic reason, *opsis*, and witness.

NOTES

1. Martin Luther King, Jr. "Beyond Vietnam—A Time to Break Silence," accessed January 15, 2019, https://www.americanrhetoric.com/speeches/mlkatimetobreaksilence.htm.

2. Glenn Hughes, *Transcendence and History* (Columbia: University of Missouri Press, 2003), 36.

3. See, for example, https://www.usatoday.com/story/news/nation/2016/02/07/black-history-month-violence/79837270/, Kehinde Andrews, "Racism is still alive and well, 50 years after the UK's Race Relations Act." *The Guardian*, Dec. 8, 2015, accessed March 1, 2019, https://www.theguardian.com/commentisfree/2015/dec/08/50-anniversary-race-relations-act-uk-prejudice-racism; Matthew Weaver, "Hate crime surge

linked to Brexit and 2017 terrorist attacks," *The Guardian*, October 16, 2018, accessed 3.1.2019; https://www.theguardian.com/society/2018/oct/16/hate-crime-brexit-terrorist-attacks-england-wales; Statista, "Racist incidents recorded by the police in England and Wales from April 2015 to March 2018, by region," accessed March 1, 2019, https://www.statista.com/statistics/624038/racist-incidents-in-england-and-wales/; Abigail Hauslohner, "Hate crimes jump for fourth straight year in largest U.S. cities, study shows," *Washington Post,* May 11, 2018, https://www.washingtonpost.com/news/post-nation/wp/2018/05/11/hate-crime-rates-are-still-on-the-rise/?utm_term=.4eb245cf04ae, accessed March 1, 2019; Jessica Schneider, "Hate crimes increased by 17% in 2017, FBI report finds," *CNN.com*, December 11, 2018, accessed March 1, 2019; https://www.cnn.com/2018/11/13/politics/fbi-hate-crimes-2017/index.html; and Federal Bureau of Investigation, "Uniform Crime Statistics: Hate Crimes Statistics, 2017," accessed March 1, 2019, https://ucr.fbi.gov/hate-crime/2017/resource-pages/hate-crime-summary.pdf; Oliver Holmes, "Antisemitic incidents in US soar to highest level in two decades," *The Guardian* (February 27, 2018), accessed March 1, 2019, https://www.theguardian.com/society/2018/feb/27/antisemitism-us-rises-anti-defamation-league. See also Antidefamation League, "U.S. Anti-Semitic Incidents Spike 86 Percent So Far in 2017 After Surging Last Year, ADL Finds," April 24, 2017, accessed March 1, 2019, https://www.adl.org/news/press-releases/us-anti-semitic-incidents-spike-86-percent-so-far-in-2017; and Yosef Govrin, "Anti-Semitic Trends In Post-Communist Eastern European States," ed. Dore Gold and Manfred Gerstenfeld, Co-Publishers. Zvi R. Marom, Editor. Joel Fishman and Chaya Herskovic, Associate Editors (Jerusalem Center for Public Affairs) *Jewish Political Studies Review* 15:3–4 (Fall 2003) http://www.jcpa.org/phas/phas-govrin-f03.htm; accessed March 1, 2019, http://www.jcpa.org/phas/phas-govrin-f03.htm; and Thomas Cullen, "Hate Crimes on the Rise. *The Roanoke Times: Opinion,* March 11, 2019, 3.

4. BBC News, "Europe and Nationalism: A Country by Country Guide," (Sept. 10, 2018), accessed March 1, 2019. https://www.bbc.com/news/world-europe-36130006.

5. See, for example, Robin Wright, "The New Tribalism," *Los Angeles Times,* June 8, 1992 as cited in Miroslav Volf, *Exclusion and Embrace: A Theological Exploration of Identity, Otherness, and Reconciliation* (Nashville: Abingdon Press, 1996), 15; Samuel Kronen, "Neo-Tribalism," accessed February 12, 2019, https://medium.com/@samuelkronen/modern-tribalis-and-the-danger-of-identity-politics-33150fd257f2; Robert Reich, "Tribalism Is Tearing American Apart," accessed February 12, 2019, https://www.salon.com/2014/03/25/robert_reich_tribalism_is_tearing_america_apart_partner/; Cass Sunstein, # *Republic: Divided Democracy in the Age of Social Media* (Princeton University Press, 2018). Kindle edition; Arlie Russell Hochschild, *Strangers in Their Own Land: Anger and Mourning on the American Right* (The New Press, 2018). Kindle edition; and Jonah Goldberg, *The Suicide of the West: How the Rebirth of Tribalism, Populism, and Identity Politics is Destroying American Democracy* (New York: Crown Forum, 2018).

6. Miroslav Volf, *Exclusion and Embrace: A Theological Exploration of Identity, Otherness, and Reconciliation* (Nashville, TN: Abingdon Press, 1996), 18.

7. Cormac McCarthy, *Cities of the Plain* (New York: Alfred A. Knopf, 1998), 281.

8. Cormac McCarthy, *The Crossing* (New York: Vintage Books, 1998), 143.

9. Hochschild, 4. See also, Joe Bageant, *Deer Hunting with Jesus: Dispatches from America's Class War* (New York: Three Rivers Press, 2007).

10. Id.

11. David Hume, *3 David Hume: Philosophical Works*, ed. T. H. Green and T. H. Gross (London: Scientia Verlag Aalen, 1964). See also David Hume, *An Enquiry Concerning the Principles of Morals* (LaSalle, IL: Open Court Books, 1966).

12. Arendt, *Men in Dark Times* (Harcourt, Brace, & World, Inc., 1968), 24.

13. Nnedi Okorafor, *Who Fears Death* (DAW Books, Inc., 2010), 391. Hereafter abbreviated as WFD.

14. King, 2.

15. Nnedi Okorafor, N. K. Jemison, and Noelle Stevenson Zwillich, "Science Fiction's New Reality: Interview with Todd Zwillich," produced by Paige Osburn. *1A.*

Monday, Sep. 10, 2018. https://the1a.org/shows/2018-09-10/scifi-fever. Accessed March 7, 2019.

16. Nnedi Okorafor, *The Book of Phoenix* (DAW Books, Inc., 2015), 136. Hereafter abbreviated as TBOP.

17. Ibid., 2.
18. King, 11.
19. TBOP, 98.
20. Ibid., 179.
21. Ibid., 180.
22. Ibid., 95.
23. Ibid, 66.
24. Ibid., 108.
25. Ibid., 192.
26. Ibid., 130.
27. Ibid., 203.
28. Ibid., 207.
29. Ibid., 221.
30. Ibid., 224.
31. Ibid., 226.
32. Ibid., 227.
33. Ibid., 228.
34. Ibid., 162.
35. Okorafor, WFD, 203.
36. Ibid., 218.
37. Ibid., 254.
38. Ibid., 105.
39. Ibid., 111.
40. Ibid., 178.
41. TBOP, 98.
42. WFD, 218.
43. Ibid., 94.
44. Ibid., 283.
45. Id.
46. Ibid., 288.
47. Ibid., 291.
48. Ibid., 292.
49. Id.
50. Ibid., 119.
51. Ibid., 383.
52. Ibid., 385.
53. Ibid., 381.
54. TBOP, 105
55. For Okorafor's preference for border stories see Miriam Pahl, "Time, Progress, and Mutidirectionality in Nnedi Okorafor's *Who Fears Death*," *Research in African Literature* Vol. 49, No. 3 (Fall 2018): 207–222. Accessed February 12, 2019. DOI: 10.2979/reseafrilite.49.3.12, and Adam Savage's interview with Nnedi Okorafor cited in footnote 21 of this chapter.

56. TBOP, 109.
57. Ibid., 121.
58. Ibid., 61.
59. WFD, 153.
60. For more on possibility in Okorafor and Afrofuturism see, Miriam Pahl and Ytasha L. Womack, *Afrofuturism: The World of Black Science Fiction and Fantasy* (Chicago: Lawrence Hill Books, 2013). Kindle edition.

61. WFD, 140.

62. Michael Sandel, *Democracy's Discontent* (Cambridge, MA: The Belknap Press of Harvard University Press, 1996), 323.

63. Charles Taylor, *The Ethics of Authenticity* (Cambridge, MA: Harvard University Press, 1991).

64. Margaret Hrezo, "The Reinforcement of Social Cohesion: Humean Philosophy, the Therapeutic State, and the Exclusion Ritual," *The Journal of Psychiatry and Law* (Fall, 1978): 377–402.

65. Sheldon Wolin, *Politics and Vision: Continuity and Innovation in Western Political Thought* (Princeton, NJ: Princeton University Press, 2004), 258.

66. Ibid., 263.

67. Ibid., 250.

68. Ibid., 295.

69. Ibid., 282.

70. Eric Voegelin. "Anxiety and Reason" in *The Collected Works of Eric Voegelin, Vol. 28: What Is History and Other Late Unpublished Writings*, ed. Thomas Hollweck and Paul Caringella. Baton Rouge: University of Louisiana Press, 1990), 71.

71. See, for example, Jonah Goldberg, *Suicide of the West: How the Rebirth of Tribalism, Populism, Nationalism, and Identity Politics is Destroying American Democracy* (Crown Forum, 2018); John Von Heyking and Richard Avramenko, ed. *Friendship and Politics: Essays in Political Thought* (Notre Dame, IN: Notre Dame University Press); William E. Connolly, *Identity/Difference* (Minneapolis: University of Minnesota Press, 1991); and Cass Sunstein, # Republic: Divided Democracy in the Age of Social Media (Princeton, NJ: Princeton University Press, 201). Kindle edition.

72. Sunstein, ix.

73. Connolly, *Identity/Difference*. Agonistic democracy is one in which everyone has their own identity but recognizes that having an identity also means affirming a difference. Individuals need to understand the implications of the complexity of the identity/difference relationship in themselves and apply that to their relationship with other "Others." That recognition allows one to work "cautiously" on "modest shifts" in both one's own ideas and that of one's group (xiv).

74. Geoffrey Galt Harpham, *Getting It Right: Language, Literature, and Ethics* (Chicago: University of Chicago Press, 1999), 2.

75. Hannah Arendt, "Introduction *into* Politics" in *The Promise of Politics*, ed. Jerome Kohn (New York: Schocken Books, 2005, 93.

76. Sandel, 323.

77. Ibid, 89.

SEVEN

What Can I Do?

Stories and Possibility

At nine Kai, observing that the world is cruel and a mess, asked: "What can I do to change it? I'm just one person?" Here he echoed the question that Dartisse, HeLa's love asked Phoenix, Saeed, and Mmuo in *The Book of Phoenix*. It is another basic human question. How can one answer a nine-year old except to say: "Try not to make the mess worse? Do the best you can with your little corner of the world?" He is twelve now, and a more complicated answer is appropriate: Foster and live possibility. Heed the advice of Neil Gaiman that "We have an obligation to imagine. It is easy to pretend that nobody can change anything. . . . But the truth is . . . individuals make the future and they do it by imagining that things can be different."[1] It is interesting how far ahead of his grandparent he is. These days, on the way home from school, he talks about the mythology he is creating and the origin myths he is developing. He is imagining possibility.

Good stories, good myths suggest what to foster and what may be possible. In the past, there were parents, grandparents, aunts, uncles, and cousins who gathered in kitchens or on back porches to talk about their lives growing up, the history they had seen, the family members who made good role models and those who made poor choice after poor choice. Family Bibles almost burst with stories—family as well as biblical. The Bible once was a family's most important possession, and not only for religious reasons. The family Bible was the family. It housed the family's laughter, fears, successes, and tears in its lists of marriages, births, and deaths, in the newspaper clippings, citizenship papers, and locks of hair. Opening an old family Bible was as much a treasure hunt and a mystery story as it was a religious experience.

129

In those Bibles it was easy to see that human beings are their stories. That simple truth applies to political communities as well as to families and to individuals. Stories reflect and inform human beings—both individually and communally—about whom they are, what they believe, where they came from and why. They incorporate human understandings of justice, equality, freedom, power, order and disorder. In other words, they summarize humanity's individual and communal politics.

The stories chosen for this book are all of humanity's stories. They offer insights into what it means to be an ordered individual and an ordered community. They do so by example, not by argument, just as did the stories heard in kitchens and on porches at family gatherings, just as did the stories that emerged from the contents of an old family Bible. Just as do many family stories and political events, they contain elements of the fantastic and bizarre. They are mythic in their scope and form.

The authors of this book believe that such stories are an essential part of the study of politics, and particularly of the study of political philosophy. Yes, stories like theses "tend to produce private mythologies" rather than "public myths" capable of grounding a culture in the *metaxy*. However, as Hughes argues, "The content of our public myth owes much to the quality and content of those symbols that, although developed privately . . . evoke a shared experience of openness to the ground. Private does not necessarily mean totally subjective. Nor does it mean illusory."[2] These stories encompass all aspects of human life and thought. They are neither "totally subjective" nor "illusory." They focus on and explore order and disorder. They are a tool that can help political philosophy reflect upon possibilities and use those reflections to begin writing new myths now, at the end of liberalism.

For classical liberalism, no matter what one may think, has become as hollow as the Ash and the Alder trees in *Phantastes*. It no longer provides any sense of *homonoia*, of a common experience. It constantly seeks to fill some hole at its center. In fact, as John Ranieri points out, there is no common core experience felt by all human beings in the same way. There is a common mystery that peoples have "experienced and articulated through symbols."[3] Often that experience of mystery reveals itself in feelings of awe, wonder, and participation in a play "nobody wrote" where there is "no audience but ourselves"[4] and the choice individuals make of whether to participate in that mysterious play. Individuals and cultures evoke those feelings through roughly equivalent symbols.[5]

There are as many symbolizations of the awe and wonder generated by mystery as there are peoples. The symbols differ over time and among cultures. And they evolve and change over time. As we argued in chapter 1, no myth, no evoked symbolization, is Truth. Nor does any myth accurately reflect human experience in a culture for all time. However, all those symbolizations express the mythic response of human beings searching for meaning and understanding of some mystery that transcends the material world. Contemporary Western societies need to once again encounter mystery and accept it as factual. They need to perceive the awe and wonder generated by that mystery as genuine. They need to evoke new symbols of their experience of mystery and understandings of themselves as actors in McCarthy's one tale—the tale of individual human beings participating in some universal story of humanity.

The books chosen for inclusion in this volume are critical of the continued viability of the classical liberal myth. They hint at new directions. Further, these novels assist in the task of holding together life's multiple planes political, social, religious, family, work, friendship and community. They suggest ways of achieving a balanced consciousness—of mediating between the pull of the immanent material world and that of some ineffable transcendent reality. They recognize the importance of *homonoia* and might agree with Ranieri that "refusal to acknowledge what is common is to imagine that one's consciousness is private." [6] By withdrawing into themselves, they become McCarthy's *huerfano* (orphan). At the same time, these authors understand that myths must be inclusive, "pluralist and multicultural." [7] Like the postmoderns, they reject totalizing myths. However, they also reject the postmodern assertion that any search for meaning and any questioning of what exists is fruitless. They believe in life's contingency without accepting that participation in its mystery is useless or that contingency is all there is. [8] Human choice is important in each work examined here.

Only by grounding existence in something beyond the self is communal life possible. Only if communal life and some sense of responsibility for one's fellow human beings exists, can there be public space and a political realm. Otherwise human beings exist in a world of isolated orphans. All the works examined here understand that basic fact. They hint at how to balance authority and community and the content of the political sphere. They contain glimpses of important aspects of a functioning democracy—or at least of the things such a democracy would want to avoid. The stories shared in this book open doors to re-establishing an independent political sphere and establishing a balance between authority and community.

What the stories included in this book teach is possibility. The child's world is one of possibility. As Neil Gaiman wrote concerning Hope Mirrlees' *Lud-in-the-Mist* and Tolkien's Ring Trilogy, human beings need both the mundane and the miraculous. [9] The trick is reconciling them. The adult world is full of possibility as well, if adults remember that possibility exists and that more than time and chance rule the world. The stories we chose to include here link possibility to certain characteristics: understanding of consciousness as two-fold, acceptance of the ubiquitous presence of ineffable mystery in the world, the need for noetic reason in order to appreciate the paradox of consciousness and presence, the importance of *opsis* and witness if human beings are to turn possibility into reality. The search for possibilities also must "critically emphasize the distinction between, on the one hand, the many types and domains of human knowledge of finite reality and, on the other hand, stories, myths or visions of the Whole that orient us in relation to transcendence through the articulation of a common drama."[10] It must include all of Reality, not just one aspect. By extending its understanding of the real, the search for new understandings mandates that a political community must take care of all its members, that there are obligations to one another that go further than "do no harm."

We did not make up these links; they are in the books we included. We merely point them out. They may not be realistic—certainly they are not in contemporary liberal societies. However, they make it clear that postmodernism no more answers the questions posed by Kai than does Lockean liberalism.

It is important to remember that these stories do not ask human beings to go back to some time in the past when things were better. Nor do they point the way to any religion, even a "weak" one. Instead, they suggest that political philosophy find new ways to incorporate insights such as those discussed in this book into innovative thinking that might be better suited to humane communal life than what exists today. Stories point out possibilities. Human beings never achieve all the possibilities open to them. Perhaps though, belief in and work toward accomplishing some of the possibilities these mythopoets offer will spark the movement of political philosophy in new and more productive directions. The life, the world, and the universe, especially the search for meaning and order, are endlessly complicated, mysterious, fascinating, and worthy of exploration. Political philosophy is exploring new directions. Currently those directions seem unable to untether themselves from the essence of the Lockean liberal tradition. The works discussed here argue that political philosophy needs a more radical break from classical liberalism in order to include and foster new possibilities. It, as well as stories, needs to become the parent of creative possibilities in the never-ending search for order.

NOTES

1. Neil Gaiman, "Why Our Future Depends on Libraries, Reading and Daydreaming: The Reading Agency Lecture, 2013," in *The View from the Cheap Seats* (New York: William Morrow *an imprint of* HarperCollins *Publishers*, 2016), 14.

2. Glenn Hughes, *Transcendence and History* (Columbia and London: University of Missouri Press, 2003), 37.

3. John Ranieri, "Grounding Public Discourse" in Glenn Hughes, ed. *The Politics of the Soul* (Lanham, MD: Rowman & Littlefield Publishers, 1999), 38.

4. Susan Cooper, *Silver on the Tree* (New York: Aladdin Paperbacks, 2000), 139.

5. Ranieri, 38.

6. Ibid., 39.

7. Hughes, *Transcendence and History*, 36.

8. See, for example, Richard Rorty, *Irony, Contingency, and Solidarity* (Cambridge University Press, 1989). Rorty argues that human beings are surrounded only by contingency--by power and pain. Thus, there is no inherent meaning to human beings or life. Individuals create themselves when they create sentences. This means the true creators of contemporary time are the poet and the revolutionary. Both recognize that Truth is not "out there," but, rather, must be made. Thus, intellectual and moral progress is the history of increasingly useful metaphors, rather than of discovering truth. Humanity then will no longer worship God, or truth, or itself. Instead it will realize that everything is the product of time and chance.

9. Neil Gaiman, *"Lud-in-the-Mist,"* in *The View from the Cheap Seats*, 437.

10. Hughes, *Transcendence and History*, 36.

Glossary

Agonistic democracy: As described by William E. Connolly, agonistic democracy accepts that every individual has their own identity. However, it also recognizes that having an identity also means affirming one's difference from all others. Individuals need to understand the implications of the fact that they are both similar to and different from others. That recognition allows for increased democratic discussion of policy. It also allows one to re-think their own identity and to work toward making small shifts in their own outlooks and the outlook of their group(s), shifts that would promote inclusiveness.

Alusi/going alu: Going *alu* means to go into the wilderness. The *Alusi* are wilderness spirits. In Okorafor's work. The wilderness is an experience of the spiritual, including the spirits of the dead.

Ani: In Okorafor, Ani is the goddess of the earth and natural things. She also is the sister of the creator of all things.

Anxiety of existence: The feeling of powerlessness in the face of time and space. Human beings will never know exactly how they as particular human beings came to be or why they exist. Humanity lives in ignorance of both the totality of the knowable immanent (material) and the unknowable transcendent. The anxiety of existence is more than a fear of death; it is fear of losing their place within the community of being.

Architecture of serendipity: Created spaces in which chance encounters among different classes, races, religions, ethnicities, nations, genders, etc. can meet and exchange ideas. Cass Sunstein sees the creation of such spaces as possible using the Internet. This architecture, he believes, can change minds and create an enhanced sense of political community.

Attunement: The ability to take experiences and imagine the truths about reality they may represent.

Balance of consciousness: Openness to all of reality, both to the immanent (the here and now) and the transcendent (see transcendence in this glossary) and an attempt to bring both experiences into equilibrium. Balance depends on faith, hope, and love.

Biblical polity: Government rooted in the Christian New Testament that is both civil and ecclesiastical.

Classical Liberalism (Lockean Liberalism): Classical liberalism as it developed over hundreds of years came to mean that human beings are physical beings composed of matter and ruled by their passions and appetites. They are individuals who often are competitive and self-interested. They possess rights to life, liberty, and property. Human beings owe each other respect and should not harm one another. Society is the center of real life, not politics, and citizenship is not important. Human beings attempt to accumulate as much property as possible. Reality is what humans can observe and test. It is composed of matter and functions as a machine. Human beings can control some parts of reality by understanding natural laws and bending them to human use. There may or may not be gods. There is no way to prove their existence scientifically. If the gods do exist, they have nothing to do with the human world.

Communitarian: The Communitarians are an eclectic group of reform liberals, strong democrats, Neoconservatives, and independents who believe contemporary America is shattered, materialistic, and morally empty. They often disagree with one another, but tend to argue that politics contains no conception of the common good; consumerism rules and citizens no longer possess a sense of social coherence and civic mindedness. To the Communitarians, Americans are fragmented selves without attachments, commitments, or duties. They trace the origins of this problem to liberalism and an exaggerated preoccupation with rights.

Community of being: The community of being consists of transcendence (some unknowable and mysterious beyond), human beings, the universe, and society. Every human being and society must make decisions about the nature of the four parts of the community of being and how they will address questions related to that community.

Covenant of Grace: A binding agreement between the community and God, such as the Old Testament covenant between God and Abraham stating, "I will be your God and you will be my people." Mutual obligation is an essential element. It was the founding principle of the second wave of Puritan emigrants. If the congregational community faithfully followed God's will, as stated in the Bible, God would favor and support the community.

Deconstructionism: This school of contemporary political philosophy most often is associated with Jacques Derrida who came to it late in life. It tends to question all traditional ideas about identity and truth. It seeks to ferret out the underlying assumptions behind concepts and ideas.

Demon: In Greek thought a demon is not necessarily a devil. It is the passion or motivating force of an individual's life.

Diké: Justice, righteousness.

Drama of being/drama of existence: Human existence is historical and dramatic. Events occur. Some are stirring; some horrific; some wondrous. However, history is not just a string of events on a time line. History, because it includes human choice, also is the story of human participation in the community of being. Overall, human life, that drama of being, takes place in the world transcendent.

Eshu: In Okorafor's novels, an individual capable of deep magic.

Ewu: In Okorafor's novels, A child born out of violent rape.

Existence out of nothing: Because there exists a community of being, there is no point outside that community from which an individual can stand as an outside observer. Yet there also is no certainty of the meaning of that community or what one's role in it is. Existence out of nothing is humanity's essential ignorance of its purpose and origin and of the purpose and origin of the community of being.

Falling out of time: Human beings worry that they will fall from being to nothingness. It is more than the fear of personal death. Falling out of time includes the worry that death also will end their partnership in being. It is the result of lack of attunement to the order of being.

Ground of being or existence: The search for some anchor in life that can provide meaning and a sense of permanent order; some comprehensive reality. Voegelin argues that reason is humanity's ground, but that reason requires inclusion of some ultimate end or purpose which is not a means to some further end.

Historiogenesis: Speculation on the origins of society that result in a founding myth.

Homo economicus: Economic man.

Hypostatize: To hypostatize is to turn an idea or value into part of the fundamental substance of reality; for example, deciding that one pole or the other of consciousness (either the reality of physical or of nonphysical things) is all of reality rather than part of it.

Immanentize: The attempt to build heaven on earth.

Immortalizing: Living into whatever is immortal in the universe.

Instrumental reason: Using the mind to set goals and achieve them.

It-Reality: It-Reality is a reality filled with things that exist but that cannot be touched. It-Reality is ineffable (mysterious and beyond human understanding) and cannot be controlled by human will and intention.

Jeremiad: A lamentation over the state of society and a call to repentance and change.

Kinesis: Upheaval; total social, political, and spiritual disintegration of a society.

Krees (or Kris): A dagger most associated with Indonesia and sometimes thought to possess magical power.

Libertarianism: There are many forms of libertarianism. For Robert Nozick, the most important right is self-ownership (particularly ownership of one's labor). Self-ownership is the only way to implement the idea that every person must be treated with equal human dignity and assure that human beings are not used as means to other people's ends. Under this view, human beings are individuals with distinct claims of their own. There are things about a person—that person's rights—with which no one may interfere. These rights relate to the individual's self-ownership and are so strong that there is little that government may morally do to limit them. Nozick holds freedom higher than obligation and self-ownership higher than community. He believes that any attempt to reconcile individual liberty with community will result in a kind of slavery to the whole.

Logos: Word, story or tale.

Mana: The power of the elemental forces of nature embodied in an object or person.

Masquerade: A Masquerade is a physical presence in an elaborate costume that evokes deep feelings. Masquerades serve a variety of purposes in West African culture. In *Who Fears Death*, they are Alusi (wilderness spirits) who mask themselves in a costume to appear on earth. A Masquerade may be a warning, a threat to evildoers, or a bringer of peaceful tidings.

Metalepsis: To Eric Voegelin, *metalepsis* is the joint participation of God and man in the *metaxy*.

Metaxy: Experiencing life as both a subject in a world that human beings can control, a world of will and intention, and as an actor in a play that takes place in a mystery one cannot understand. *Metaxy* is an experience, not a place; it is the experience of living in the middle between life and death, lasting and passing, one phase of life and another, etc.

Modern Project/Modernity: Underlying the Modern Project is the idea that the desires for wealth, power, and survival are the sole goals of human life and action. Human beings are motivated only by self-interest, fear, and the will to power. Isolated and inwardly directed, they are morally neutral creatures who seek meaning in the world. Under this model the State exists to provide its citizens with the means of achieving these goals. The myth of modernity rests upon a certain type of consciousness—the belief that human beings can order their physical and personal environment according to will (intent) and that progress is the result of the imposition of human will on the world and on social relations. Freedom, thus, is the ability to impose one's will and achieve one's desired ends. Justice is a convention. Designed to mask the harsh realities of power politics, it consists in the practice of actions useful to the greatest number and the decisions made according to accepted procedures. There is no "Good." God is either a human artifact or the deists' clock winder.

Mythopoesis: The use of the myth to communicate ever more differentiated experiences of the truth of existence. Rather than a literal interpretation of a myth, the term suggests the use of myth to explore the ground of human existence and the interaction of the human and transcendent in the world. It includes such themes as coming-of-age, heroes and quests, encounters with the preternatural, a weakening of the boundaries between existent and nonexistent reality, and a bending or breaking of modernity's notions of time and space.

Muthos: For most scholars of the subject, myth is *muthos*, or *logos*—a word, statement, or tale.

Neutral Administrative State: The belief that unbiased, well-trained, professional competence will lead to effective, just, and ethical decisions. Politics is about the administration of resources.

Noetic reason: Noetic reason is reason that relies on both aspects of the mind, both finding ways to achieve goals and evaluating the ends sought in terms of the Good. It helps individuals navigate life in the *metaxy* and achieve a balanced, healthy consciousness through a constant interaction of both the passions and the *Agathon* (Good, True, Just). It is not a set group of ideas. It is the conscious use of intellect to seek the transcendent good.

Nous: *Nous* is mind or intellect that assists human beings in understanding the true or the real. In choosing noetic reason human beings acknowledge they are not wholly autonomous and do not carry the meaning and origins of life within themselves. The political philosopher Eric Voegelin calls this "reason in the classic sense."

Nsibidi: Ancient script used in West-Central Africa.

Numinous: Evoking awe and wonder.

Nuru: In Okarafor's novels these are golden-skinned people descended from the Arabs.

Obligations of solidarity: Those obligations to other citizens that are inherent in the idea of a political community. They are not subject to individual choice. See Michael, J. Sandel, *Justice* (New York: Penguin Books, 2009).

Okeke: In *The Book of Phoenix*, Okeke means all human beings. In *Who Fears Death*, it had come to mean dark-skinned people born to be slaves of the Nuru.

Opsis: Clear-sightedness.

Paradox of consciousness: The feeling of being a subject in a world of will and intention *and* an actor in a play that takes place within a mystery one cannot understand.

Postmodernism: Postmodernism can mean several different things, many of which are contradictory. They do share some commonalities, however, because they all acknowledge being influenced by Nietzsche, Marx, and Heidegger. Commonalities include: (1) Human beings are thrown in to the world; (2) Life is random; (3) There is nothing "out there" but power and pain—thus, there is no transcendence; (4) Human beings must develop an aesthetic morality—their role models should be the poets and revolutionaries; (5) Human beings must remember they are creatures containing both limit and possibility; and (6) There are no universal essences, foundations, or natures. Human beings are neither rational reflective subjects nor consciously self-determining agents.

Post-Structuralism: There is no such thing as a unified and coherent self. A reader's understanding of a text is more important than any meaning intended by the text's author. The reader replaces the author in determining a text's meaning. In *The Book of Phoenix*, this is the method Sunuteel uses when he copies and re-writes Phoenix's recording of her life.

Preterite: Those passed over for salvation.

Parousia: Presence

Reflective distance: Attunement to the order of being (or Plato's World Soul). Remembrance of participation in the *metaxy*, composed of both Thing-Reality and It-Reality, and use of that memory as an experience and a source of order; attunement to the fact that life takes place within ineffable and transcendent meaning (or It-Reality).

Reform Liberalism: John Rawls begins with the premise that society is a system of fair social cooperation between free and equal persons. In such a society cooperation is guided by procedures that all those involved recognize and regulate their conduct. Fair terms include ideas about reciprocity and mutuality. Social cooperation requires an idea of each participant's rational advantage (or good). Persons possess (1) a capacity for a sense of justice and (2) a capacity for a conception of the good. This, Rawls argues, is a political conception of a person rather than a moral one. Rawls urges human beings to leave any comprehensive moral doctrines they believe at the door of public space and cooperatively agree to a definition of justice that will serve all of everyone, no matter what their moral doctrine.

Situated Self: A sense of self identity that is at least partially formed by and connected to a community. For more, see Michael J. Sandel "The Procedural Republic and the Unencumbered Self." *Political Theory* 12 (Feb. 1984): 81–96.

Social Covenant: An agreement with God for a binding relationship that is both civil and ecclesiastical. The main function of government is to foster a pure biblical polity. With this goal the determining factor in all policy, then social solidarity would be inevitable. Social classes would always exist. However, individuals would consider the maintenance of biblical purity more important than the accumulation of individual wealth and would take care of those less fortunate. There would be no conflict among different interests or classes because all would share the same goal.

Structuralism: Structuralists believe all human activity, even perception, are the product of our experiences with culture, society, schooling, etc. They believe that structure is embedded into any system or society. Structure is the reality lying underneath appearance. In addition, the embedded structure gives everything its meaning and everyone their "place."

Subjunctivity: Possibility, especially possibility for change. Something that is contingent or possible.

"The right is prior to the good": This phrase was used by the political philosopher John Rawls to mean that although rights existed before society, understandings of the social/moral Good did not. Further, because everyone does not share the same understanding of what is Good, everyone must have the right to define and pursue their own understanding of the Good.

Thing-Reality: A world filled with physical objects that human beings can manipulate to meet their personal needs and desires; the reality human beings intend or will.

To slip: In *Who Fears* Death, to slip means to move through time, space, and dimension at will.

Transcendence: Following Eric Voegelin and Glenn Hughes, the transcendent is the ineffably mysterious that goes beyond the "conditions of space and time and our direct or substantive understanding." See Hughes, *Transcendence and History* (Columbia and London: University of Missouri Press, 2003), 20.

Unencumbered Self: Seeing oneself as alone in the universe, unrooted to anything beyond the self and one's personally chosen goals and group. See Michael J. Sandel. *Democracy's Discontent: America in Search of a Public Philosophy*. Cambridge: Cambridge University Press, 1996 and Michael J. Sandel "The Procedural Republic and the Unencumbered Self," *Political Theory* 12 (Feb. 1984): 81–96.

Bibliography

Adams, Guy B. "Reply to Professor Koven." *Public Integrity*. Vol, 14, no. 1 (Winter 2011–2012): 93–94.

Adams, Guy B. and Balfour, Danny L. "The Problem of Administrative Evil in a Culture of Technical Rationality." *Public Integrity*, Vol. 54, no. 4 (Summer 2011): 275–285. Accessed January 10, 2019. DOI: 10.2753/PIN1099-9922130307.

Adams, Guy B. and Balfour, Danny L. "'Open Secrets: The Masked Dynamics of Ethical Failures and Administrative Evil." *Research in Social Problems and Public Policy* vol. 19 (2011): 403–419. Accessed January 15, 2019. DOI: 10.1108/S0196-115r2(2011)0000019025.

Adams, Kelly. "Acts Without Agents: The Language of Torture in J.M. Coetzee's Waiting for the Barbarians." *Ariel: A Review of English Literature* vol. 46, no. 3 (2015): 165–177. Accessed January 10, 2019. No DOI.

Alexander, Lloyd. "Fantasy and the Human Condition." *The New Advocate* 1, no. 2 (1988): 75–83. Accessed April 3, 2018. ERIC Number: EJ374829.

Allen, Diogenes and Eric O. Springsted. *Spirit, Nature, and Community: Issues in the Thought of Simone Weil*. Albany: State University of New York Press, 1994.

Al-Saidi, Afaf Ahmed Hasan. "Post-Colonialism Literature the Concept of Self and the Other in Coetzee's Waiting for the Barbarians: An Analytical Approach." *Journal of Language Teaching and Research* vol. 5, no. 1 (January 2014): 95–105.

Alter, Alexandra. "Nnedi Okorafor and the Fantasy Genre She Is Helping Redefine." *New York Times Books*. Oct. 6, 2017. Accessed March 7, 2019. https://www.nytimes.com/2017/10/06/books/ya-fantasy-diverse-akata-warrior.html.

Ančič, Andrijana. "The Ambivalence of Colonial Discourse: Waiting for the Barbarians in the Gaze of the Other." *Bulletin of the Institute of Ethnography of the Serbian Academy of Arts and Sciences* (May 19, 2015): 383–394. Accessed November 11, 2018. DOI: 10.2298/GEI1502383A.

Andrews, Kehinde. "Racism is still alive and well, 50 years after the UK's Race Relations Act." *The Guardian*. Dec. 8, 2015. Accessed March 1, 2019. https://www.theguardian.com/commentisfree/2015/dec/08/50-anniversary-race-relations-act-uk-prejudice-racism.

Antidefamation League. "U.S. Anti-Semitic Incidents Spike 86 Percent So Far in 2017 After Surging Last Year, ADL Finds." April 24, 2017. Accessed March 1, 2019. https://www.adl.org/news/press-releases/us-anti-semitic-incidents-spike-86-percent-so-far-in-2017.

Arendt, Hannah. *Between Past and Future*. Viking Press, 1968.

Arendt, Hannah. *Men in Dark Times*. Harcourt, Brace, & World, Inc., 1968.

Arendt, Hannah. *Eichmann in Jerusalem: A Report on the Banality of Evil*. Penguin Classics, 1977.

Arendt, Hannah. "Introduction *into* Politics" in *The Promise of Politics*. Edited by Jerome Kohn. New York: Schocken Books, 2005.

Arnold, Edwin T. and Dianne C. Luce, ed. *A Cormac McCarthy Companion: The Border Trilogy*. Jackson: University Press of Mississippi, 2001.

Auerbach, Erich. *Mimesis: The Representation of Reality in Western Literature*. Translated by Willard R. Trask. Princeton University Press, 1953.

Baker, Daniel. "Within the Door: Portal Quest Fantasy in Gaiman and Miéville." *Journal of the Fantastic in the Arts*. 27, no. 3 (2016): 470–493. Accessed October 22, 2018.

https://lib-proxy.radford.edu/login?url=http://search.ebscohost.com/lo-gin.aspx?direct=true&db=hlh&AN=124769634&site=eds-live&scope=site.

Bateson, Gregory. *Steps to an Ecology of Mind*. University of Chicago Press, 1972. BBC News. "Europe and Nationalism: A Country by Country Guide." Sept. 10, 2018. Accessed March 1, 2019. https://www.bbc.com/news/world-europe-36130006.

Bealer, Tracy, Rachel Luria, and Wayne Yuen, ed. *Neil Gaiman and Philosophy: Gods Gone Wild*. Chicago and LaSalle, IL: Open Court Press, 2012.

Berressem, Hanjo. *Pynchon's Poetics: Interfacing Theory and Text*. Urbana and Chicago: University of Illinois Press, 1993.

Bidney, David. "Myth, Symbolism, and Truth." 68 *Journal of American Folklore* (Oct.-Dec. 1955): 379–92. Accessed 29-01-2013. DOI: 10.2307/536765. https://www-jstor-org.lib-proxy.radford.edu/stable/536765.

Bilbro, Jeffrey. "Phantastical Regress: The Return of Desire and Deed in *Phantastes* and *The Pilgrim's Regress*." *Mythlore* 28, no. ¾ (Spring/Summer 2010): 21–37. Accessed October 22, 2018. https://lib-proxy.radford.edu/login?url=http://search.ebsco host.com/login.aspx?direct=true&db=edsglr&AN=edsgcl.227196956&site=eds-live& scope=site.

Blomqvist, Rut. "The Road of Our Senses: Search for Personal Meaning and the Limitations of Myth in Gaiman's *American Gods*." *Mythlore* 30, no. 3|4 (Spring/Summer 2012). Accessed October 22, 2018. https://lib-proxy.radford.edu/login?url=http:// search.ebscohost.com/login.aspx?direct=true&db=edsglr&AN=edsgcl.288689245& site=eds-live&scope=site.

Bloom, Harold. *The Anxiety of Influence: A Theory of Poetry, 2 nd edition*. New York: Oxford University Press, 1997.

Bloom, Harold, ed. *Cormac McCarthy*. Infobase Publishing, 2009.

Bloomfield, Morton W., ed. *Allegory, Myth, and Symbol*. Cambridge: Harvard University Press, 1981.

Booth, Wayne C. *The Company We Keep*. Berkeley: University of California Press, 1988.

Boudway, Matthew. "Children of God? Cormac McCarthy's Misfits." *Commonweal* 11, no.11 (2016): 18–23. Accessed November 2, 2017. https://www.common wealmagazine.org/children-god.

Bowie, Fiona. *The Anthropology of Religion: An Introduction*. Blackwell Press, 2006.

Brown, Paula. "*Stardust* as Allegorical 'Bildungsroman': An Analogy for Platonic Idealism." *Extrapolation* 51, no. 2 (2010): 216–234. Accessed October 22, 2018. https:// lib-proxy.radford.edu/login?url=http://search.ebscohost.com/login.aspx?direct =true&db=edsglr&AN=edsgcl.243526092&site=eds-live&scope=site.

Burdge, Anthony S. "So Long and Thanks for All the Dents! A Guide for the Hitchhiker Through the Worlds of Douglas Adams and Neil Gaiman." In *The Mythological Dimensions of Neil Gaiman*, edited by Anthony Burdge, Jessica Burke, and Kristen Larsen, 79–93. Kitsune Books, 2012 and CreateSpace, 2013.

Burke, Jessica. "Women of Magic: Witches and the Work of Neil Gaiman." In *The Mythological Dimensions of Neil Gaiman*, edited by Anthony Burdge, Jessica Burke, and Kristen Larsen, 140–172. Kitsune Book, 2012 and CreateSpace, 2013.

Burt, Michael. "Phantastes and the Development of the Imagination." *North Wind: A Journal of George MacDonald Studies* 33 (January 1, 2016): 89–103. Accessed October 24, 2018. https://digitalcommons.snc.edu/northwinds/vol35/iss1/31.

Campbell, Joseph. *Creative Mythology: The Masks of God*. New York: Penguin, 1968.

Campbell, Joseph with Bill Moyers. *The Power of Myth*. Edited by Betty Sue Flowers. New York: Anchor Doubleday, 1988.

Camus, Albert. *The Plague*. Translated by Stuart Gilbert. Vintage Press, 1991.

Camus, Cyril. "The 'Outsider': Neil Gaiman and the Old Testament." *Shofar: An Interdisciplinary Journal of Jewish Studies* 29, no. 2 (2011): 77–99. Accessed October 22, 2018. https://lib-proxy.radford.edu/login?url=http://search.ebscohost.com/login.as px?direct=true&db=edsglr&AN=edsgcl.247740562&site=eds-live&scope=site.

Carinae, Tanya and Jones, Pell. "It Starts with Doors: Blurred Boundaries and Portals in the World of Neil Gaiman." In *The Mythological Dimensions of Neil Gaiman*, edited by Anthony Burdge, Jessica Burke, and Kristen Larsen, 207-222. Kitsune Books, 2012 and CreateSpace, 2013.

Cassirer, Ernst. *The Myth of the State*. Yale University Press, 1961.

Cassirer, Ernst. *The Philosophy of Symbolic Forms, Vol. 2: Mythical Thought*. Yale University Press, 1965.

Chase, David. "Myth as Literature," in *Myth and Method: Modern Theories of Fiction*. Edited by James Miller. University of Chicago Press, 1960.

Chesterton, G. K. *The Everlasting Man*. Watchmaker Publishing, 2013.

Clerc, Charles. Mason & Dixon *and Pynchon*. Lanham: University Press of America, 2000.

Cohen, Samuel. "*Mason & Dixon* & the Ampersand." *Twentieth Century Literature* 48 (Autumn 2002): 264–91. Accessed 04-07- 2007. DOI: 10.2307/3176029 https://www-jstor-org.lib-proxy.radford.edu/stable/3176029.

Coleman, Christian A. "Interview with Nnedi Okorafor." *Lightspeed Magazine*, Issue 82 (Mar. 2017):5525. Accessed March 7, 2019. http://www.lightspeeb btg3dmagazine.com/nonfiction/interview-nnedi-okorafor/.

Connolly, William E. *Identity/Difference*. Minneapolis: University of Minnesota Press, 1991.

Cooper, Lydia R. *No More Heroes*. Louisiana State University, 2011.

Coraghessan, Boyle. T. "The Great Divide." *The New York Times Book Review* (May 18, 1997): p NA. Academic OneFile. Thomson Gale. Radford University Library.

Cowart, David. *Thomas Pynchon: The Art of Illusion*. Carbondale: Southern Illinois University Press, 1980.

Cowart, David. "The Luddite Vision: Mason and Dixon." *American Literature* 71 (June 1999): 341-63. Accessed 04-07-2007. https://www-jstor-org.lib-proxy.radford.edu/stable/2902814.

Creed, Daniel. "Connecting Dimensions: Directions, Location, and Form in the Fantasies of George MacDonald. *North Wind: A Journal of George MacDonald Studies* 33 (2014): 1-20. Accessed October 24, 2018. https://digitalcommons.snc.edu/north-winds/vol35/iss1/1.

Crocker, Thomas P. "Constitutive Visions: Sovereignty, Necessity, and Saramago's Blindness." *Constellations* vol. 24, no. 1 (November 2017): 63–75. Accessed January 10, .2019. DOI: 10.1111/1467-8675.12260.

Crossan, John Dominic. *The Dark Interval: Towards a Theology of Story*. Sonoma, CA: Polebridge Press, 1988.

Cullen, Thomas. "Hate Crimes on the Rise." *The Roanoke Times: Opinion*. March 11, 2019, 3. Print.

Dahl, Robert and Stinebrickner, Bruce. *Modern Political Analysis*. Prentice Hall, 2003.

Danzinger, James. *Understanding the Political World*. Durham, NC: Duke University Press, 2001.

Deneen, Patrick J. and Romance, Joseph. *Democracy's Literature: Politics and Fiction in America*. Lanham: Rowman & Littlefield, 2005.

Deneen, Patrick. *Why Liberalism Failed*. Yale University Press, 2018.

Denham, Robert D., ed. *Northrop Frye—Myth and Metaphor: Selected Essays, 1974–1988*. Charlottesville: University of Virginia Press, 1990.

Derrida, Jacques. *Of Hospitality*. Translated by Rachel Bowlby. Stanford, CA: Stanford University Press, 2000.

Derrida, Jacques. *Before the Law: The Complete Text of Préjugés*. Translated by Sandra Van Reenen. University of Minnesota Press, 2018.

Derrida, Jacques. *The Politics of Friendship*. Translated by George Collins. London: Verso, 2005.

Dickinson, Matthew and Rudalevige, Andrew. "Worked Out in Fractions: Neutral Competence, FDR, and the Bureau of the Budget." *Congress and the Presidency* vol. 34, no. 1 (Spring 2007): 1–26. Accessed January 10, .2019. DOI: 10.1080/07343460709507665.

Drury, Leslie. "Gaiman: The Teller of Tales and the Fairy Tale Tradition." In *The Mythological Dimensions of Neil Gaiman*, edited by Anthony Burdge, Jessica Burke, and Kristen Larsen. Kitsune Books, 2012 and CreateSpace, 2013.

Durrant, Sam. *Postcolonial Narrative and the Work of Mourning*. State University of New York Press, 2004

Duriez, Colin. *The C.S. Lewis Handbook*. Grand Rapids: Baker Book House, 1990.

Duyfhuizen, Bernard. "Review: Taking Stock: 26 Years since "V." (Over 26 Books on Pynchon." *NOVEL: A Forum on Fiction* 23 (Autumn, 1989): 75–88. Accessed 04-07-2007. DOI: 10.2307/1345580.

Edwards, Brian. "Surveying 'America': in the Mnemonick Deep of Thomas Pynchon's *Mason & Dixon*." *Australian. Journal of American Studies* 23, no. 2 (December 2004): 21–30. Accessed 23-08-2018. Stable URL: https://jstor.org/stable/41416003.

Eliade, Mircea. *Myth and Reality*. Introduction by Ruth Nanda Anshen. New York: Harper and Row, 1963.

Ellwood., Robert. *The Politics of Myth: A Study of C.G. Jung, Mircea Eliade, and Joseph Campbell*. Albany: SUNY Press, 1999.

Epstein, Richard A. "The Perilous Position of the Rule of Law and the Administrative State." *Harvard Journal of Law and Public Policy* vol.36, no. 1 (Winter 2003): 5–20. Accessed January 10, 2019. No DOI.

Estelrich, Bartolomeu. "Simone Weil's Concept of Grace," *Modern Theology* 25, no. 2 (April 2009): 231–259. Accessed November 2, 2017. https://doi.org/10.1111/j.1468-0025.2008.01518.x.

Eve, Martin Paul. "Whose Line is It Anyway? Enlightenment, Revolution, and Ipseic Ethics in the Works of Thomas Pynchon." *Textual Practice* 26, no. 5 (2012): 921–939. Accessed 23-08-2018. DOI: 10.1080/0950236X.2012.709877. https://www.tandfonline.com/doi/abs/10.1080/0950236X.2012.709877.

Federal Bureau of Investigation, "Uniform Crime Statistics: Hate Crimes Statistics, 2017." Accessed March 1, 2019. https://ucr.fbi.gov/hate-crime/2017/resource-pages/hate-crime-summary.pdf.

Florensky, Pavel. *Ikonostasis*. Trans. Donald Sheehan and Olga Andrejev. Crestwood, New York: St. Vladimir's Seminary Press, 1996.

Frazer, Sir James George. *The Golden Bough, Vol. I*. New York: The MacMillan Company, 1951.

Freibel, Robert M. and Arch, Jennifer. "Perspective: Cuban Endemic Optic Neuropathy (1991-1993) and José Saramago's Novel *Blindness*." *American Journal of Opthamology* vol. 193 (September 2018): xxiii–xxvii. Accessed January 10, 2019. DOI.org/10.1016/j.ajo.2018.06.006.

Frye, Steven. *Understanding Cormac McCarthy*. The University of South Carolina Press, 2009.

Gaarden, Bonnie. Review of *Divine Carelessness and Fairytale Levity* by Daniel Gabelman. *Christianity and Literature* 64, no. 2 (2015): 221–224. Accessed October 24, 2018. https://doi.org/10.1177%2F0148333114566770.

Gaiman, Neil. *The Sandman, Vol. 3: Dream Country*. DC Comics, 1995.

Gaiman, Neil and Terry Pratchett. *Good Omens*. Ace Books, 1996.

Gaiman, Neil. *Stardust*. Harper, 1999.

Gaiman, Neil. *American Gods*. HarperTorch, *an imprint of* HarperCollins *Publishers*, 2001.

Gaiman, Neil. *Anansi Boys*. HarperTorch, *an imprint of* HarperCollins *Publishers*, 2005.

Gaiman, Neil. *The Graveyard Book*. Harper, 2008.

Gaiman, Neil. *The Ocean at the End of the Lane*. HarperCollins *Publishers*, 2013.

Neil Gaiman, "Why Our Future Depends on Libraries, Reading and Daydreaming: The Reading Agency Lecture, 2013." In *The View from the Cheap Seats*, 5–16. New York: William Morrow *an imprint of* HarperCollins *Publishers*, 2016.

Gaiman, Neil. "Lud-in-the-Mist." In *The View from the Cheap Seats*, 436–437. New York: William Morrow *an imprint of* HarperCollins *Publishers*, 2016, 437.

Gaiman, Neil. "Lou Reed, In Memoriam: 'The Soundtrack to My Life'." In *The View from the Cheap Seats,* 397–401. New York: William Morrow *an imprint of* HarperCollins *Publishers,* 2016.

Neil Gaiman, "A Speech Given to Professionals Contemplating Alternative Employment, Given at PROCON, April 1997." In *The View from the Cheap Seats,* 238–252. New York: William Morrow *An imprint of* HarperCollins *Publishers,* 2016.

Geland, Lynn. "The End of the World as We Know It: Neil Gaiman and the Future of Mythology." In *The Mythological Dimensions of Neil Gaiman,* edited by Anthony Burdge, Jessica Burke, and Kristen Larsen, 222–237. Kitsune Books, 2012 and CreateSpace, 2013.

Gerth, H.C. and Mills, C. Wright. *From Max Weber: Essays in Sociology.* New York: Oxford University Press, 1946.

Girard, René. *Deceit, Desire, and the Novel.* Baltimore: Johns Hopkins University Press, 1976.

Girard, René. *Violence and the Sacred.* W.W. North & Company, 1979.

Girard, René. *The Scapegoat.* Baltimore: Johns Hopkins University Press, 1989.

Girard, René. *I See Satan Fall Like Lightning.* Orbis Books, 2001.

Glendinning, Simon. *Derrida: A Very Short Introduction.* Oxford: Oxford University Press, 2011.

Goldberg, Jonah. *The Suicide of the West: How the Rebirth of Tribalism, Populism, and Identity Politics is Destroying American Democracy.* New York: Crown Forum, 2018.

Govrin, Yosef. "Anti-Semitic Trends in Post-Communist Eastern European States." Jerusalem Center for Public Affairs. *Jewish Political Studies Review* 15:3–4 (Fall 2003), accessed March 1, 2019. http://www.jcpa.org/phas/phas-govrin-f03.htm.

Green, Melody. "Librarians, Ravens, and Beautiful Ladies: Bakhtinian Dialogueism." In *The Mythological Dimensions of Neil Gaiman,* edited by Anthony Burdge, Jessica Burke, and Kristen Larsen, 47-63. Kitsune Books, 2012 and CreateSpace, 2013.

Greenblatt, Stephen. *The Swerve: How the World Became Modern.* New York: W.W. Norton & Company, 2011.

Griffin, Jasper. *The Mirror of Myth: Classical Themes and Variations.* Boston: Faber and Faber, 1986.

Grigsby, Ellen. *Analyzing Politics.* Belmont, CA: Wadsworth Press, 2002.

Habermas, Jurgen. *The Inclusion of the Other: Studies in Political Theory,* edited by Ciarin P. Cronin and Pablo de Greiff. Cambridge, MA: MIT Press, 2000.

Hage, Erik. *Cormac McCarthy: A Literary Companion.* McFarland and Company, 2010.

Hall, Wade and Rick Wallach, ed. *Sacred Violence: Vol. 2, Cormac McCarthy's Western Novels.* El Paso: Texas Western Press, 2002.

Harari, Yuval Noah. *Sapiens: A Brief History of Humankind.* Harper, 2015.

Harpham, Geoffrey Galt. *Getting It Right: Language, Literature, and Ethics.* Chicago: University of Chicago Press, 1999.

Hatab, Lawrence J. *Myth and Philosophy: A Contest of Truths.* LaSalle, IL: Open Court Press. 1990.

Hauslohner, Abigail. "Hate crimes jump for fourth straight year in largest U.S. cities, study shows." *Washington Post.* May 11, 2018. Accessed March 1, 2019. https://www.washingtonpost.com/news/post-nation/wp/2018/05/11/hate-crime-rates-are-still-on-the-rise/?utm_term=.4eb245cf04ae.

Hawkins, Ty. *Cormac McCarthy's Philosophy.* Palgrave Macmillan, 2017.

Head, James G. and Linda MacLea. *Myth and Meaning.* Evanston, IL: McDougal, Littell & Company, 1976.

Heilke, Thomas. "The Politics of Space: Wolin, Voegelin, and Arendt Compared." *Voegelin View.* Accessed 29-05-2017. https://voegelinview.com/space-politics-wolin-voegelin-arendt-compared/.

Hein, Roland. *George MacDonald: Victorian Mythmaker.* Nashville, TN: Starsong Publishing Group, 1993.

Hein, Roland. *The Heart of George MacDonald.* Wheaton, IL: Harold Shaw Publishers, 1994.

Hinds, Elizabeth Jane Wall. "Thomas Pynchon, Wit, and the Work of the Supernatural." *Rocky Mountain Review of Language and Literature* 54, no. 1 (2000): 23–40. Accessed 04-07-2007. http://www.jstor.org/stable/1348417.

Hinds, Elizabeth Jane Wall ed. *The Multiple Worlds of Pynchon's* Mason & Dixon. Rochester: Camden House, 2005.

Hite, Molly. *Ideas of Order in the Novels of Thomas Pynchon.* Columbus: Ohio State University Press, 1983.

Holmes, Oliver. "Antisemitic incidents in US soar to highest level in two decades." *The Guardian.* February 27, 2018. Accessed March 1, 2019, https://www.theguardian.com/society/2018/feb/27/antisemitism-us-rises-anti-defamation-league.

Horvath, Brooke and Irving Malin, ed. Pynchon and Mason & Dixon. Newark: University of Delaware Press, 2000.

Howard, Jeffrey. "The Anarchist Miracle and Magic in *Mason & Dixon*." *Pynchon Notes.* 52-53 (Spring-Fall 2003): 166–184. Accessed 23-08-2018. DOI: 10.16995/pn.58.

Howard, Susan. "In Search of Spiritual Maturity." *Extrapolation* 30, no. 3 (1989): 280–292. Accessed May 15, 2011. DOI:10.3828/extr.1989.30.3.280.

Hrezo, Margaret. "The Reinforcement of Social Cohesion: Humean Philosophy, the Therapeutic State, and the Exclusion Ritual." *The Journal of Psychiatry and Law* (Fall, 1978): 377–402.

Hrezo, Margaret S. "Composition on a Multiple Plane: Simone Weil's Answer to the Rule of Necessity." In *Feminist Approaches to Social Movements, Community, and Power, Vol I: Conscious Acts and the Politics of Social Change*, edited by Robin Teske and Mary Ann Tétreault, 91–106. Columbia: University of South Carolina Press, 2000.

Hrezo, Margaret S. "Wisdom, Strength, and Courtesy: Graveyard Favor Go with Thee." In *Neil Gaiman in the 21st Century*, edited by Tara Prescott, 83–96. McFarland and Company, Inc., 2015.

Hrezo, Margaret S. "Toni Morrison and Thomas Pynchon: Inspiring our Imaginations." *Voegelin View.* (Sept 2, 2012): https://voegelinview.com/preferring-miracles-to-magic.

Hughes, Glenn. *Mystery and Myth in the Philosophy of Eric Voegelin.* Columbia: University of Missouri Press, 1993.

Hughes, Glenn, ed. *The Politics of the Soul.* Lanham, MD: Rowman & Littlefield Publishers, 1999.

Hughes, Glenn. *Transcendence and History.* Columbia and London: University of Missouri Press, 2003.

Hume, Kathryn. *Pynchon's Mythography: An Approach to 'Gravity's Rainbow'.* Carbondale: Southern Illinois University Press, 1987.

Hume, David. *3 David Hume: Philosophical Works.* Edited by T. H. Green and T. H. Gross (London: Scientia Verlag Aalen, 1964).

Hume, David. *An Enquiry Concerning the Principles of Morals.* LaSalle, IL: Open Court Books, 1966.

Hunt, Caroline. "Form as Fantasy—Fantasy as Form." *Children's Literature Association Quarterly* 12, no. 1 (Spring 1987): 7–10. Accessed April 3, 2014. https://muse.jhu.edu/.

Jarrett, Robert L. *Cormac McCarthy.* New York: Twayne Publishers, 1997.

Jenkins, Ruth. "Imagining the Abject in Kingsley, MacDonald, and Carroll: Disrupting Dominant Values and Cultural Identity in Children's Literature." *The Lion and the Unicorn* 35, no. 1 (January 2011): 67–87. Accessed April 1, 2014. DOI:10.1353/uni.2011.0003.

Katsiadas, Nick. "Mytho-Autobiography: Neil Gaiman's *Sandman*, the Romantics, and Shakespeare's *The Tempest. Studies in Comics* 6, no. 1 (2015): 61–84. Accessed October 22, 2018. DOI: 10.1386/stic6.1/61_1/.

Keren, Michael. "The Original Position in José Saramago's *Blindness*." *The Review of Politics* vol. 69 (2007): 447–463. Accessed January 10, 2019. DOI: 10.1017/S0034670507000769.

Khalifa, Muhammed A., Jennings, Michael E., Briscoe, Felecia, Oleszweski, Ashley M. and Abdi, Nimo. "Racism? Administrative and Community Perspectives in Data-Driven Decision Making: Systemic Perspectives Versus Technical Rational Perspectives." *Urban Education* vol. xx, no. x (2013): 1–35. Accessed January 13, 2019. DOI: 10.1177/0042085913475635.

King, Martin Luther, Jr. "Beyond Vietnam—A Time to Break Silence." Accessed January 15, 2019. https://www.americanrhetoric.com/speeches/mlkatimetobreaksilence.htm.

Kirk, G.S. *Myth: Its Meaning and Functions in Ancient and Other Cultures.* Berkeley: University of California Press, 1970.

Klapcsik, Sendor. "The Double-Edged Nature of Neil Gaiman's Perspectives and Liminal Fantasies." *The Journal of the Fantastic in the Arts* 20, no. 2 (2009): 193–209. Accessed October 22, 2018. https://lib-proxy.radford.edu/login?url=http://search.ebscohost.com/login.aspx?direct=true&db=hlh&AN=48657467&site=eds-live&scope=site.

Kolakowski, Leszek. *The Presence of Myth.* Translated by Adam Czerniawski. Chicago: University of Chicago Press, 1989.

Koven, Steven G. "Revisiting Administrative Evil: Is It Consistent with Principles of Administration? Does It Move the Discipline Forward?" *Public Integrity* vol. 14, no. 1 (Winter 2011–2012): 85–92. Accessed January 10, 2019. DOI: 10.2753/PIN1099-9922140106.

Kronen, Samuel. "Neo-Tribalism." Accessed February 12, 2019. https://medium.com/@samuelkronen/modern-tribalis-and-the-danger-of-identity-politics-33150fd257f2.

Kundera, Milan. *The Curtain*, trans. Linda Asher. New York: HarperCollins, 2005.

Kunsa, Ashley. "Mystery and Possibility in Cormac McCarthy." *Journal of Modern Literature* 35, no. 2 (2012): 146–152.

Kurkjian, Catherine, Livingstone, Nancy, Young, Terrell, and Avi. "Worlds of Fantasy." *The Reading Teacher* 59, no. 5 (Feb. 2—6): 492–503. Accessed April 3, 2014. Doi:10.1598/RT.59.5.10.

Lambek, Michael A., ed. *A Reader in the Anthropology of Religion.* Boston: Blackwell Publishing, 2002.

Lee, Daniel. "The Politics of Fairyland: Neil Gaiman and the Enchantments of Anti-Bildungsroman Critique." Accessed April 3, 2014." *Studies in Contemporary Fiction.* http:/tandfonline.com/loi/ocrt 57, no. 5 (2016): 552–564. DOI: 10.1080/.00111619.2016.1138444.

Lehr, Susan. "Inner Journey for Today's Child." *Publishing Research Quarterly.* 7 (1991): 91–101. Accessed April 3, 2014. https://doi.org/10.1007/BF02678164.

Lessa, William A. and Evon Z. Vogt ed. *Reader in Comparative Religion: An Anthropological Approach.* New York: HarperCollins, 1979.

Lévi-Strauss, Claude. *Myth and Meaning.* New York: Schocken Books, 1978.

Levine, Herbert M. *Political Issues Debated.* Englewood Cliffs, NJ: Prentice Hall, 1992.

Lewis, C.S. *An Experiment in Criticism.* London: Cambridge University Press, 1961.

Lilley, James D. *Cormac McCarthy: New Directions.* Albuquerque: University of New Mexico Press, 2002.

Lincoln, Kenneth. *Cormac McCarthy: American Canticles.* Palgrave-Macmillan, 2009.

Litten, Jonathan. "*Phantastes*: All Mirrors are Magic Mirrors." *North Wind: A Journal of George MacDonald Studies* 35, no. 32 (2016): 104–125. Accessed October 24, 2018. http://digitalcommons.snc.edu/northwind/vol35/iss1/32.

Lochner, Liani. "Power and the Subject in J. M. Coetzee's *Waiting for the Barbarians.*" *Ariel: A Review of International English Literature* vol. 47, no. 4 (2016): 103–134. Accessed 1.10.2019. ISSN: 00041327. No DOI.

Lowi, Theodore J. "Where Do We Go from Here?" *International Political Science Review* vol. 32, no. 2 (March 2011): 223–230. Accessed January 10, 2019. DOI: 10.1177/0192512.111405787.

MacDonald, George. *Phantastes.* Mineoloa, New York: Dover Publications, 2005.

MacDonald, George. *Discovering the Heart of God*, Michael R. Phillips, ed. Minneapolis, MN: Bethany House Publishers, 1989.

MacDonald, George. *A Dish of Orts*. CreateSpace Independent Publishing Platform, 2012.

MacIntyre, Alasdair. *After Virtue*. Notre Dame, IN: University of Notre Dame Press, 1984.

Madsen, Deborah L. *The Postmodernist Allegories of Thomas Pynchon*. New York: St. Martin's Press, 1991.

Malpas, Simon and Andrew Taylor. *Thomas Pynchon*. Manchester: Manchester University Press, 2013.

Manlove, Colin. "The Circle of the Imagination: George MacDonald's *Phantastes* and *Lilith*." *Studies in Scottish Literature* 17, no. 1 (1982): 55–80. Accessed 12-3-2018.

Mattessich, Stefan. *Lines of Flight*. Durham: Duke University Press, 2002.

May, Rollo. *The Cry for Myth*. New York: W.W. Norton, 1991.

McCarthy, Cormac. *All the Pretty Horses*. New York: Vintage Books, 1993.

McCarthy, Cormac. *The Crossing*. New York: Vintage Books, 1994.

McCarthy, Cormac. *Cities of the Plain*. New York: Vintage Books, 1998.

McClure, John. *Partial Faiths: Postsecular Fiction in the Age of Pynchon and Morrison*. University of Georgia Press, 2007.

McEntee, Jason T. "Pynchon's Age of Reason: *Mason & Dixon* and America's Rise of Rational Discourse." *Pynchon Notes* 52–53 (Spring-Fall 2003): 186–207. Access date 23-08-2018. Literature Resource Center, http://link.galegroup.com.lib-proxy.radford.edu/apps/pub/1UJW/LitRC?u=viva_radford&sid=LitRC.

McGillis, Roderick, ed. *George MacDonald: Literary Heritage and Heirs*. Wayne, PA: Zossima Press, 2008.

McMahon, Robert. "Eric Voegelin's Paradoxes of Consciousness and Participation." *The Review of Politics."* 6f1, no. 1 (Winter, 1999): 117–139. Accessed 26-11-2017. Stable URL: http://www.jstor.org/stable/1408650.

Meletinsky, Eleazar M. *The Poetics of Myth*. Translated by Guy Lanoue and Alexandre Sadetsky. New York: Garland Publishing, 1998.

Mendelson, Michael. "The Fairy Tales of George MacDonald and the Evolution of a Genre." In *For the Childlike*. Edited by Roderick McGillis, 67–74. Zossima Press, 1992.

Metcalf, Robert "Religion and the 'Religious': Cormac McCarthy and John Dewey." *Journal of Speculative Philosophy* 31, no. 1 (2017): 135–154. Project Muse access provided by Radford University & (VIVA). Accessed November 2, 2017. https://muse.jhu.edu/.

Miller, Hugh T. "Post-Progressive Public Administration: Lessons from Policy Networks." *Public Administration Review* vol. 54, no. 4 (July/August 1994): 378–386. Accessed January 10, .2019. DOI: 10.2307/977386.

Miller, James E., ed. *Myth and Method: Modern Theories of Fiction*. University of Nebraska Press, 1960.

Miller, Perry. *The New England Mind: The Seventeenth Century*. Cambridge: Belknap Press of Harvard University Press, 1939.

Miller, Perry. *The New England Mind: From Colony to Province*. Cambridge: Belknap Press of Harvard University Press, 1953.

Miller, Perry. *Errand into the Wilderness*. Cambridge: Belknap Press of Harvard University Press, 1956.

Moore, Thomas. *The Style of Connectedness: Gravity's Rainbow and Thomas Pynchon*. Columbia: University of Missouri Press, 1987.

Morris, John S. "Fantasy in a Mythless Age." *Children's Literature* 2 (1973): 77–86. Accessed 01.04.14. DOI: 10.1353/ch1.0.0065.

Murdoch, Iris. *Existentialists and Mystics*. New York: Penguin Books, 1977.

Nashef, Hania A. M. "Becomings in J. M. Coetzee's Waiting for the Barbarians and José Saramago's *BlindnessM*." *Comparative Literature Studies* vol. 47, no. 1 (2010):21–41. Accessed January 13, 2019. DOI: 10.5325/complitstudies47.10021.

Nashef, Hania A. M. "Spectors of Doom: Saramago's Dystopias in *Blindness* and *The Cave.*" *Orbis Litterarum* vol. 70, no. 3 (April 15, 2015): 206–233. Accessed January 10, 2019. https://11001-org-lib.proxy.radford.edu/10.1111/0li.12067.

Newell, Philip J. *Listening to the Heartbeat of God: A Celtic Spirituality.* Paulist Press, 1997.

Niemi, Minna. "Totalitarian Politics and Individual Responsibility: Revisiting Hannah Arendt's Inner Dialogue through the Notion of Confession in J. M. Coetzee's *Waiting for the Barbarians.*" *South African Journal of Philosophy* vol. 36, no. 2 (Jun 2017): 223–238. Accessed January 13, 2019. DOI: 10.1080/02580136.2016.1219210.

Noll Mark A. "Wee Shall be as a City upon a Hill': John Winthrop's Non-American Exceptionalism." *The Review of Faith and International Affairs* (Summer 2012): 5–11. Accessed 14-10-2018.

Nussbaum, Martha. *The Fragility of Goodness.* Cambridge: Cambridge University Press, 1988.

Nussbaum, Martha. *Love's Knowledge.* New York: Oxford University Press, 1990.

Nussbaum, Martha. *Poetic Justice.* Boston: Beacon Press, 1995.

Olson, Alan M. ed. *Myth, Symbol, and Reality.* Notre Dame: Notre Dame University Press, 1980.

Olster, Stacey Michele. "A 'Patch of England, at a three-thousand mile off-set'? Representing America in *Mason & Dixon.*" *Modern Fiction Studies* 50, no. 2 (Summer 2004): 283–302. Accessed 23-08-2018. DOI: https://doi.org/10.1353/mfs.2004.0037.

O'Connor, Karen and Sabato, Larry J., ed. *Essentials of American Government: Continuity and Change.* Longman Publishing, 2009.

Okorafor, Nnedi. *Who Fears Death.* DAW Books, Inc., 2010.

Okorafor, Nnedi. *The Book of Phoenix.* DAW Books, Inc., 2015.

Owens, Barclay. *Cormac McCarthy's Western Novels.* Tucson: University of Arizona Press, 2000.

Pahl, Miriam. "Time, Progress, and Mutidirectionality in Nnedi Okorafor's *Who Fears Death.*" *Research in African Literature* Vol 49, No. 3 (Fall 2018): 207–222. Accessed February 12, 2019. DOI: 10.2979/reseafrilite.49.3.12.

Panichas, George A. *The Politics of Twentieth Century Literature.* New York: Hawthorn Books, Inc., 1971.

Patai, Raphael. *Myth and Modern Man.* Englewood Cliffs, NJ: Prentice-Hall, 1972.

Patel, Cyrus R. K. *Negative Liberties.* Durham: Duke University Press, 2001.

Pearse, Richard. *Critical Essays on Thomas Pynchon.* Boston: G.K. Hall & Co., 1981.

Pederson, Joshua. "The Gospel of Thomas (Pynchon): Abandoning Eschatology in *Gravity's Rainbow.*" *Religion and the Arts* 14 (2010): 139–160. Accessed 23-08-2018. DOI: 10.1163/107992610X125913031865.

Pendergast, John. "Six Characters in Search of Shakespeare: Neil Gaiman's *Sandman* and Shakespearian Mythose." *Mythlore* 26, no. ¾ (Spring/Summer 2008): 185–197. Accessed October 24, 2018. https://lib-proxy.radford.edu/login?url=http://search.ebscohost.com/login.aspx?direct=true&db=edsglr&AN=edsgcl.178795469&site=eds-live&scope=site.

Pionke, Albert. "The Art of Manliness: EKPHRASIS and/as Masculinity in George MacDonald's Phantastes." *Studies in the Novel* 43, no. 1 (2011): 21–37. Accessed April 3, 2014. http://www.jstor.org.lib-proxy.radford.edu/stable/41203499.

Plato. *Phaedrus* Translated by Benjamin Jowett. *Vol. I: The Dialogues of Plato.* New York: Random House, 1937.

Plato. *Symposium.* Trans. W.H.D. Rouse. (New York: Mentor Book, 1984), 204–211.

Plato. *The Republic.* Translated by Allan Bloom. New York: Basic Books, 1968.

Plato. *Gorgias.* Trans. Donald J. Zeyl. Hackett Books, 1987.

Polybius. *The Histories: Vol. II* (Cambridge: Harvard University Press, 1922), XXXVIII 22.1–3.

Potts, Matthew. "There is no god and we are his prophets: Cormac McCarthy's Christian Faith *Christianity and Literature* 63, no. 4 (Summer 2014): 489–501. Accessed November 2,-2017. https://doi.org/10.1177/014833311406300409.

Potts, Matthew. *Cormac McCarthy and the Signs of Sacrament: Literature, Theology, and the Moral of Stories*. New York: Bloomsbury Press, 2015.

Prickett, Stephen "The Two Worlds of George MacDonald." In *For the Childlike: The Two Worlds of George MacDonald*, edited by Roderick McGillis, 17–29. Scarecrow Press, 1992.

Pridemore, John. "George MacDonald's Estimate of Childhood." *International Journal of Children's Spirituality*" 12, no. 1 (April 2009): 61–74. Accessed April 1, 2014. doi:10.1080/13644360701266168.

Pynchon, Thomas. "Is It O.K. to be a Luddite?" *New York Times* (October 28, 1984). https://archive.nytimes.com/books/97/05/18/reviews/pynchon-luddite.html.

Pynchon, Thomas. *Slow Learner*. New York: Bantam Books, 1985.

Pynchon, Thomas. *Mason and Dixon*. New York: Henry Holt and Company, 1997.

Pynchon, Thomas. *Against the Day*. New York: Penguin Press, 2006.

Raeper, William. *George MacDonald*. Tring, Herts, England: A Lion Book, 1987.

Ranieri, John. "Grounding Public Discourse: The Contribution of Eric Voegelin." In Glenn Hughes, ed. *The Politics of the Soul*, 33–64 (Lanham, MD: Rowman & Littlefield Publishers, 1999).

Rauch, Stephen. *Neil Gaiman's The Sandman and Joseph Campbell: In Search of Modern Myth*. Wildside Press, 2003.

Reich, Robert. "Tribalism Is Tearing America Apart." Accessed February 12, 2019, https://www.salon.com/2014/03/25/robert_reich_tribalism_is_tearing_america_apart _partner/.

Ricouer, Paul. *Time and Narrative*. Translated by Kathleen McClaughlin and David Pellauer. Chicago: University of Chicago Press, 1984.

Rigsbee, Sally Adair. "Fantasy Places and Imaginative Belief: *The Lion, the Witch, and the Wardrobe* and *The Princess and the Goblin*." *Children's Literature Association Quarterly* 8, no. 1 (Spring 1993): 10–11. Accessed 03.04.14. DOI: 10.1353//chq.0.0431.

Robbins, Tom. *Wild Ducks Flying Backwards*. New York: Bantam, 2005.

Roukema, Aren. "The Shadow of Anodos: Alchemical Symbolism in *Phantastes*." *North Wind: A Journal of George MacDonald Studies* 31, art. 5 (2012): 48–63. Accessed. 24.10.18. http://digitalcommons.snc.edu/northwind/vol13/1ss1/5.

Rozelle, Lee. "'What Phantom Shape, Implicit in the Figures?': Liminal Monsters, Paranormal Places in Thomas Pynchon's *Mason & Dixon*." *South Central Review* 30, no. 1 (Spring 2013): 155–172. Accessed 23-08-2018. DOI: https://doi.org/10.1353/ scr.2013.0000.

Russell, Danielle. "'You heard her, you ain't blind': The 'Haunting' Presence of *Their Eyes Were Watching God*." In *Neil Gaiman in the 21st Century*, edited by Tara Prescott, 52–64. McFarland and Company, Inc., 2015.

Russell, Ford. *Northrop Frye on Myth*. New York: Garland Publishing, 1998.

Sahlins, Marshall. "The Sadness of Sweetness" *Current Anthropology* 37, no. 3 (June 1996):395–428. Accessed 19-12-2018. DOI: 10.2307/536765 https://www-jstor-org.lib-proxy.radford.edu/stable/536765.

Sahlins, Marshall. "The Western Illusion of Human Nature," *Michigan Quarterly Review* XLV, no. 3 (Summer 2006). No page numbers. Accessed December 19, 2019. Permalink : http://hdl.handle.net/2027/spo.act2080.0045.306.

Salvey, Courtney "Riddled with Evil: Fantasy as Theodicy in George MacDonald's Phantastes and Lilith." *North Wind: A Journal of George MacDonald Studies*. 27, Art.2 (2008): 16–34. Accessed October 24, 2018. http://digitalcommons.snc.edu/northwind/vol27/iss1/2.

Sandel, Michael J. *Democracy's Discontent*. Belknap Press, 1996.

Sanders, Scott. "Pynchon's Paranoid History." *Twentieth Century Literature* 21, no. 2 (May 1975): 177–92. Accessed 04-07-2007. Stable URL: http://links.jstor.org/ sici?sici=0041-462X%28197505%2921%3A2%3C177%3APPH%3E2.0.CO%3B2-N.

Saramago, José. *Blindness*. Translated by Giovanni Pontiero. Harcourt, Brace & Company, 1997.

Saramago, José. *Seeing*. Translated by Margaret Jull Costa. Harcourt Inc., 1994.

Saramago, José. *The Cave*. Mariner Books, 2003.

Savage, Adam. "SUYFY 25: Origin Stories." Interview by Adam Savage. SYFY WIRE. Sept. 5, 2017. https://www.syfy.com/syfywire/listen-adam-savage-interviews-nne-di-okorafor. Accessed March 7, 2019.

Savvas, Theophilus. "Pynchon Plays Dice: *Mason & Dixon* and Quantum History." *Literature and History* 20, no. 2 (Fall 2011): 51–67. Accessed 23-08-2018. ISSN: 0306-1973 OR 03061973.

Schell, David. "Engaging Foundational Narratives in Morrison's *Paradise* and Pynchon's *Mason & Dixon*. *College Literature: A Journal of Critical Literary Studies* 41, no. 3 (Summer 2014): 69–94. E-ISSN: 1542-4286. Accessed 23-08-2018. https://lib-proxy.radford.edu/login?url=http://search.ebscohost.com/login.aspx?direct=true&db=edsglr&AN=edsgcl.377529930&site=eds-live&scope=site.

Schmidt, Peter. "Line, Vortex, and Mound: On First Reading Thomas Pynchon's *Mason & Dixon*." Accessed 04-07-2007. http://www.swarthmore.edu/Humanities/pschmid1/essays/pynchon/mason.html.

Schneider, Jessica. "Hate crimes increased by 17% in 2017, FBI report finds." CNN.com. December 11, 2018. Accessed March 1, 2019. https://www.cnn.com/2018/11/13/politics/fbi-hate-crimes-2017/index.html.

Scott, Kyle. *The Limits of Politics: Making the Case for Literature in Political Analysis*. Lexington Books, 2016.

Sebeok, Thomas A., ed. *Myth: A Symposium*. Bloomington: University of Indiana Press, 1958.

Seed, David. *The Fictional Labyrinths of Thomas Pynchon*. Iowa City: University of Iowa Press, 1988.

Segal, Robert. *Myth: A Very Short Introduction*. Oxford University Press, 2004.

Sherman, Cordelia. "The Princess and the Wizard: The Fantasy Worlds of Ursula K. LeGuin and George MacDonald." *Children's Literature Association Quarterly* 12, no.1 (Spring 1987): 24–28. Accessed April 1, 2014. DOI: 10.1353/chq./0.0163.

Sims, Harly J. "Consorting with the Gods: Exploring Gaiman's Pan-Pantheism." In *The Mythological Dimensions of Neil Gaiman*, edited by Anthony Burdge, Jessica Burke, and Kristen Larsen, 93–172. Kitsune Books, 2012 and CreateSpace, 2013.

Sklar, Robert. "The New Novel, USA: Thomas Pynchon." *The Nation* (September 25, 1967): 277–80. Accessed 2007. https://lib-proxy.radford.edu/login?url=http://search.ebscohost.com/login.aspx?direct=true&db=edb&AN=13135139&site=eds-live&scope=site.

Slabbert, Mathilda and Viljoen, Leonie. "Sustaining the Imaginative Life: Mythology and Fantasy in Neil Gaiman's *American Gods*." *Liberator* 27, no. 3 (December 2006): 135–155. Accessed October 22, 2018. ISSN 0258-2279. https://lib-proxy.radford.edu/login?url=http://search.ebscohost.com/login.aspx?direct=true&db=edsglr&AN=edsgcl
.172907865&site=eds-live&scope=site.

Slade, Joseph W. *Thomas Pynchon*. Warner Paperback Library, 1974.

Slochower, Harry. *Mythopoesis*. Detroit: Wayne State University Press, 1970.

Soto, Fernando. "Kore Motifs in the Princess Books: Mythic Threads Between Irenes and Eirinys." In *George MacDonald: Literary Heritage and Heirs*, edited by Roderick McGillis.65–79. Zossima Press, 2008.

Spicer, Michael W. "Neutrality, Adversary Argument, and Constitutionalism in Public Administration." *Administrative Theory & Praxis* vol. 37 (2015): 188–202. Accessed January 10, 2019. DOI: 10.1080/10841806.2015.1053363.

Spiridon, Monica. "Holy Sinners: Narrative Betrayal and Thematic Machination in Thomas Mann's and Thomas Pynchon's Novels." *Neohelicon* 40 (2013): 199–208. Accessed 23-08-2018. DOI: 10.1007/s11059-013-0174-0.

Statista, "Racist incidents recorded by the police in England and Wales from April 2015 to March 2018, by region," accessed March 1, 2019, https://www.statista.com/statistics/624038/racist-incidents-in-england-and-wales.

Steiner, George. *Real Presences*. Chicago: University of Chicago Press, 1991.

Stelle, Ginger. "Phantastic Parallels in George MacDonald's *Phantastes* and *St. George and St. Michael*. In *George MacDonald: Literary Heritage and Heirs*, edited by Roderick McGillis.139–151. Zossima Press, 2008.

Straub, Peter. "Neil Gaiman: An Introduction." *Journal of the Fantastic in the Arts*. 24, no. 3 (2013): 399–400. Accessed October 22, 2018. Retrieved from https://lib-proxy.radford.edu/login?url=http://search.ebscohost.com/login.aspx?direct=true&db=hlh&AN=110028906&site=eds-live&scope=site.

Strenski, Ivan. *Four Theories of Myth in the Twentieth Century: Cassirer, Eliade, Lévi-Strauss, and Malinowski*. Iowa City: University of Iowa Press. 1987.

Sunstein, Cass. *# Republic: Divided Democracy in the Age of Social Media*. Princeton University Press, 2018. Kindle edition.

Tatar, Maria. "Mirrors and Webs: Fairy Tales, Cultural Memory, and Trauma in Helen Oyeyenii's *Boy, Snow, Bird* and Neil Gaiman's *Anansi Boys*." *Book 2.0* 7, no. 2 (2017): 177–190. Accessed 24.10.18. DOI: 10.1386/btwo.7.2.177!.

Taylor, Charles. *The Ethics of Authenticity*. Harvard University Press, 1991.

Tegla, Emanuela. "*Waiting for the Barbarians*: The Journey from Duty to Moral Choice." *English* vol. 60, no. 228 (2011): 68–91. Accessed January 10, 2019. DOI: 10.0193/english/efq024.

Tolkien, J.R.R. *Tree and Leaf*. London: HarperCollins, 2001.

Van Baal, J. *Symbols for Communication*. The Netherlands: Koninklijke Van Gorcum & Company, 1971.

Veena, Das. "The Boundaries of the We: Cruelty, Responsibility, and Forms of Life." *Critical Horizons* vol. 17, no. 2 (May 2016): 168–185. Accessed January 10, 2019. DOI: 10.1080/14409917.2016.1153888.

Vico, Giambattista. *New Science*. Penguin Classics, 2000.

Voegelin,Eric. *Order and History, Vol. I: Israel and Revelation*. Baton Rouge: Louisiana State University Press, 1956.

Voegelin, Eric. *Order and History II: The World of the Polis*. Baton Rouge: Louisiana State University Press, 1957.

Voegelin, Eric. *Order and History III: Plato and Aristotle*. Baton Rouge: Louisiana State University Press. 1957.

Voegelin, Eric. *Order and History IV: The Ecumenic Age*. Baton Rouge: Louisiana State University Press. 1974.

Voegelin, Eric. *Order and History V: In Search of Order*. Introduction Ellis Sandoz. Baton Rouge: Louisiana State University Press, 1987.

Voegelin, Eric. "A Formal Relationship with Puritan Mysticism." In *The Collected Works of Eric Voegelin, Vol. I: On the Form of the American Mind*. Translated by Ruth Hein, Edited by Jürgen Gebhardt and Barry Cooper. Baton Rouge: Louisiana State University Press, 1995.

Voegelin, Eric. "The New Science of Politics" in *The Collected Works of Eric Voegelin, Vol. 5: Modernity Without Restraint*. Edited by Manfred Henningsen. Translated by Virginia Ann Schildhauer. Columbia: University of Missouri Press, 2000.

Voegelin, Eric. "In Search of the Ground." In *The Collected Works of Eric Voegelin, Vol. 11: Published Essays 1953–1966*. Edited by Ellis Sandoz, 224–251. Baton Rouge: Louisiana State University Press, 2000.

Voegelin, Eric. "Immortality: Experience and Symbol." In *The Collected Works of Eric Voegelin, Vol. 12: Published Essays 1966–1985*. Edited by Ellis Sandoz. Baton Rouge: Louisiana State University Press, 1990.

Voegelin, Eric. "Locke." In *The Collected Works of Eric Voegelin, Vol. 25: The New Order and Last Orientation*, edited by Jürgen Gebhardt and Thomas A. Hollweck, 137–152. Baton Rouge, Louisiana: *Louisiana State University Press*,1999.

Voegelin, Eric. *The Collected Works of Eric Voegelin, Vol. 26: History of Political Ideas VIII: Crisis and the Apocalypse of Man*. Edited by David Walsh. Columbia: University of Missouri Press, 1999.

Voegelin, Eric. "Anxiety and Reason." In *The Collected Works of Eric Voegelin, Vol. 28: What Is History and Other Late Unpublished Writings*. Edited by Thomas Hollweck and Paul Carringella. Baton Rouge: University of Louisiana Press, 1990.

Voegelin, Eric. "The Beginning and the Beyond: A Meditation on Truth." In *The Collected Works of Eric Voegelin, Vol. 28: What Is History? And Other Late Unpublished Writings*. Edited by Thomas Hollweck and Paul Caringella. Baton Rouge: University of Louisiana Press, 1990.

Von Czarnowsky, Laura-Marie. "'The Old Man was Gone': The Problematic Unity of Tricksters, Gods, and Fathers in *Anansi Boys* and *American Gods*." In *Neil Gaiman in the 21st Century*, edited by Tara Prescott. McFarland and Company, Inc., 2015.

Von Heyking, John and Avramenko, Richard, ed. *Friendship and Politics: Essays in Political Thought*. Notre Dame, IN: University of Notre Dame Press, 2008.

Wagner, Hank, Golden, Christopher, and Bissette, Stephen R., ed. *Prince of Stories*. St. Martin's Griffin, 2008.

Wallach, Rick, ed. *Myth, Legend, Dust: Critical Responses to Cormac McCarthy*. Manchester: Manchester University Press, 2000.

Weaver, Matthew. "Hate crime surge linked to Brexit and 2017 terrorist attacks." *The Guardian*. October 16, 2018. Accessed 3.1.2019. https://www.theguardian.com/society/2018/oct/16/hate-crime-brexit-terrorist-attacks-england-wales.

Weil, Simone. *Gravity and Grace*. London: Routledge, 1992.

Weil, Simone. *The Need for Roots*. New York: Harper-Colophon, 1971.

Weil, Simone. *Waiting for God*. New York: Harper and Row, 1973.

Weil, Simone. *On Science, Necessity and the Love of God,* trans. R. Reece. Oxford: Oxford University Press, 1968.

Whalen-Bridge, John. *Political Fiction and the American Self*. Champaign-Urbana: University of Illinois Press, 1998.

Williamson, James T. "The Fourfold Myth of Death and Rebirth in George MacDonald's *Phantastes*." *North Wind: A Journal of George MacDonald Studies*. Accessed October 24, 2018. http://digitalcommons.snc.edu/northwind/vol33/iss1/3.

Wilson, James Q. *American Government: Brief Edition*. Wadsworth Publishing, 2008.

Winthrop, John. *A Modell of Christian Charity* (1630).

Wolin, Sheldon. *Politics and Vision: Continuity and Innovation in Western Political Thought*. Princeton: Princeton University Press, 2004.

Womack, Ytasha L. *Afrofuturism: The World of Black Science Fiction and Fantasy*. Chicago: Lawrence Hill Books, 2013. Kindle edition.

Worthington, Leslie Harper. *Cormac McCarthy and the Ghost of Huck Finn*. New York: McFarland and Company, 2012.

Wright, Robin. "The New Tribalism." *Los Angeles Times*. June 8, 1992 as cited in Volf, Miroslav. *Exclusion and Embrace: A Theological Exploration of Identity, Otherness, and Reconciliation*. Nashville: Abingdon Press, 1996.

Zipes, Jack. "Why Fantasy Matters Too Much." *The Journal of Aesthetic Education* 43, no. 2 (Summer 2009): 77–91. Accessed April 1, 2014. DOI: 10.1353/jae.0.0039.

Zwillich, Todd, "Science Fiction's New Reality: Interview with Nnedi Okorafor, N. K. Jemison, and Noelle Stevenson." Produced by Paige Osburn. *1A*. Monday, Sep. 10, 2018. Accessed March 7, 2019. https://the1a.org/shows/2018-09-10/scifi-fever.

Index

About the Authors

Nick Pappas played football at and graduated Phi Beta Kappa from Shepherd College, served as a Marine lieutenant in Vietnam where he earned a bronze star, spent a year in Bethesda Naval Hospital, taught high school, worked for the Youth Conservation Corps, and earned his PhD in international relations theory at the University of Virginia. He taught political philosophy and international relations theory for over thirty years. His knowledge of Eric Voegelin's work was encyclopedic. Nick's scholarship focused on the importance of Voegelin's work for international relations theory. He also wrote extensively on Cormac McCarthy. Nick died prior to the completion of this book; however, his impact on it was profound.

Margaret Hrezo graduated Phi Beta Kappa from Saint Louis University in Missouri and received her PhD in political theory and constitutional law from the University of Maryland. Prior to her hire as a tenure track professor of political science at Radford University, she conducted survey research for Pulaski County, Virginia, worked as an administrator and researcher on water law and drought management for one of the Water Resources Research Centers at a state land-grant university, and taught community college, college, and middle school and high school students. She is co-editor with John M. Parrish of *Damned If You Do: Dilemmas of Moral Action in Literature and Popular Culture*. Her primary research interests are in the sub-field of politics, film, and literature. However, she also has published in other areas of political science and political philosophy.

Milton Keynes UK
Ingram Content Group UK Ltd.
UKHW021711080324
439172UK00002B/7